Luminos is the Open Access monograph publishing program
from UC Press. Luminos provides a framework for preserving and
reinvigorating monograph publishing for the future and increases
the reach and visibility of important scholarly work. Titles published
in the UC Press Luminos model are published with the same high
standards for selection, peer review, production, and marketing as
those in our traditional program. www.luminosoa.org

Migration and Hybrid
Political Regimes

Migration and Hybrid Political Regimes

Navigating the Legal Landscape in Russia

Rustamjon Urinboyev

UNIVERSITY OF CALIFORNIA PRESS

University of California Press
Oakland, California

Suggested citation: Urinboyev, R. *Migration and Hybrid Political Regimes: Navigating the Legal Landscape in Russia*. Oakland: University of California Press, 2021. DOI: https://doi.org/10.1525/luminos.96

Library of Congress Cataloging-in-Publication Data
Names: Urinboyev, Rustamjon, author.
Title: Migration and hybrid political regimes : navigating the legal
    landscape in Russia / Rustamjon Urinboyev.
Description: Oakland, California : University of California Press, [2020] |
    Includes bibliographical references and index.
Identifiers: LCCN 2020019267 (print) | LCCN 2020019268 (ebook) |
    ISBN 9780520299573 (paperback) | ISBN 9780520971257 (epub)
Subjects: LCSH: Migrant labor—Legal status, laws, etc.—Russia
    (Federation)—Case studies. | Foreign workers—Legal status, laws,
    etc.—Russia (Federation)—Case studies. | Uzbekistan—Emigration
    and immigration—Case studies. | Asia, Central—Emigration and
    immigration—Case studies. | Russia (Federation)—Emigration
    and immigration—Government policy.
Classification: LCC HD5856.R8 U75 2020 (print) | LCC HD5856.R8
    (ebook) | DDC 331.5/4408994325047—dc23
LC record available at https://lccn.loc.gov/2020019267
LC ebook record available at https://lccn.loc.gov/2020019268

30 29 28 27 26 25 24 23 22 21
10 9 8 7 6 5 4 3 2 1

CONTENTS

The completion of this book marks the end of my exciting adventures and transnational experiences in Moscow, Russia, and Fergana Valley, Uzbekistan, and I would like to acknowledge the support and encouragement of a great number of people and institutions without whom it would not have been possible.

The initial idea emerged in January of 2014 when I was doing fieldwork in various construction sites in Moscow and Moscow province. Muhiddin, my childhood friend and fieldwork assistant in Moscow, suggested that I should introduce myself to informants as an author (*yozuvchi*) writing a book on Uzbek migrants' adventures in Moscow. This way of introducing myself made my informants more eager to participate in my project as "book heroes" and eventually convinced me that I should indeed write a book on Uzbek migrants' adventures in Russia. Not only did Muhiddin help me with conducting the fieldwork, but he also taught me how to behave correctly by showing respect and expressing appreciation when visiting migrants' workplaces and accommodations, which are often far below normal working and living standards. I would like to express my sincere gratitude to Muhiddin for his valuable support and coaching, which enabled me to collect a rich stock of ethnographic data in Moscow. I am grateful to hundreds of Uzbek migrant workers in Moscow and their left-behind families and communities in Fergana Valley who participated in my research and generously shared their feelings, experiences, and life histories with me.

My special thanks goes to Måns Svensson, my mentor and dear friend, who has supported me from the early stages of my academic career until now. Thanks to his support and encouragement, especially during my post-PhD years, I was able to keep my affiliation with the Department of Sociology of Law, Lund University (where I am employed now), as well as receive the prestigious international post-doctoral grant from the Swedish Research Council that made this book possible. I am very thankful to Måns for his never-ending support, honesty, and friendship.

I am grateful to my colleagues Anna-Liisa Heusala, Kaarina Aitamurto, and Sherzod Eraliev, from the University of Helsinki research project "MISHA: Migration, Shadow Economy and Parallel Legal Orders" (funded by the Kone Foundation), with whom I conducted ethnographic fieldwork and expert interviews in Moscow in 2017. This book has greatly benefited from the illuminating conversations we had during our project meetings and field trips, as well as from the expert interview data we collected within the project.

For insightful conversations at different stages of my research I would also like to thank Sergey Abashin, Judith Pallot, Rano Turaeva, Abel Polese, Jeremy Morris, Agnieszka Kubal, Håkan Hydén, Markku Kivinen, Caress Schenk, Per Wickenberg, Karsten Åström, Matthias Baier, Patrik Olsson, Isabel Schoultz, Ida Nafstad, Reza Banakar, John Woodlock, Chris Thornhill, Elena Maslovskaya, and Erhan Dogan. I extend a special thanks also to my colleague Sevara Usmanova, who has recently joined the Department of Sociology of Law at Lund University and has organized four international workshops in Lund, which have provided an interdisciplinary venue and enabled me to receive valuable feedback from migration and area studies scholars. I am also thankful to Umid Bobomatov, Radio Free Europe Uzbek Service (Ozodlik Radiosi) correspondent in Moscow, who acted as a gatekeeper to key informants and regularly updated me on the lives of Uzbek migrants in Russia. I am also grateful to a number of migrant rights lawyers, activists, and experts in Moscow, namely, Botirjon Shermatov, Zarnigor Omonillayeva, Valentina Chupik, Izzat Amon, Vyacheslav Postavnin, and Vasiliy Kravtsov, who shared their experiences on migrant rights situation in Russia.

The book took its initial form during my visiting fellowship at the Cambridge Central Asia Forum (CCAF), University of Cambridge, where I benefited from informal conversations with Siddharth Saxena (CCAF director), as well as comments at the CCAF Seminar by Diana Kudaibergenova and Vsevolod Samokhvalov. I would also like to express my gratitude to Madeleine Reeves for commenting on the initial version of my book proposal and sharing her experience on publication strategies. I would also like to thank a number of anonymous reviewers for their constructive and helpful comments on an earlier version of the book.

At the University of California Press, I am grateful to Maura Roessner for her enthusiasm, professionalism, promptness, and patience, and to Madison Wetzell for her excellent administrative and technical support. I am indebted to Vanessa Fuller, language editor at the University of Helsinki, for editing and proofreading all chapters of the book, especially during June and July of 2019, when she worked full-time and intensively with me, without taking any break during the summer holidays.

I would like to express my sincere gratitude to my employers, the Department of Sociology of Law at Lund University and the Aleksanteri Institute, University of Helsinki, for providing facilities, resources, and an atmosphere conducive to quality research. Several funding agencies and institutions have provided financial and administrative support that made this book possible. From 2014 to 2019, research and fieldwork for this book was funded by the Swedish Research Council (dnr D0734401), European Commission (MSCA IF Project 751911), Kone Foundation, and University of Helsinki (Three-Year Grants Programme).

I would like to thank my father, Uktamjon, my mother, Yoquthon, and my siblings, Rohatoy, Ravshanbek, and Abdurasul, for their love, encouragement, and support. I wish also to pay tribute to the memory of my late uncle, Adhamjon, who has been a great role model in our *urug'* (extended family) and taught us how to be good persons in life. I am immensely grateful to my wife, Shahnoza, for her love and care and for standing by me through good times and bad. It is actually her support and sacrifices that have made this book possible. The book would also not have been possible without the support of my mother in-law, Ozodakhon, who traveled all the way from rural Fergana to Sweden, stayed with us for two years in Lund, and took care of her grandchildren while I spent many days at the university writing. Shahnoza and I are grateful to her for her unconditional help, love, and care. Finally, I would like to thank my son Abdurahim (Abbe) and my daughter Aysel for making my life meaningful and for giving me the motivation and inspiration that made this book possible. It is to them that I dedicate this book.

Rustam Urinboyev
Lund, Sweden, March 2020

Throughout this book I have changed the names of my informants, even in those instances where they specifically asked me to use their real names. Furthermore, to protect my informants' confidentiality, I have changed the names of the villages and *mahallas* in the Fergana Valley of Uzbekistan referred to in the text. All Uzbek and Russian terms are spelled according to standard literary forms. Their use is based on two criteria: (1) whether an Uzbek or Russian word or phenomenon is central to this study; (2) if an English translation inadequately or incompletely captures the meaning of the Uzbek or Russian word or phenomenon. Uzbek and Russian words appear in italics. Where an appropriate English word exists for particular terms and phenomena, I have used the regular English version rather than the transliterated term.

Understanding Migrants' Legal Adaptation in Hybrid Political Regimes

As a part of my transnational ethnography among Uzbek migrant workers in Moscow, Russia, and in their home village in Uzbekistan, on August 6, 2014, I traveled to the Fergana Valley of Uzbekistan, to a village I call "Shabboda," from whence the majority of Uzbek migrants I met in Moscow originated. Shabboda is one of the many remittance-dependent villages in rural Fergana, where labor migration has become a widespread livelihood strategy in the post-Soviet period, a norm for young and able-bodied men. During the "migration season" (March to November) the majority of village inhabitants consist of elderly people, women, and children. In the words of villagers, Shabboda is a "Moscow village," since the majority of villagers work in Moscow given the existence of village-specific networks there. Several villagers work as intermediaries in Moscow's construction sector, serving as gatekeepers for villagers seeking access to the labor market. Young men who prefer to stay in the village during the migration season are usually viewed as lazy and abnormal by villagers, whereas those who work in Russia and regularly send money home enjoy higher social status and greater respect.

My field trip to Uzbekistan coincided with the introduction of the entry ban (*zapret na v'ezd*) legislation in Russia (2013–14), under which any foreign citizen who committed two administrative offenses within a three-year period received a three-year entry ban. By September of 2014, more than 1 million foreigners had already been banned from reentering Russia; the majority of those foreigners were citizens of Uzbekistan (Bobylov 2014). The effects of these legal interventions were already felt in Shabboda, since many migrants were stranded in the village and could not return to Russia after being issued an entry ban. I observed that daily conversations in the village's "gossip hotspots" (e.g., the mosque, teahouse, at regular get-togethers, and weddings) revolved primarily around entry-banned migrants (*zapreti borlar*) and various informal strategies and tactics devised by

FIGURE 1. Everyday life in Shabboda village, rural Fergana, Uzbekistan. June 2016. Photo by author.

migrants to reenter Russia. I was truly intrigued by these daily conversations and became interested in learning more about the informal strategies adopted by entry-banned migrants. I wondered whether it was indeed possible for entry-banned migrants to reenter Russia and, if so, how that process works, what informal strategies and tactics are employed to navigate around the entry-ban system, and the implications of these strategies and processes for understanding the functioning of the Russian migration regime.

Reflecting on these questions, I was particularly interested in the informal strategies of three entry-banned migrants in the village—Alish (male, 32), Mamir (male, 35), and Tillo (male, 37)—individuals who were well-connected to different formal and informal institutions in Russia. Between 2008 and 2014, Alish worked as a caretaker at a *dacha* (summer cottage) in Rublevka, a prestigious residential area in the western suburbs of Moscow where many high-level Russian state officials, oligarchs, and successful businessmen reside. The owner of the *dacha* (Alish's boss) was a high-level state official within the Russian Federal Security Service (FSB), the most powerful organization in the country. Owing to his six years of *halol* (honest) work at the *dacha*, Alish was able to establish a good relationship with his FSB boss and family members. When I asked Alish if his FSB connection could solve his entry-ban problem, he replied confidently that he had already contacted his boss, who assured him that his entry ban would be lifted quite soon. Once lifted, he could return to Moscow and continue working at the *dacha*.

Mamir's case also intrigued me, given his connections to immigration officials. From 2009 until 2014 Mamir worked as a *registraysiyachi* (an informal intermediary in residence registration) at an air ticket office located near a metro station in the north of Moscow. In that position he primarily acted as a bridge between (a) migrant workers who needed a residence registration certificate and other immigration papers and (b) immigration officials who always sought opportunities to generate informal benefits from their "oily position." This was where Mamir became acquainted with immigration officials who could, for an informal fee of US$700, help him enter Russia despite the existence of an entry ban. When I asked Mamir how his entry ban problem would be resolved, he replied that, in some cases, immigration officials might suspend someone's entry-ban case for a few months by referring to ongoing legal proceedings or by appealing the ban in court. In such circumstances the entry ban is suspended in the databases of both the immigration service and the border control service, allowing the entry-banned migrant to enter Russia. Mamir believed that this strategy would work and enable him to reenter Russia in the near future.

Unlike Alish and Mamir, Tillo was not well-connected with Russian state officials but had strong connections with "street institutions," such as racketeers, intermediaries, and smugglers. Between 2005 and 2014 Tillo worked at a wholesale bazaar in Moscow, selling Uzbek fruits and vegetables. Owing to his daily interactions with people from diverse backgrounds and social statuses Tillo also had friends from the "street world" who could put him in touch with reliable human smugglers operating at the Russia-Kazakhstan border. These smugglers would help him enter Russia through roundabout means. Given his contacts, Tillo appeared quite well-informed about how things work at the border, relaying that Russian border guards and human smugglers act as accomplices and jointly organize migrants' illegal border crossings. Tillo even knew about the existence of the so-called plan system, where Russian border guards ignored and facilitated illegal border-crossing operations during the first two weeks of each month (from the first until the 15th), while those migrants who cross the border illegally during the second half of the month were usually caught and arrested to serve as indicators of the effectiveness of border control measures. In Tillo's words Russian border guards worked for the well-being of their "families and children" during the first two weeks of each month, and after the 15th of the month they worked for the government, catching all migrants illegally entering Russia. Owing to his influential "street contacts," Tillo was confident that he would be able to return to Russia within a few months.

After a nine-month break I returned to Moscow for a follow-up fieldwork visit from July 19 through August 15, 2015. On arriving in Moscow, I first determined whether the three entry-banned migrants I had met in Fergana were actually able to return to Moscow. Much to my surprise, all three of them—Alish, Mamir, and Tillo—were already back in Moscow and working at the same jobs they had held before being banned from entry. Eager to learn more about their adventures, I invited them for dinner at an Uzbek café in Moscow's Medvedkovo district. During my conversation with them I learned that the strategies they mentioned to me a year previously did actually work and helped secure their reentry into Russia. Following their reentry into Russia via semilegal or illegal channels, all three of them "legalized" their work and residence status through the *Kazansky vokzal*, a very popular "migrant legalization" site situated in Moscow's Kazansky railway station. At this site it is possible to obtain virtually all types of illegal and semilegal documents, including fake (*fal'shivka*), "clean fake" (*chistaya fal'shivka*), and "almost clean" (*pochti chistiy*) residence registrations and work permits, as well as fake Russian and Kyrgyz, Tajik, and Uzbek passports. Since all three of these migrants lacked authentic immigration documents, I wondered how they organized their daily life and avoided surveillance from police officers and immigration officials scattered across Moscow. When I asked them whether they ran the risk of being deported if they were caught by the authorities, they laughed sarcastically and said, "Russia is a land of opportunities if you know the street rules and have the right amount of money when stopped by police officers." Yet, seeing my puzzled face, they quickly noticed my poor understanding of the "street life" and shared an anecdote about "Putin and the golden fish." This anecdote slyly hinted at the near impossibility of immigration control in the Russian legal context, a context predicated on ubiquitous corruption and a weak rule of law:

> There is an anecdote widely circulated among Uzbek migrants in Russia. Once upon a time, Putin, the President of Russia, went fishing. Putin cast his net and luckily pulled out a golden fish. Not wanting to die, the golden fish pled for its life, promising three wishes in return. But Putin laughed and said that he wanted neither wealth nor power and said that he had just one wish. He promised to let the fish go if it fulfilled his wish. The golden fish became happy and asked for his wish. Putin said, "I neither need wealth nor power. I want you to send all Uzbek migrants to their homeland. All organizations responsible for immigration control—that is, immigration service, the police, and the border guards—are corrupt and want to keep migrants in Russia because migrants are the source of wealth for them. If you help me get rid of Uzbek migrants, I will free you and you can enjoy your life." The golden fish's heart sank when it heard Putin's wish, and it fell into deep thought. "I am very sorry, but I cannot fulfill this wish, brother Putin," said the golden fish. Putin became angry and asked why the fish could not fulfill it. The golden fish replied, "It's because I am a migrant too. Originally, I am from Syrdaryo, the second largest river in Uzbekistan."

To my mind, my field observations refined many of my initial assumptions about how migrants establish a relationship with the law in Russia. The above empirical examples suggest that migrants' legal adaptation to weak rule-of-law migration contexts such as Russia's should not be merely understood in terms of migrants' knowledge of immigration laws, their legal status, and legalization strategies. Instead, that adaptation should also be examined in terms of their knowledge of the informal rules, street laws, and their capacity to negotiate with informal channels. Despite the existence of draconian immigration laws and border control infrastructure, combined with ever-increasing antimigrant sentiments within Russian society, I found that migrant workers continued to live and work under the conditions of a shadow economy. Even the behavior of state officials overseeing immigration laws and policies (e.g., immigration officials, border guards, and the police) was driven more by informal norms and practices than by state law. Consequently, rather than complying with immigration laws that are rarely followed by Russian state officials, migrants have actually produced new forms of informal governance and a legal order that provides alternative means of legal adaptation. These alternatives allow migrants to regulate their working lives and navigate around structural constraints, such as complicated residence registration and work permit rules, racism, and the lack of a social safety net. Furthermore, this navigation implies that informal and illegal practices in weak rule-of-law migration contexts may actually enable migrants to escape the constraints imposed by the immigration laws and policies (Garcés-Mascareñas 2010; Reeves 2013; Dave 2014a; Urinboyev and Polese 2016; Schenk 2018).

The above field observations thus lead us to the main goal of this book, which is intended to contribute new theoretical and empirical insights into scholarly debates on migrants' legal adaptation and integration. In doing so, this study is conceived as a critical reflection on the dominant migrant legal adaptation and integration literature (and, more generally, migration studies scholarship), which is still based largely on case studies of immigrant communities in Western-style democracies, such as Australia, Canada, France, Germany, the United Kingdom, and the United States (Castles and Miller 2013). While the dominant frameworks provide useful insight toward understanding migrants' experiences in a new legal environment, they have limited utility when applied in the context of non-Western, nondemocratic migrant-receiving contexts. Consequently, in spite of the large diversity of scholarly explanations for, and approaches to, explaining the diverse patterns of migrant legal adaptation and incorporation, we know relatively little about how migrants adapt to a new legal environment in the ever-growing hybrid political regimes that are neither clearly democratic nor conventionally authoritarian (Diamond 2002; Levitsky and Way 2002; Goode 2010a). As Reeves (2013) maintains, this lacuna can be explained in part by the ongoing legacies of the "three-worlds division" of social-scientific labor (Pletsch 1981; Chari and Verdery 2009) that tend to focus on Global South–North migrations, whereas migration processes in hybrid regimes such as Russia ("non-Western migration regimes," broadly conceived) remain underrepresented in comparative and theoretical debates about contemporary migration regimes. At the same time, hybrid political regimes have been traditionally viewed as exporters of migrant workers to Western Europe, North America, and Australia (Castles and Miller 2013); their role as a recipient of migrant workers from other countries has been obscured. Addressing this research gap is especially important when considering the fact that hybrid regimes such as Russia, Kazakhstan, Malaysia, Singapore, and Turkey, as well as other nondemocratic contexts such as the Gulf States, have become key "migration hotspots" worldwide because of their improved economic conditions, receiving an increasing number of migrants with either low qualifications, no legal right to work or stay, or simply lacking the skills to quickly integrate into local job markets (Garcés-Mascareñas 2010; Anderson and Hancilová 2011; Tolay 2012; Heusala and Aitamurto 2016). The need for empirically grounded knowledge of these relatively understudied migratory flows, as well as the necessity to understand their implications for (Western-centric) migration theories, is thus, from this perspective, substantial.

Migrant legal adaptation is not uniform everywhere but rather holds different meanings, forms, and functional roles depending on sociopolitical context, legal environment, economic system, and various cultural factors. The comparative political-regimes literature demonstrates the rapid proliferation of hybrid political regimes worldwide, stretching from postcommunist Eurasia to sub-Saharan Africa (Diamond 2002). Unlike classic authoritarian regimes, such as North Korea or Turkmenistan, which brutally suppress any form of opposition, hybrid regimes display some elements of political competition and regularly hold presidential and parliamentary elections. But unlike Western-style liberal democracies in which culture of the rule of law is strong and presumed to be the standard of governance, political competition under hybrid regimes remains heavily shaped by an authoritarian culture, the rule of law remains quite weak, formal institutions are dysfunctional, informal governance and corruption are prevalent, and independent civil society institutions are heavily controlled or banned altogether (Robertson 2007; Wigell 2008; Gilbert and Mohseni 2011).

Given the differences in state-society relations, governance, and legal cultures, we cannot assume that immigrant integration and adaptation frameworks constructed in Western contexts apply within the context of hybrid political regimes, where migrants do not experience the "rule-of-law" and functional institutions but must navigate around the corrupt legal system and produce new forms of informal governance and legal orders. A closer empirical investigation of these processes may lead to new theoretical insights on migrants' legal adaptations to non-Western migration locales and, more broadly, on the functioning of the social fabric involving state actors, nonstate legal orders, and migrants in the law-and-order chain. Ultimately, this book argues that in hybrid-regime contexts migrants are not passive entities; instead, migrants do have agency, and they use that agency and the opportunities provided by a weak rule of law and a corrupt political system to navigate the legal landscape using informal channels to access employment and other opportunities that are limited (to those with legal status) or hard to obtain in the current legal framework of the host country. Based on these propositions,

I explore the following questions in this book: How do migrants build relationships with the law and law-like informal orders in hybrid political regimes? What factors incite them to disengage from the formal legal system and, thereby, produce new forms of informal governance and legal order to organize their daily lives? How does migrants' legal culture (e.g., premigratory social norms, religious values, daily transnational practices, attitudes toward the law, and interpretations of legality and illegality) shape their legal adaptation patterns and strategies in a new environment? How, why, and when do migrants resort to informal channels and adaptation strategies? What theoretical implications do such "outside the nation-state law" processes have for the dominant [Western-centric] immigrant integration and adaptation frameworks in general and, more specifically, for the sociolegal perspectives on migrants' legal adaptation and incorporation?

I investigate these questions through a multisited transnational ethnography of Uzbek migrant workers in Moscow, Russia, and in their home village in Uzbekistan's Fergana Valley. I focus on Russia because it represents the archetypal hybrid political regime (Diamond 2002; Levitsky and Way 2002) and because it is one of the five largest recipients of migrants worldwide. Yet Russia remains relatively underrepresented in comparative and theoretical debates about contemporary migration regimes. Hence, analyzing migrant legal adaptation in a context of this type is of huge importance, given our need to bridge the knowledge gap on the topic, whereby current studies are limited to the analysis of immigration communities in Western-style democracies. The novel sociolegal lens put forth in this book—that is, that we must examine not only the limitations of the legal system but the unintended consequences of it that empower the agency of migrants to navigate the system—enables us to go beyond the Western-centric scholarship on contemporary migration regimes. With these considerations in mind, I provide in the next section of this chapter a review of dominant (Western-centric) frameworks and approaches to understanding migrants in a new legal environment. I focus on (1) assimilation, acculturation, and integration; (2) transnationalism; (3) premigratory cultural legacies as a factor in understanding migrants in their new environment; and (4) sociolegal perspectives on studying migrants in the host country. Emphasizing the relevance and usefulness of these frameworks for explaining migrants' integration into and adaptation to a new legal environment, I argue that their analytical applicability is limited in terms of fully understanding migrants' legal adaptation to nondemocratic, weak rule-of-law contexts.

UNDERSTANDING MIGRANTS IN A NEW LEGAL ENVIRONMENT: DOMINANT FRAMEWORKS AND APPROACHES

As outlined in the previous section, much of the scholarly literature on migrant adaptation and integration (both historical and current literature) relies on case studies of immigrant communities living in Western-style democracies. This is especially true for the United States, which represents the main source of research on the theme of immigrant incorporation and adaptation (Gordon 1964; Park 1964; Portes and Zhou 1993; Portes and Rumbaut 2006; Alba and Nee 2009). Extensive literature also focuses on immigrant adaptation in Australia, Canada, continental Europe (e.g., France, Germany, Italy, and Spain), and the United Kingdom (Sayegh and Lasry 1993; Brubaker 2003; Colic-Peisker and Walker 2003; Robinson 2005; Alencar and Deuze 2017). These trends can be explained by the fact that Australia, Canada, and the United States have long stood as the "established countries of immigration," while many countries of Western Europe received large numbers of immigrants because of their colonial legacy and guest worker programs in the post–World War II period (Castles and Miller 2013). Given these circumstances, it is not surprising that the dominant frameworks of immigrant adaptation—namely, assimilation, acculturation, and integration—were originally constructed with reference to the experiences of immigrant communities in Western-style democracies.

The assimilation theory, based on the American experience of immigration, represents one of the most dominant perspectives in the literature on immigrant adaptation (Park 1928; Stonequist 1937; Gordon 1964; Portes and Böröcz 1989; Portes and Zhou 1993; Zhou 1997; Alba and Nee 2009). The early models of assimilation theory, developed by Park (1928) and Stonequist (1937), were based on the assumption that immigrants, constrained by various biotic and social pressures, gradually abandon their premigratory cultural legacies and ways of life, eventually "melting" into the host society through processes of residential integration and occupational achievement. In the 1960s, however, classical assimilation approaches were challenged by Gordon (1964), who argued that cultural assimilation (adaptation to a new country through cultural adjustment) is a precondition for successful immigrant adaptation but does not automatically lead to other forms of assimilation (e.g., economical, structural, marital, and civic). In Gordon's view immigrant groups' full assimilation depends largely on the degree to which they gain acceptance from the dominant population. Gordon's insights were further refined by new theoretical perspectives developed in the 1990s and 2000s, which focused on non-European and second-generation immigrant groups (Portes and Zhou 1993; Zhou 1997; Alba and Nee 2009). Unlike the earlier assimilation models, which predicted the eventual convergence of immigrant groups into the dominant population, new frameworks such as the "segmented assimilation" (Portes and Zhou 1993; Zhou 1997) and "new assimilation theory" (Alba and Nee 2009) illustrate the diverse patterns and outcomes of adaptation among immigrant groups. These new frameworks pose an important theoretical question regarding what makes some groups prone to downward mobility and what enables them to escape stagnant positions. In addition, these new frameworks have been particularly useful in determining various (alternative) paths and outcomes of immigrant incorporation, shaped by immigrants' economic, human, and social capital, as well as by structural factors such as poor urban schools, racialization, job market inequalities, and immigration laws.

Another mainstream framework to understanding migrants' adaptation to a new environment lies in acculturation (Redfield, Linton, and Herskovits 1936; Ward and Kennedy 1994; Berry 1997, 2005; Bhattacharya 2008; Sam and Berry 2010). The classic definition of acculturation presented by Redfield, Linton, and Herskovits (1936, 149–52) is based on the understanding that acculturation represents one phase within the broader processes of culture change: "acculturation comprehends those phenomena which result when groups of individuals having different cultures come into continuous first-hand contact, with subsequent changes in the original culture patterns of either or both groups. . . . Under this definition, acculturation is to be distinguished from culture change, of which it is but one aspect." Although this definition depicts *acculturation* as a rather neutral term, highlighting that a change may occur in either or both groups, in reality acculturation leads to further change in nondominant or immigrant groups rather than in the dominant group (Berry 2005). Various terms describe those changes resulting from firsthand contact with groups of individuals from different cultural backgrounds, such as "adjustments and behavioral shifts" (Berry 1997), "culture learning" (Brislin, Landis, and Brandt 1983), and "social skills acquisition" (Furnham and Bochner 1986). We must note, however, that acculturation does not necessarily lead to assimilation. Rather, acculturation should be distinguished from assimilation—that is, one of the initial phases of change in cultural patterns toward those of the host society (Gordon 1964; Berry 2005). A similar argument was also made by Portes and Bach (1985, 23–24), who maintain that "greater knowledge of the core language and culture by new immigrants and greater familiarity with members of the dominant group do not necessarily lead to more positive attitudes and more rapid assimilation."

The third dominant framework for understanding migrants in a new legal environment relates to integration (Hansen 2000; Joppke and Morawska 2003; Lucassen, Feldman, and Oltmer 2006; Tubergen 2006; Schneider and Crul 2010). While immigrant adaptation discourse in the USA is dominated by assimilation and acculturation paradigms, European immigration debates are largely shaped by the integration framework (Schneider and Crul 2010). As Joppke and Morawska (2003, 3) assert, the very notion of integration originally rested on the premise of an already integrated, bounded, consensus-based society composed of domestic individuals and groups (as the antipode to "immigrants"), which faced the risk of disintegrating and unbinding owing to immigration. This means that the notion of immigrant integration is a political construction without academic roots. It is not surprising, therefore, that the emergence of various ethnic enclaves and mosque communities in Western Europe is perceived as an indication of "parallel legal orders" rather than an alternative pathway to integration. While the American understanding of "successful assimilation" does not preclude variety and diversity (especially in the area of economic activities), European integration carries the implicit ideal of cultural homogeneity, where "ethnic enclaves" or economic success within the ethnic community are not positively valued as a possible pathway to "integration" (Schneider and Crul 2010). Therefore, integration, as opposed to assimilation, implies the introduction of active welfare measures targeting immigrant groups to provide extensive opportunities for their successful adaptation (Joppke and Morawska 2003). High levels of immigrant representation in education and the labor market serve as an indicator of successful integration. Thus, in the European context immigrant integration is understood with regard to structural aspects of adaptation into society, particularly in relation to one's legal status, educational achievements, and access to the labor market (Schneider and Crul 2010).

While the aforementioned three dominant frameworks provide useful insight toward understanding migrants' experiences in a new environment, they remain insufficient to fully understand the complexity of immigrant adaptation in the contemporary globalized world. As previously outlined, these frameworks were constructed with reference to the experiences of immigrant groups in Western-style democracies, implying that they may not necessarily translate well into nondemocratic migration contexts because of differences in sociopolitical contexts and legal environments. Additionally, these frameworks, as Kubal (2013a, 20–21) argues, suffer from at least three important shortcomings. First, they do not account for the diversity of migrants' premigration experiences (e.g., demographic factors, economic performance, motivation and cultural distance, and personal factors), possibly facilitating or hindering immigrant adaptation. Second, these frameworks tend to portray the host society as a unitary, homogenous entity, thereby ignoring historical conditions, cultural pluralism, and diverse attitudes that may affect the responses and experiences of migrants. Third, they do not consider the role and implications of transnational ties beyond the first generation. Another factor adding to this complexity lies in the ever-growing use of new media, such as smartphones and social media tools among migrants, likely shaping their everyday lives and their left-behind families and communities in many parts of the world. Undoubtedly, continuity exists between "older" and new media, but the question remains as to whether and how these new technologies shape the nature and forms of immigrant adaptation.

Reflecting on these complexities and global tendencies, several new frameworks were developed to better understand immigrant adaptation in the digital era. In this regard classical frameworks (assimilation, acculturation, and integration) confined to the study of immigrant adaptation to the territory of a single nation-state have been challenged by the growing literature on migrant transnationalism (e.g., Schiller, Basch, and Blanc-Szanton 1992; Portes, Guarnizo, and Landolt 1999; Vertovec 1999; Levitt 2001a). While acknowledging the usefulness of classical frameworks, migrant transnationalism scholarship argues that migrants' daily lives and experiences differ from earlier forms because of rapid developments in information and communication technologies (ICTs) enabling migrants to be "simultaneously incorporated" into both their host country and their society of origin (Foner 1997a; Morawska 1999; Portes, Guarnizo, and Landolt 1999; Vertovec 2001). Hence, the concept of migrant transnationalism rests on the idea that migrants, living their lives in two (or more) nation-states, remain a part of the fabric of everyday life and social relations in their home country; simultaneously, they become a part of the socioeconomic processes in their receiving country, thereby rendering home and host society a single arena for social action (Schiller, Basch, and Blanc-Szanton 1995; Portes, Guarnizo, and Landolt 1999; Levitt and Schiller 2004; Dahinden 2005). These transnational linkages are multistranded (e.g., economic, social, cultural, political, institutional, and emotional) and entwined in the lived experiences of migrants and their left-behind families and communities (Levitt 2001b; Espiritu 2003; Kelly and Lusis 2006).

An extensive literature also focuses on migrants' premigratory experiences and cultural codes as a lens to understanding various pathways to immigrant adaptation in the host society (Hondagneu-Sotelo 1994; Kibria 1995; Foner 1997b; Lim and Wieling 2004; Niekerk 2004; Read 2004; Bhattacharya 2008). The bulk of these studies have shown that migrants' premigratory cultural codes and the social practices they brought with them continued to shape their behavior in the host society, serving as some sort of "tool kit" or repertoire (Hannerz 1996). Using this tool kit, migrants made sense of their new experiences and constructed different "strategies of action" (Swidler 1986). Simultaneously, these studies have demonstrated that migrants' premigratory cultural norms, beliefs, and behavioral patterns may undergo a change or become "reinvented" in their new environment as a result of new circumstances. Premigratory cultural legacies shape migrants' actions, choices, and behaviors across all aspects of life, be it family life, gender relations, relationships with the legal institutions, social mobility, educational performance, labor market, or welfare behavior (Beger and Hein 2001; Niekerk 2004; Read 2004; Bhattacharya 2008; Hook and Bean 2009).

The cultural scholarship discussed above also gave rise to a sociolegal literature on "migration and legal culture/pluralism." This literature is based on the understanding that migrants carry their own "legal baggage" (values, attitudes toward the law, entrenched behavioral patterns, accustomed social practices, and informal norms) to their host country and continue to draw on them when constructing different adaptation strategies in new legal environments (Menski 1993, 2008; Shah 2005, 2009; Ballard 2006; Kubal 2013a, 2013b). Studies have described the implications of culturally mediated understandings of the law on immigrants' behavior when they come into contact with the legal system of the host society (Bauer 1999; Ta 1999; Beger and Hein 2001; Kubal 2013a). For instance, Bauer's (1999) study demonstrated how a Ukrainian immigrant's prior legal experiences and phobias toward the legal system led him to refuse a court-appointed lawyer, fearing that a court-appointed attorney was part of the KGB. Another body of scholarly work examined how migrants preserved and reinvented their premigratory social practices and norms, developing various adaptive responses to their new legal environment (Ballard 2007; Menski 2008; Shah 2009). In his study of South Asian immigrant communities in Britain, Menski (2008) showed how South Asians simultaneously followed English law and their premigratory traditional laws, leading to the emergence of new forms of hybrid legal rules in the UK. All in all, these sociolegal insights on migrant legal adaptation provided nuanced accounts of how immigrant groups interpret and relate themselves to state law and reproduce their own "legal order" and community life in a new environment. Ultimately, this leads to the formation of a pluralistic legal environment in the host country.

As this section shows, dominant immigrant adaptation frameworks were constructed with regard to the experiences of immigrant communities in Western-style democracies. Moreover, the frameworks presented above tend to describe migrants as passive, agencyless actors who are gradually expected to abandon their premigratory cultural legacies and ways of life, eventually "melting" into the host society. One exception lies in "migration and legal culture/pluralism" scholarship, which has demonstrated that migrants *do* carry their own legal culture to their host society and rely on it when devising different adaptation strategies. But, again, legal culture scholarship primarily concerns the experiences of immigrant communities in the context of Western countries, whereas little scholarly investigation of similar issues in relation to non-Western, nondemocratic migration contexts exists. Given the sociopolitical and cultural differences between Western-style democracies and nondemocratic contexts, it is rather naive to assume that one analytical lens remains sufficient to understand migrant legal adaptation in corrupt or weak rule-of-law environments. These arguments, in turn, necessitate a review of the state-of-the-art on migrant legal adaptation such that parallels and differences among various immigration legal regimes can be identified. With this in mind the next section provides a review of migrant legal adaptation scholarship.

MIGRANT LEGAL ADAPTATION DEBATES

Two central (and interlinked) themes emerge in the literature on migrant legal adaptation. First, an extensive amount of literature focuses on the legal environment (immigration laws and institutions within the legal system) as a key factor determining the quality and character of immigrant adaptation (e.g., Coutin 2003a; De Genova 2004; Bloch and Schuster 2005; Menjívar 2006; Menjívar and Abrego 2012; Sigona 2012; Kubal 2013a; Hallett 2014). Building on the segmented assimilation model (Portes and Zhou 1993), studies have shown that immigration laws critically shape daily life and adaptation among immigrants by creating legal categories and statuses that delimit their chances in the labor market (Gleeson 2010), wages (Takei, Saenz, and Li 2009), health-seeking behavior (Viladrich 2012), educational opportunities (Gonzales 2011), and access to social services (Fujiwara

2008) and housing (McConnell 2013). Most of these studies illustrate that the state of being undocumented becomes embedded in the lives of immigrants and gradually permeates their lifeworlds, rendering them physically present and socially active yet legally nonexistent. Drawing on her empirical study of Salvadoran and Guatemalan immigrants in the United States, Coutin (2003b) shows that such legally nonexistent migrants are vulnerable to deportation, confined to low-wage jobs, and denied basic rights including access to decent housing, education, food, and health care. Another relevant study comes from Menjívar and Abrego (2012), who showed that Central American immigrants lacking legal recognition also experienced "legal violence," a legally sanctioned structural and symbolic violence embedded in legal practices, actively enforced through formal mechanisms, and, therefore, viewed as "normal" and legitimate because it "is the law." A similar "law-first" approach can also be found in the European context, where researchers affiliated with the Migrant Integration Policy Index (MIPEX)[1] project define migrant integration by referring to the factors associated with the legal immigration regime, which includes migrants' legal status, residence rights, citizenship, and access to rights, goods, services, and resources (Huddleston 2008).

A wide array of research also explores how immigration laws produce various forms and categories of "migrant illegality" (Calavita 1998; De Genova 2002; Jordan and Düvell 2002; Menjívar 2006; Willen 2007b; Goldring, Berinstein, and Bernhard 2009; Kubal 2013c; Ngai 2014). Much of this research argues that migrant illegality is legally constructed since immigration laws restrict the entry and movement of some noncitizens, while allowing the admission of others, thereby producing documented, undocumented, and "in-between" statuses. Based on a review of the migration illegality literature, Kubal (2013c, 556–57) presents a diversity of terms and categories used to conceptualize legal statuses and categories: in-betweens (Schuck 1998), mixed-status households (Chavez 1998), liminal migrants (Menjívar 2006), learning to be illegal (Gonzales 2011), deportees with unrecognized claims (De Genova and Peutz 2010), semicompliant (Ruhs and Anderson 2010), legally illegal (Rigo 2010), civically stratified (Morris 2003), precarious (Goldring, Berinstein, and Bernhard 2009), quasi-legal (Düvell 2008), a-legal (Lindahl 2010), or semilegal (Kubal 2009). Since these legal categories grant or limit immigrants' access to resources, rights, and benefits in the host society, immigration laws create a new form of stratification and significantly shape immigrants' daily lives and adaptation paths. De Genova (2002) argues that immigration laws should be viewed as a deliberate strategy that nation-states deploy to produce cheap and legally unprotected undocumented migrants so that they can be included in the labor market under a condition of "enforced and protracted vulnerability." In her study of immigration laws in Spain, Calavita (1998) also found that immigration laws were written and enforced in a way that made it nearly impossible for immigrants to retain legal status over time. This implied that Spanish immigration laws aim primarily to control the lives of immigrants rather than control immigration. Thus, migrant illegality represents not simply a form of legal status or sociopolitical condition but also "a mode of being-in-the-world" (Willen 2007a).

The above analysis of migrant legal adaptation debates generates two important conclusions. First, although "the cake is sliced in different ways," one idea emerges as consistent across studies: they emphasize the enduring power of the legal environment (that is, the immigration laws and institutions of the legal system) as a key factor shaping the nature and forms of immigrant adaptation. Yet overemphasizing the host country's legal framework may result in underestimating the role of the migrants' agency, including their capacity to navigate any legal restrictions. Second, and connected to the first point, while the aforementioned studies uncovered how and why migrant illegality is produced, not much has been said about the agency of undocumented migrants and how they organize their daily lives and develop alternative adaptation paths. Rather than focusing on migrants' agency, as Ruhs and Anderson (2010) observe, many studies tend to portray undocumented migrants either as "victims" of exploitation or as "villains" who break laws. Even those studies that argue for the necessity of considering migrants' agency emphasize the importance of institutional and legal factors. Indeed, notable exceptions demonstrate that migrants are not merely passive actors constrained by structural factors but are also capable of negotiating and challenging the legal system (Delgado 1993; Hagan 1994; Coutin 2003c; Zlolniski 2006; Chimienti and Achermann 2007; Ellermann 2010; Sigona 2012; Kubal 2013a). Focusing on immigrant legalization strategies in the United States, Coutin (2003a) showed that migrants have agency and can respond to authorities' political maneuverings. Another example can be found in Hagan's (1994) book *Deciding to Be Legal*, in which she illustrates how Mayan immigrants creatively interpret and respond to the loosely specified documentation requirements of the US Immigration Reform and Control Act of 1986. Yet, despite their focus on migrant agency, these accounts also seem to reinforce the law-first perspective and stress the role of the legal environment by focusing on migrants' efforts aimed at following or challenging immigration law in their struggle to change their legal status. Consequently, migrant legal adaptation is primarily understood in reference to the legal status of migrants, underscoring the role of the nation-state and its immigration laws as key analytical features to understanding various paths, as well as the quality and timescale of immigrant adaptation.

The persistence of law-first perspectives is understandable, given that they reflect the sociolegal context of Western-style democracies, where the rule of law is embedded in the national culture. But insights developed in Western contexts may not adequately explain how migrants build relationships with the law in hybrid political regimes characterized by corruption and a weak rule of law. While recognizing the importance of law-first perspectives, I respond to Twining's call, proposed in his seminal paper "Globalization and Comparative Law" (1999), to move beyond the Western-centric paradigm. In doing so, I put forth new theoretical insights for understanding migrant legal adaptation in non-Western migration regimes. Building on this previous research, particularly Sigona's (2012) suggestion that we develop a historically and geographically differentiated analysis of migration regimes, I aim in this book to extend the state of the art by investigating (1) how the effects and manifestations of "undocumentedness" (or illegality) depend on geographical, political, and historical factors and (2) whether undocumented migrants are not just passive actors constrained by structural barriers but can also invent strategies and maneuver around the system. Hence, we need a more context-sensitive understanding of "migrant undocumentedness" that takes into account how lacking a legal status intersects with, on the one hand, the broader sociolegal environment, economic system, and type of political regime and, on the other hand, migrants' agency, informal strategies, experiences, and premigration cultural codes. Thus, migrant "undocumentedness" or "illegality" does not automatically deprive migrants of their agency, but it may actually entice them to resort to alternative avenues, thereby allowing them to avoid constraints imposed by draconian immigration laws and policies (see, e.g., Garcés-Mascareñas 2010; Donato and Armenta 2011; Urinboyev and Polese 2016). Drawing from the transnational sociolegal ethnography of Uzbek migrants in Russia and their home village in Uzbekistan, this book moves away from treating migrants as passive actors and identifies migrants' agency in how they negotiate and cope with structural barriers and labor market uncertainties through their interactions with informal "legal orders" and street-based adaptation channels. Hence, an examination of how migrants organize their daily lives and build relationships with the law and informal "legal orders" in a corrupt and weak rule-of-law context (i.e., hybrid political regimes) can lead to nuanced theorizing about migrant legal adaptation. Before presenting the framework for understanding migrant legal adaptation in hybrid political regimes, in the sections that follow I present a brief review of the literature on hybrid political regimes. This review provides contextual information for understanding my perspective on migrant agency and legal adaptation in hybrid regime contexts.

UNDERSTANDING HYBRID POLITICAL REGIMES

Following the collapse of the Soviet Union, and the subsequent rise of democracy as a legitimate form of governance in the global political discourse, the number of political regimes that are neither fully democratic nor conventionally authoritarian has steadily increased. Understandably, these developments led to extensive discussions in academic circles regarding how to understand and conceptualize regimes that do not fit within conventional classifications (Diamond 2002; Levitsky and Way 2002; Howard and Roessler 2006; Munck 2006; Wigell 2008; Brownlee 2009; Morlino 2009; Gilbert and Mohseni 2011). Different terms and names have been proposed to conceptualize these regimes: hybrid political regimes, competitive authoritarianism, electoral authoritarianism, partially liberalized regimes, semidemocracy, pseudo-democracy, illiberal democracy, semiauthoritarianism, soft authoritarianism, defective democracy, or Freedom House's "partly free" (Zakaria 1997; Carothers 2002; Diamond 2002; Levitsky and Way 2002; Schedler 2015). Regardless of the label we choose, one thing is clear: such "in-between" regimes have become a common and resilient phenomenon to the extent that nearly one-third of all states fall into the "political gray zone," straddling full-fledged democracy and outright dictatorship (Diamond 2002; Levitsky and Way 2002). The proportion of such "in-between" regimes, in Diamond's (2002) view, may further increase if a highly demanding standard of democracy is used, which covers not only democratic elections but also the solid protection of civil liberties under a strong rule of law.

As discussed above, the present era is characterized by a global proliferation of hybrid polities that necessitate new approaches and tools to understand development trajectories and institutional configurations in such "in-between" regimes. Archetypal hybrid political regimes, such as those in Malaysia, Russia, Turkey, Ukraine, and Zambia remain stable and resilient (Levitsky and Way 2002). As a result, classic taxonomies and concepts no longer capture the authoritarian regimes plugged into global economies that are becoming highly innovative in their legitimacy building and image making, thereby obscuring the role of democratic rules and procedures, institutions, and multicultural lifestyles. This is further exacerbated by the emergence of authoritarian leaders in liberal democracies, who use legal means, economic regulation, and anti-immigrant sentiments to discredit democratic governance and coerce populations into particular lifestyles. Reflecting on these complexities, Wigell (2008, 236–42) presented a list of electoral and constitutional criteria to distinguish liberal democracies from nondemocratic regimes. These criteria are (1) free elections, (2) fair elections, (3) competitive elections, (4) inclusive elections, (5) freedom of organization, (6) freedom of expression, (7) the right to alternative information, (8) freedom from discrimination, (9) electoral empowerment, (10) electoral integrity, (11) electoral sovereignty, (12) electoral irreversibility, (13) executive accountability, (14) legal accountability, (15) bureaucratic integrity, and (16) local government accountability. In truth the weakness or absence of these criteria serves to distinguish Western-style liberal democracies from hybrid political regimes. These points lead me to question the applicability and validity of existing migrant legal adaptation frameworks in the context of hybrid political regimes, characterized by a weak rule of law, dysfunctional institutions, corruption, large shadow economies, a poor human rights record, and a weak civil society.

CONCEPTUALIZING MIGRANT LEGAL ADAPTATION IN A HYBRID POLITICAL REGIME CONTEXT

As outlined in the previous sections, the sociolegal context of hybrid political regimes is characterized by a weak rule of law, dysfunctional institutions, and widespread corruption and informality. Under these circumstances we can assume that migrants do not experience the rule-of-law system but rather invent various tactics and strategies to adapt to the existing "unrule-of-law" environment to "get things done." This means that migrants may produce various informal "legal orders" that provide alternative (to state law) means to regulate their working lives and seek redress for their problems. In the legal anthropological scholarship such a normative pluralism is referred to as "legal pluralism" (Merry 1990; Griffiths 2003). Legal pluralism emphasizes the coexistence and clash of multiple sets of rules that mold people's social behavior: the law of the nation-state, indigenous customs and rules, religious decrees, moral codes, and practical norms for social life (Nuijten and Anders 2007). Classic legal anthropology studies and the more recent legal pluralism scholarship documented the emergence of "semi-autonomous social fields" or "non-state forms of normative ordering," with their own forms of regulation and informal norms, many of which contradict state law (Moore 1973; Tamanha 2000; Roberts 2005; Pirie 2006). From this point of view state law merely represents one among many other normative orders within society. Thus, no single, integrated set of rules in any society exists, whether codified in law, sanctified in religion, or established as the rules of daily social behavior. Quite simply, there is no uncontested universal normative code that guides people's lives and actions; the very nature of the legal order is determined by the outcomes of the struggles and the interplay among plural normative orders.

Russia, as an archetypal hybrid regime with a weak rule of law, rampant corruption, and a large shadow economy (Ledeneva 2006; Cameron and Orenstein 2012; Petrov, Lipman, and Hale 2014), provides an excellent context in which to more closely examine migrant legal adaptation from a legal pluralism perspective. Accordingly, within the context of hybrid regimes such as Russia, where millions of migrants are concentrated in a shadow economy, the study of migrant legal adaptation should account for the interplay between (a) migrants' agency and the "legal baggage" that migrants carry to their host country and (b) an informality and a weak rule-of-law environment, possibly creating an avenue for informal, innovative adaptation practices. Migrants' "legal baggage" may contain different values, different attitudes, and different patterns of behavior toward state law and its institutions (Kurkchiyan 2011; Kubal 2013b). Thus, the host country's legal environment may become even more legally plural with the arrival of new legal cultures. The combination of these two features—migrants' agency and the specifics of a hybrid regime—may produce new forms of informal governance and legal order. Hence, the legal pluralism perspective allows us to move debates about the legal incorporation of immigrants beyond national frameworks of state law to open up the concept of the law along those lines suggested in the legal pluralism scholarship.

While acknowledging the importance of existing migrant legal adaptation frameworks, I propose a framework that incorporates "informality and a weak rule of law" as key analytical factors to understand migrant legal adaptation in hybrid political regimes. The core argument is that the legal adaptations of migrant workers in hybrid political regimes such as Russia should be understood not only through migrants' legalization efforts and involvement with state institutions but also in terms of their knowledge of street law and informal rules, connections to street institutions, and their capacity to integrate into the corrupt and weak rule-of-law environment. Thus, drawing on the legal pluralism perspective, this book proposes a new framework, suggesting that the law and legal adaptation should be defined more broadly, beyond state immigration laws, policies, and institutions, and encompass informal "legal orders." These informal legal orders include (1) migrants' agency and their "legal baggage" (i.e., informal [and nonlegal] practices, rules, strategies, networks, and structures used by migrants to follow, avoid, or maneuver around the laws); (2) informal, rent-seeking behaviors and practices among state officials (e.g., immigration officers, policemen, and border guards) in charge of enforcing immigration laws and policies; (3) street institutions (e.g., racketeers, intermediaries, and former law-enforcement officers) used to enforce contracts and legalization; and (4) transnational networks, interactions, and pressures that shape migrants' experiences in the host society.

METHOD, APPROACH, AND FIELDWORK

This book is based on a multisited transnational ethnography of Uzbek migrant workers in Russia and in their home village in Uzbekistan. I collected the ethnographic material during 14 months of fieldwork in Moscow, Russia, and the Fergana Valley, Uzbekistan, between January of 2014 and August of 2018. These field sites were chosen because Moscow is the capital city and largest megapolis in Russia, featuring the highest number of migrant workers. Therefore, Moscow's attitudes and policies regarding labor migration greatly influence developments in other regions of Russia, where local officials, politicians, and journalists reproduce Moscow's policies in their home territory (Abashin 2016; Schenk 2018). Likewise, I chose the Fergana Valley because it is the primary migrant-sending region in Uzbekistan, given its population density and high unemployment rate (Laruelle 2007). In addition, I myself hail from a village in the Fergana Valley, a reality that enabled me to participate in the daily life of migrants and their home village, thereby becoming *svoi* ("one of us, those who belong to our circle"), a term widely used in the post-Soviet context to refer to a person who has internalized the norms and values of a particular social group. Thus, owing to my Uzbek ethnicity, village origin, cultural competence, and language skills (Uzbek and Russian), I was well-connected to the Uzbek migrant worker community in Moscow and their left-behind families and communities in the Fergana Valley.

The ethnographic material was primarily collected through observations and informal interviews, supplemented with regular contact with informants over smartphone-based instant messaging applications such as Telegram Messenger, WhatsApp, and IMO. Because I collected ethnographic material in two different locations, I present it separately for each locale. This allows me to provide a detailed and clear description of my fieldwork, including the data-collection strategies and the selection of informants and fieldwork sites.

First, in Moscow I conducted observations and interviews at construction sites, bazaars, *dachas* (cottages), farms, dormitories, shared apartments, cafés, railway stations, and on the streets of Moscow, where Uzbek and other Central Asian migrants work, live, and socialize. My observations frequently turned into informal chats and interviews owing to the numerous questions that arose on the spur of the moment. I focused primarily on migrants' everyday lives, informal adaptation strategies, knowledge of the state and street laws, and their interactions with their employers, state institutions (e.g., police, immigration, and border officials), and street actors (e.g., racketeers and middlemen). In addition, I applied various strategies during my fieldwork. These strategies included renting mattress space in shared apartments where migrants lived, being present at migrants' workplaces at different times, participating in migrants' daily lives, accompanying migrants on the streets and via public transportation where they are often stopped and frisked by police officers, inviting migrants for lunch or dinner in cafés, and "hanging out" with migrants in bars. In addition, I maintained regular contact with informants via smartphone-based social media applications, where they share various news items, videos, and photos; update one another with Moscow and village news; and spread gossip and rumors when someone acts unfairly toward other villagers. Rigorous procedures and techniques for collecting data were applied: observation and informal interviews were documented in field diaries in addition to audio recordings.

Second, and simultaneously, to keep up with the pace of developments in Uzbek migrants' lives in Moscow, I conducted observations and informal interviews in the Fergana Valley of Uzbekistan, in the village of Shabboda, from whence most migrants I met in Moscow originated. My primary aim was to explore the processes of everyday material, emotional, social, and symbolic exchanges between Shabboda and Moscow and how these transnational interactions shaped the everyday lives and adaptation of Uzbek migrants in Moscow. Given my *svoi* status, I enjoyed direct access to all social spaces within the village, enabling me to gather firsthand information about Uzbek migrants' and their left-behind families' and communities' daily transnational interactions. The role of smartphones was crucial in transnational relationships. Many villagers I met possessed smartphones (Artel, Huawei, Samsung, Sony Xperia, and even the latest iPhone) running the Android

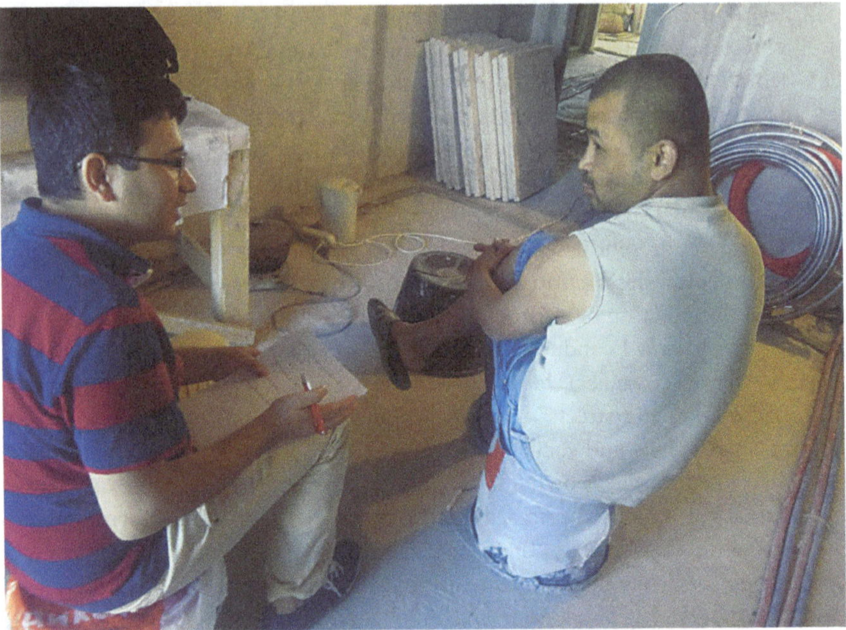

FIGURE 2. The author interviews an Uzbek migrant worker at a construction site in Moscow province. July 2015. Photo by Muhiddin Yursunaliev.

operating system (or iOS), thanks to remittances sent from Moscow. During my fieldwork I regularly visited migrants' left-behind families and carried out observations and informal interviews at the village "gossip hotspots" such as the *guzar* (community socializing space), *choyxona* (teahouse), *gaps* (regular get-togethers), and life-cycle events (e.g., weddings and funerals) where many villagers, including women, children, and religious leaders, came together on a daily basis and conducted the bulk of the village's information exchanges. Because I met more than ten villagers on a daily basis during various social events, situations, and spaces, it is difficult to pinpoint the exact number of individuals with whom I chatted during these site visits. Instead, the narrative I provide in the subsequent chapters can be understood as a composite of the voices of the hundreds of villagers I encountered during daily visits to the *guzar, choyxona, gaps*, wedding feasts, circumcision ceremonies, and funerals.

In addition to transnational ethnography, between July and August of 2015 I also conducted one hundred semistructured (in-depth) interviews with Central Asian (Kyrgyz, Tajik, and Uzbek) migrant workers. I aimed to investigate to what extent the findings from this ethnographic study (observations and informal interviews) are common among Central Asian migrants in Russia, so as to add more depth and detailed information to the ethnographic material and allow for some degree of generalization. I conducted interviews face-to-face, through a conversational process, which lasted from 35 minutes to an hour. The interview questionnaire consisted of 91 open-ended questions and covered 15 different themes: (1) background and demographic questions; (2) migrant labor market and working conditions; (3) immigration laws, actors, and legal protection; (4) work permit and residence registration; (5) reentry ban and deportations; (6) street institutions, such as racketeers; (7) middlemen; (8) relations between migrant workers and the police; (9) corruption and bribes; (10) relations between migrant workers and immigration officials; (11) migrant workers' legal culture and their knowledge and experiences of immigration and labor laws; (12) migrant workers' informal coping strategies; (13) discrimination and racism; (14) migrants' social networks; and (15) migrants' transnational ties and practices. In selecting migrants for in-depth interviews, I paid special attention to diversity across ethnicity, country of origin, citizenship, age, gender, social status, occupation, educational background, Russian-language skills, legal status, and migration experiences (experienced or newly arrived migrant). Regarding sampling, I used random, snowball, and purposive sampling techniques to increase the diversity of my informants. I conducted interviews at 15 different locations in Moscow city and the Moscow province, in diverse settings and situations such as Uzbek cafés and *choyxonas*, bazaars, shared apartments, construction sites, *dachas*, parking garages, auto service centers, dormitories, furniture workshops, and random street interviews in localities known for high migrant clustering.

Eleven expert interviews were conducted in Moscow in 2017 in collaboration with my colleagues Anna-Liisa Heusala and Kaarina Aitamurto from the University of Helsinki research project "Migration, Shadow Economy and Parallel Legal Orders" (the project of which I am also part), funded by the Kone foundation.[2] The interviewed experts included migration lawyers, human rights activists, journalists, representatives from migrant rights' nongovernmental organizations, and representatives of the Trade Union of Migrant Workers and the Federation of Migrants in Russia. During these interviews, questions focused on the history and evolution of Russian immigration laws and policies, migrants' working conditions and relationships with employers, migrants' legal culture and the relationship with the law, migration and the shadow economy, residence registration and work permit rules, the culture of informality, administrative developments, and the specifics of the Russian legal system.

The use of multiple data collection methods (observation, informal interviews, semistructured interviews, and expert interviews) generated a rich stock of empirical material about migrants' legal adaptation strategies. More specifically, I was able to collect original empirical data on (1) migrants' knowledge and experiences of immigration and labor laws; (2) factors that incite migrants to disengage from the formal legal system; (3) migrants' agency, which consisted of alternative adaptation strategies and techniques migrants employ to comply with, avoid, or maneuver around the law; (4) migrants' interactions with immigration officials, policemen, and border guards; (5) migrants' labor arrangements, including the informal, parallel labor market, and everyday life under the conditions of the shadow economy; and (6) the street world, including how, why, and when migrants approach middlemen and racketeers. In addition, I collected data on (7) the role of civil society in migration processes; (8) the impact of corruption and a weak rule of law on migrant labor market and adaptation strategies; (9) migrants' smartphone-based transnational environments, including the various collective and individual coping strategies they employed within that environment, the ways they managed and maintained transnational relationships with their left-behind communities, and the ways they reproduced and enacted their village-level practices, norms, and identities in their daily lives in Moscow; and (10) the nuances and specifics of the Russian migration regimes in a global, comparative perspective. Although the empirical material presented in this book focuses largely on Uzbek migrants' legal adaptation strategies, it is important to emphasize that these adaptation and survival strategies are common to all Central Asian migrants in Russia and resonate with the experiences of other migrants from Azerbaijan, Armenia, Syria, Moldova, and Ukraine (see, e.g., Laruelle 2007; Malakhov 2014; Reeves 2015; Kubal 2016a, 2016b; Kuznetsova and Round 2018; Schenk 2018; Markovska, Serdyuk, and Sokurenko 2019).

Despite my efforts to ensure diversity, most interviewees were male; I was able to locate only a few female informants. This limitation can be explained in part by the actual gender composition of Central Asian migrants (Uzbeks and Tajiks) in Russia: 80 percent are male. Almost half of migrants from Kyrgyzstan are female, however, owing to historical and cultural factors. Historically, Uzbeks and Tajiks are considered the sedentary nations of Central Asia, with resilient community-based traditional institutions (*mahalla*) that survived Soviet cultural interventions and still preserve strong social and gender hierarchies, whereas nomadic nations of the region such as Kazakh and Kyrgyz were more receptive to Soviet modernization policies (Levi 2007). This explains why the majority of Uzbek and Tajik migrants are male, while women in Kyrgyzstan enjoy more mobility as a result of a less patriarchal social structure. Having said this, I want to emphasize that the legal adaptation and survival strategies of female Central Asian migrant workers do not differ significantly from those of male migrants in terms of their experiences of the shadow economy, weak rule of law, and corrupt legal system when interacting with labor market actors (employers, intermediaries) and state institutions and actors (police officers, immigration officials, and border guards). These observations have been confirmed by a growing body of literature that covers the experiences of Central Asian female migrant workers in Russia (Tyuryukanova 2011; Agadjanian and Zotova 2012; Agadjanian, Gorina, and Menjívar 2014; Gabdulhakov 2019).

During my field research I strived for spontaneity and sudden discoveries and treated migrants as experts on the migration situation in Russia. In other words I focused on their daily experiences with both formal and informal institutions as a lens through which to understand the functioning of the Russian migration regime. My position in relation to my informants remained fluid, sliding between "insider" and "outsider." I was an "insider" when relations between migrants, their left-behind families, middlemen, and Russian employers were smooth, but I became an "outsider" when conflict arose among parties. In such circumstances I approached each actor privately and maintained the confidentiality of information. This research took place with informants who were fully informed about its purpose, methods, and the use of the data. To ensure maximum anonymity, the names and whereabouts of informants have been changed, and only the most general information about the informants and fieldwork sites are provided.

TERMS AND CONCEPTS

As illustrated in the previous sections, I use a variety of terms and concepts to define the regimes that combine democratic and authoritarian elements. In line with Gilbert and Mohseni (2011) I employ the phrase *hybrid political regime* to refer to nondemocratic, nonauthoritarian regimes rather than using *democracy* or *authoritarianism* qualified by adjectives, which may lead to conceptual confusion and conceptual stretching.

The term *legal culture* is also frequently used in this book. A legal culture is one of the most central concepts in the sociology of law. There are many interpretations of this concept, as evidenced by the ongoing tension between legal positivists and sociolegal scholars. As described by Nelken (2004), most scholarly work continues to identify a legal culture within a nation-state, thereby focusing on facts about institutions, such as the number and role of lawyers, law enforcement, various forms of behavior such as litigation and prison rates, and how judges are appointed and controlled. Another account gleaned from scholarly works maintains that researchers must distinguish between the legal culture of "those members of society who perform specialized legal tasks" (internal legal culture) and that of other citizens (external legal culture). For example, Friedman (1975, 194) asserts that a legal culture may also represent "bodies of custom organically related to the culture as a whole." In this book I utilize the concept of "legal culture" in broader terms, encompassing not only the (state) legal system and traditional legal institutions but also various informal (nonlegal) forms of normative ordering, such as unofficial laws or customary practices based on religious and cultural values.

I frequently refer to "migrant agency" when discussing migrant legal adaptation processes. My understanding of migrant agency relies on Emirbayer and Mische's (1998, 963) conceptualization of human agency as the "temporary embedded engagement by actors of different structural environments through the interplay of habit, imagination, and judgment which both reproduces and transforms those structures in interactive response to the problems posed by changing situations." I also rely on Sewell's (1992, 20) definition of *human agency*: "To be an agent means to be capable of exerting some degree of control over the social relations in which one is enmeshed, which in turn implies the ability to transform those social relations to some degree."

We also need to define the terms in relation to noncitizens and their legal statuses. I use the terms *migrant* and *immigrant* interchangeably, given that the distinction between a permanent and temporary stay has become blurred in an increasingly transnationalized world. With regard to one's legal status, I use *undocumented* to describe people living or working in a foreign country without the documents prescribed by the host country's laws. In agreement with Kubal (2013c) I refrain from using the term *illegal migrants* because of its stigmatizing and politicized nature.

STRUCTURE OF THE BOOK

Chapter 2 discusses the impact of Russian immigration laws and policies on the formation of a shadow economy characterized by a large-scale migrant labor force. The chapter shows that Russian immigration laws and policies have produced unintended consequences; that is, rather than reducing the number of undocumented migrants, those laws and policies further pushed migrants into a shadow economy. This resulted from the Russian legal environment—which is characterized by rampant corruption, a weak rule of law, and arbitrary enforcement. These features imply that even migrants possessing all of the required immigration papers cannot be certain that they will avoid legal problems when they come into contact with Russian authorities. Owing to the complicated legalization procedures and the arbitrariness of laws, many migrants resort to working in the shadow economy, where they can work without documents. Hence, a distinctive feature of Russia's migration regime is the rather large and continuous presence of a shadow economy heavily reliant on cheap and legally unprotected migrant labor. Thus, chapter 2 concludes by arguing for the need to consider the role of that shadow economy and the weak rule-of-law culture when investigating migrants' legal adaptation to hybrid contexts, such as that in contemporary Russia.

Chapter 3 presents the case study group—Uzbek migrant workers—on whom the empirical data and analysis focuses. I argue that focusing on only the host country's legal environment cannot explain satisfactorily the nature and quality of migrants' legal adaptation. Hence, looking beyond the host country's legal environment, we also need to understand migrants' "legal baggage," which they bring with them from their home to their host country—their attitudes toward the law, interpretations of legality and illegality, moral codes, religious values, established behavioral patterns, and the accustomed social practices that they internalized prior to their migratory experiences. Migrants import and adapt these premigratory cultural and normative repertoires to their host state, especially when they work and live under the conditions of a shadow economy. A better understanding of these processes can provide nuanced insights into migrants' adaptations to a new legal environment. Thus, chapter 3 provides the reader with the contextual information on Uzbek migrants' legal culture, which will prove instructive in understanding the empirical material in the chapters that follow.

Chapter 4 focuses on the migrant labor market in Russia and presents the ethnographic study of Uzbek migrants in the construction sector, where they work under the conditions of a shadow economy. This chapter shows that the use of a large-scale migrant labor force under these conditions led to the emergence of a "parallel world of migrants," based on its own economy, legal order, trust, and mutual aid networks. The existence of such an informal infrastructure allows migrants to devise specific integration and "legalization" strategies, create an informal job market, and establish informal social safety nets to share the livelihood risks and deal with emergency situations. At first glance these informal practices may come across as spontaneous responses; however, when we take their magnitude into consideration, they become a more or less institutionalized custom in migrants' daily lives. This chapter concludes by suggesting that the study of migrants' legal adaptation should look beyond the facade of the formal labor market and immigration laws and resituate the focus on migrants' agency and actual coping strategies under the conditions of shadow economy employment.

Chapter 5 presents empirical material on Uzbek migrants' everyday encounters with street institutions—namely, protection rackets, middlemen, and (former) employees of law-enforcement institutions who act on an informal basis as protection racketeers. I argue that street institutions are a salient feature of the Russian migrant labor market, where many migrants work without written employment contracts and experience problems securing payment for their work. Given the complete lack of security, migrants seek redress from street actors who provide alternative (to the state) forms of contract enforcement, debt recovery, and dispute settlement through threats, violence, and street law. I conclude the chapter by arguing that the legal adaptation of migrants in Russia must be understood not only through migrants' capacity to comply with immigration and labor laws but also in terms of their interactions with street-based legal orders that offer alternative forms of redress, legal adaptation, and economic security.

Chapter 6 examines Uzbek migrants' everyday encounters with two Russian state-level actors—namely, police officers and migration officials charged with the enforcement of immigration and labor laws. I argue that Russian policies of immigration control have further pushed migrants into the shadow economy rather than reducing the incentives for informal employment. This results from the vested interests of relevant Russian state-level actors (e.g., police and immigration officials), each of whom view the shadow economy as a *kormushka* (feeding-trough) and attempt to "take their own piece" of it. These patterns can be gleaned by attending to migrant workers' everyday experiences, tactics, and coping strategies when they try to negotiate the "rules of the game" with Russian migration officials and police officers. I conclude that although the processes and strategies mentioned above may come across as signs of corruption and a weak rule of law, they actually constitute a real mode of migration governance and, thus, reveal the broader sociolegal context in which migrants' legal adaptation takes place. The intrinsic message of the chapter is that the study of migrants' legal adaptation should move beyond Western-centric perspectives emphasizing the merciless application of immigration laws (e.g., "legal violence," "legal nonexistence," and "deportability"). To better understand migrants' relationships to the host state's laws and institutions in hybrid regime contexts, a new analytical lens encompassing not only legal centralistic approaches, but also legal pluralistic perspectives (i.e., informal norms, rules and practices), should be introduced.

Chapter 7 presents the life histories of three Uzbek migrants (all male) in Moscow who experienced hardships and challenges during their first five years and then successfully integrated into the migrant labor market and the host society as a result of their knowledge of street life and informal rules. These case studies illustrate how migrants, despite their undocumented status, remain resilient and resourceful and display a significant capacity to maneuver around structural constraints, such as complicated residence registration and work permit rules, punitive laws, social exclusion, racism, and the lack of a social safety net. I argue that migrants are not just passive, agencyless subjects constrained by a restrictive legal environment but that they are capable of shaping and adapting their daily routines, mundane social interactions, and "legalization" strategies to the conditions of a shadow economy, a corrupt law-enforcement system, and a weak rule of law. Hence, the meanings and everyday experiences of "illegality" are geographically, politically, and historically contingent. Illegality does not automatically deprive migrants of their agency; in fact, it may incite them to produce new forms of informal governance and legal orders (informal adaptation) enabling them to avoid constraints imposed by restrictive immigration laws and policies. I conclude the chapter by suggesting that we need a more context-sensitive understanding of "migrant undocumentedness" that takes into account how the absence of legal status intersects with, on the one hand, the sociolegal environment, broader sociopolitical context, and regime type and, on the other hand, migrants' agency, experiences, and history.

Finally, in chapter 8 I bring together the primary empirical and theoretical findings of the previous chapters and consider them against the conceptual framework outlined in this introductory chapter. Key points, the contributions toward the study of immigrant adaptation, as well as debates and avenues for future research, are discussed. I discuss the distinct framework developed in the Russian context, placing it within the broader migration and sociolegal literature on immigrant legal adaptation, as well as its relevance and the scope of applicability to the study of immigrant legal adaptation in other hybrid regimes.

Migration, the Shadow Economy, and Parallel Legal Orders in Russia

Traditionally seen as a country of emigration, Russia has become one of the main migration hubs worldwide following the collapse of the Soviet Union. Thus, two dominant trends emerge when analyzing Russia's post-Soviet immigration history. In the 1990s, migratory flows to Russia were characterized largely by forced migration, where more than 10 million people, predominantly "ethnic" Russians, returned to Russia owing to political instability and rising nationalism in the former Soviet republics (Laruelle 2007). An extensive body of scholarly literature focused on the forced migration and resettlement of ethnic Russians and other Russian-speaking communities to their ethnic homeland (Messina 1994; Pilkington 1998; Pilkington and Flynn 2006; Flynn 2007). Soon after the turn of the century, however, economic factors affected the volume, whereby large-scale labor migration became the dominant trend (Demintseva 2017). These migratory processes were driven largely by the rapidly growing Russian economy and the declining working-age population, on the one hand, and economic stagnation, poverty, high unemployment rates, and extremely low salaries in other post-Soviet republics, on the other (Denisenko and Chernina 2017). Migrant labor represented the primary source available to make up for shortages in the domestic labor force and to meet the needs of Russia's oil-fueled construction boom. Another contributing factor to the massive labor migration was the visa-free border regime under a Commonwealth of Independent States (CIS) agreement that allowed the citizens of most post-Soviet republics to enter Russia without restrictions (Abashin 2014). Thus, a distinctive feature of the migratory processes in the first decade of the new millennium, compared to the 1990s, was the massive influx of migrant labor, which transformed Russia into the world's third-largest recipient of migrants (after the United States and Germany), whereby 11.6 million foreign-born individuals resided in its territory (UNPD 2015).

International migrants are thus an integral component of the Russian labor market, contributing 16 percent to Russia's labor force (World Bank 2011). Every large-scale state-funded program—including infrastructure and construction projects such as the Moscow International Business Center (also known as Moskva-City), the 2018 FIFA World Cup Russia, or the 2014 Winter Olympic Games in Sochi—depends heavily on the migrant labor force. Large Russian cities, such as Moscow, Saint Petersburg, Novosibirsk, Krasnodar, Tyumen, and Yekaterinburg, serve as the primary magnets for migrants (Streltsova 2014). The vast majority of migrant workers come to Russia from three Central Asian countries—Kyrgyzstan, Tajikistan, and Uzbekistan (Malakhov 2014).[1] Because Russia maintains a visa-free regime with the CIS states, almost all migrants from Central Asia enter Russia legally and become undocumented only after failing to obtain a work permit and residence registration. The average Central Asian migrant is a young male with a secondary education and a poor command of the Russian language, originating from the rural areas or small towns of Central Asia where unemployment rates remain exceptionally high (Laruelle 2007; Abashin 2014). Men constitute 80 to 90 percent of migrants from Tajikistan and Uzbekistan, whereas almost half of the migrants from Kyrgyzstan are female (Marat 2009; Tyuryukanova 2011; FMS 2015). Central Asian migrants work primarily in construction, trade, transportation, service, agriculture, and housing and communal services (Malakhov 2014). Female migrants typically work in supermarkets and small shops, cafés and restaurants, and bazaars, as well as in domestic venues and the cleaning sectors (Tyuryukanova 2011). Owing to the high cost of accommodation and precarious working conditions, migrants rarely bring their family members to Russia. Members of a migrant's immediate family remain at home, and the migrant typically sends his earnings home to provide for their daily needs and other expenses, such as building a new house or purchasing a car, or to pay for life-cycle rituals, medical treatment, and education (Urinboyev 2017a).

No reliable statistics are available on the number of migrant workers in Russia. According to the General Administration for Migration Issues of the Ministry of Internal Affairs of the Russian Federation, as of November 2016, 10.2 million foreign citizens and stateless persons were legally residing in Russia (RBK 2016). Nearly 4 million of these foreigners were citizens of Central Asian countries: 1.9 million people from Uzbekistan, 1.06 million people from Tajikistan, and 620,000 people from Kyrgyzstan (RANEPA 2019a, 2019b). But Russian government statistics count only the number of foreign citizens who crossed the border and entered the country legally; they do not include the several million undocumented migrant workers currently in Russia (Denisenko 2017). Since undocumented migrants are not included, the official statistics underestimate the number of immigrants in Russia. For example, in 2016, 4 million people stated on their migration card that they were entering Russia for "employment," but only 2 million people received work permits, implying that those who did not gain work documents found

FIGURE 3. Uzbek construction workers in Moscow, Russia. September 2014. Photo by author.

employment in the shadow economy (RBK 2016). In addition, Russian government statistics are based on officially reported work permits (including migration patents), meaning citizens of member countries belonging to the Eurasian Economic Union are not included in these statistics, since they are not legally required to obtain a migration patent (Denisenko and Chernina 2017). Given these complexities, it is unsurprising that no consensus exists among migration scholars and experts regarding the number of migrants in Russia. That is, the figures vary, placing the number of migrants living in Russia at 9 to 18 million individuals depending on the source used (cf. Reeves 2015; Abashin 2016; Schenk 2018).

An analysis of labor migration trends in Russia since the early 2000s indicates that movement between Central Asia and Russia seems to be well-established and resilient. When the economic crises hit Russia in 2009 and 2014, Russian media outlets quickly announced that Central Asian migrants were leaving Russia as a result of the recession. Initially, the number of migrants indeed decreased considerably. But Russia quickly returned to its position as the primary migration hub for Central Asian migrants given the absence of reintegration policies and economic opportunities in their home countries. Even the introduction of draconian immigration laws and policies did not significantly reduce the number of migrants, instead pushing them into the shadow economy. Within that shadow economy migrants produced a parallel legal order to regulate their daily working-life and socioeconomic practices. These processes are described in the sections that follow.

DEVELOPMENT OF IMMIGRATION LAWS AND
POLICIES IN RUSSIA

The development of immigration laws and policies in Russia can be divided into two periods: (a) the 1990s and (b) 2000 to the present. An analysis of immigration laws and policies adopted during these two periods indicates that Russian migration policy underwent significant transformations from a single Soviet citizenship and identity toward increasing control over the immigration flows and the tightening of immigration laws and policies (Malakhov 2014; Abashin 2016; Schenk 2017; Kuznetsova and Round 2018).

The first migration laws adopted in the 1990s (the Federal Law on Refugees and the Law on Forcibly Displaced Persons) focused on forced migrants and refugees (predominantly "ethnic Russians") who arrived in Russia from other former Soviet republics owing to the collapse of the USSR. Those laws aimed primarily to facilitate the return of forced migrants and refugees to Russia through the introduction of simplified procedures to receive refugee status or a permanent residence permit in Russia. Another key legislative action in the 1990s focused on passing several decrees and laws on "compatriots abroad." These decrees and laws aimed to support individuals who formerly held USSR citizenship and resided in countries once a part of the USSR who wished to maintain their ties and loyalty to post-Soviet Russia. Because the concept of "compatriot" was broadly defined within the law, anyone who lived in the post-Soviet space could claim to be a "compatriot," move permanently to Russia, and eventually receive Russian citizenship (Abashin 2016). The immigration laws of the 1990s were thus ad hoc, piecemeal, and liberal in the sense that they served primarily to regulate the return of ethnic Russians and other Russian-speaking communities from the newly independent states of the former Soviet Union (Schenk 2018).

Following the onset of the massive labor migration from Central Asia to Russia in the early 2000s, Russian migration policy and the official rhetoric toward citizens of former Soviet republics shifted significantly. Given that Russia received millions of migrant workers from Central Asia and the Caucasus during a relatively short period, both the Russian public and politicians appeared largely unprepared to face the new reality of Russia becoming a country of immigration (Malakhov 2014). During the initial period of the Central Asian labor migration to Russia, no clear-cut migration policy or strategy existed, and the legal frameworks to regulate labor migration remained at an embryonic stage (Nikiforova and Brednikova 2018). These large-scale migratory processes coincided with political instability in Chechnya and global developments associated with the emerging war on terrorism, which increased security concerns among Russian policy makers and subsequently influenced the design of the resulting immigration laws and policies (Schenk 2018). The adoption of a new law in 2002, "The Law on the Legal Status of Foreign Citizens in the Russian Federation," represented one of the first serious attempts of the Russian authorities to regulate the flows of immigration based on a "preferred vs. non-preferred migrants" rationale (Abashin 2016). That law significantly tightened the ethnic and cultural requirements for foreign citizens seeking to secure a permanent residence permit and Russian citizenship. The legal status of foreign citizens was then determined based on (a) the country of origin, (b) the presence or absence of a visa, (c) the length of stay, (d) the purpose of the visit, (e) the type of employer (public, private, or individual), (f) the absence or presence of an employment contract or work permit, and (g) family status. New migration management mechanisms, such as a migration card, visa procedures, quotas for temporary residence permits and work permits for foreigners from visa countries, and requirements for registration at a place of accommodation, were introduced. These legislative changes clarified the migration status of foreign citizens and unified procedures for registering and issuing work permits (Denisenko and Chernina 2017).

Yet despite Russian authorities' attempts to coherently regulate labor migration, these new procedures for obtaining work permits emerged as too complex, unclear, and contradictory for visa-free migrants from CIS (post-Soviet) countries. While the law clearly described the procedures employers must follow to hire a worker from a visa country, no separate procedure was described for the hiring of migrants from visa-free countries. This meant that all migrant workers from CIS countries remained completely dependent on their employers to submit the documents required for legal work status (Schenk 2018). This ambiguity explains why millions of migrant workers from CIS countries resorted to the shadow economy, where they could work without any type of work permit. Another factor enabling migrants to operate in the shadow economy was the possibility of crossing the border visa-free and remaining in Russia for up to 90 days, which could be easily prolonged by leaving the country and immediately returning. Before the expiration of their 90-day stay, migrants typically traveled to the Russia-Ukraine or the Russia-Kazakhstan border to renew their migration card, thus allowing them to stay legally in Russia for another 90 days in accordance with the Law on the Rules of Entry and Exit from the Territory of the Russian Federation of 1996 (revised in 2012 and 2013). According to expert estimates, 3 to 5 million migrants worked in the shadow economy from 2002 through 2005 (Ivakhnyuk 2006; Tyuryukanova 2008; Krasinets 2009), while the number of undocumented migrants reached fewer than 1 million individuals in the period between 1999 and 2000, when labor migration remained largely unregulated (Zayonchkovskaya 2000).

These developments sent shockwaves rumbling across Russia and led to the widespread perception both among state officials and among the general public that immigration was out of control. In response the Security Council of Russia held a meeting on migration in 2005, at which Putin (2005) pointed to "notorious administrative barriers" and "chronic bureaucratic diseases" as the primary factors pushing migrants into the shadow economy. He called for a revision and modernization of Russia's immigration laws. Following Putin's critique, an interdepartmental working group was established under the leadership of the Ministry of Internal Affairs, resulting in several amendments to the "Law on the Legal Status of Foreign Citizens" in 2006 (Ivakhnyuk 2013). On the one hand, the amendments simplified the legalization procedures for migrants from CIS countries in terms of registering at the place they lived or worked, applying for a work permit on their own, and moving among different employers. On the other hand, new restrictions regarding work permit quotas were introduced for citizens of post-Soviet countries. Under this new immigration legal environment, CIS migrants had two options available to them for acquiring a work permit. The first option relied on securing a work permit through an employer, who applied for a quota allocation during the previous year. The second option required migrants to obtain a work permit independently, either by applying for a permit on their own or by applying through an intermediary. These aspects of the law were viewed as a shift toward liberalizing the Russian immigration policy, since migrants could obtain work permits on their own and move freely among employers (Schenk 2018). Owing to a quota of 6 million work permits for 2007, many migrants legalized their status, and the number of documented migrants increased from 570,000 in 2006 to 2.4 million in 2008 (Denisenko and Chernina 2017). More than half of these work permits were issued to citizens of Kyrgyzstan, Tajikistan, and Uzbekistan (Zayonchkovskaya and Tyuryukanova 2010).

Following the 2008–9 economic crisis, however, the Russian migration regime again shifted dramatically. That crisis led to a decrease in the total flow of migrant workers by approximately 15 to 20 percent (Zayonchkovskaya and Tyuryukanova 2010). Consequently, Russian authorities also reduced the work permit quota from 6 million in 2007 to 3.4 million in 2008 (Denisenko and Chernina 2017). Apparently, the decision to reduce the quota was made without a careful evaluation of the shifting demand for a foreign labor force. Because Russia quickly recovered from the economic crisis, the total flow of migrants returned to its previous levels. Yet, despite these trends, the quota continually decreased year by year (standing at 1.6 million in 2014 in its final year), pushing migrants into the shadow economy (Schenk 2018). This decrease was largely due to the legal requirement that every employer must submit applications to regional authorities by May each year, indicating their need for a certain number of foreign workers with specific skills and qualifications. Thus, the size of the yearly quota was determined in accordance with the number of applications submitted by employers. Many entrepreneurs, however, particularly small business owners, were ineligible within such quotas owing to the complicated bureaucratic procedures and legal restrictions. Even the introduction of "out-of-quota" work permits (known as a "patent") in 2010 did not significantly improve the situation, since patents were only valid for migrants entering into employment with individual citizens for personal, household, and other nonbusiness purposes. As a result, many were forced to operate in the shadow economy, hiring migrants without any work documents (Denisenko and Chernina 2017). From their side, millions of CIS migrants—predominantly Central Asian migrants—continued their established practice of prolonging their stay in Russia by renewing their migration card at a nearby border before the expiration of the 90-day grace period.

As an antidote to the constantly expanding shadow economy fueled by an undocumented migrant labor force, Russian authorities further tightened the laws, strengthened the border infrastructure, and introduced highly punitive measures. The Concept of the State Migration Policy 2025, adopted in 2012, clearly outlined the concerns of Russian authorities over continually increasing irregular migration, calling for the need to combat "illegal migration" through a refinement of the penalties for violations to migration legislation, developing the immigration control infrastructure, and improving the operation of special institutions to detain foreign nationals and stateless persons (Abashin 2016; Kondakov 2017). Consequently, between 2012 and 2015 Russian authorities adopted more than 50 laws and regulations aimed at reducing undocumented migration through severe administrative and criminal penalties for violation to migration laws (Denisenko 2017). The most visible evidence of these new tendencies was the introduction of an entry ban (*zapret na v'ezd*). In 2013 Russian authorities introduced the entry ban as an immigration law sanction and began applying it to foreign citizens who violated the conditions on the length of stay, migration, and employment regime. In July 2013 more severe amendments were made to the entry-ban legislation, according to which the three-year entry ban was to be issued to foreign citizens who had committed two or more administrative offenses within a period of three years (Kubal 2016a). Administrative law violations included offenses such as speeding or illegal parking, violations to highway codes, living in a place not indicated in the official residence registration, or not being able to present a valid identification document when stopped by the police. The three-year entry ban could be issued to a foreign citizen who committed two administrative law violations during their stay in Russia. The entry ban was typically issued by a staff member of the Main Directorate for Migration Issues of the Ministry of Internal Affairs (formerly the Russian Federal Migration Service) after cross-referencing the police databases for petty administrative offenses with the database containing information about foreign citizens' residence status in Russia (Kubal 2016a).[2] In addition to the entry ban, another new law, known as the "90–180 rule," came into effect in January of 2014, stipulating that foreigners can stay in Russia for only 90 days within any 180-day period. These restrictions made it impossible for migrants to cross the border every three months and reenter Russia beginning a new grace period. New sanctions were introduced to ensure migrants' compliance with the "90–180 rule." Accordingly, migrants who stayed illegally for more than 270 days were subsequently banned from entering Russia for 10 years, whereas those who overstayed by 170 to 270 days could not enter the country for five years, and those who overstayed less than 170 days were not allowed to enter Russia for three years (Denisenko 2017).

The Russian migration regime underwent a further significant transformation in 2014 and 2015. One of the key changes included abolishing the system of work permit quotas for citizens from visa-free countries in 2015 and the introduction of a single patent system that covered all forms of migrant employment. Until 2015, migrants could use the patent only for entering into employment with individual citizens for personal, household, or other similar purposes. As of January 1, 2015, however, patents became the main channel for legal employment for all foreign workers (including CIS citizens) entering Russia under the visa-free regime, regardless of whether they worked for an organization, individual entrepreneur, or individual.[3] To obtain a patent, migrants must complete numerous requirements within 30 days of their arrival. These include (1) holding a migration card, received at the border, upon which the purpose of entry to the Russian Federation must be indicated as "work"; (2) proof of residence registration; (3) a certificate verifying that they have passed a Russian-language, law, and history exam; (4) a medical certificate clearing them of drug addiction and infectious diseases such as tuberculosis, HIV, etc.; (5) proof of medical insurance obtained through their employers or purchased from a private insurance company approved by the regional government; (6) a receipt indicating payment of patent fees and first month's taxes; and (7) a translated and notarized copy of a valid passport. Patents are typically issued for a period of between 1 and 12 months, after which they can be renewed for another 12 months. The introduction of a single patent system was put forward as a liberal turn in the Russian immigration legislation, which would enable many migrants from Central Asian countries to legalize their work status. This would primarily benefit individuals previously unable to obtain a work permit because of the shortage of quotas and complicated bureaucratic procedures. Konstantin Romodanovski, head of the former Federal Migration Service (FMS), was quick to declare that the number of legally employed migrants exceeded the number of undocumented migrants for the first time ever (Romodanovski and Mukomel 2015).

Another significant change in the Russian migration regime features a steady move toward a "policing" approach to migration management. This is particularly visible in the transformation of the FMS from an independent civic structure to a law-enforcement agency. FMS was established in 1992 on the basis of the Committee for Migration Affairs under the Ministry of Labor and Employment of the Russian Federation. As an independent civic institution, FMS's initial task was to regulate the return of ethnic Russians and Russian-speaking refugees from the post-Soviet republics to Russia. At the beginning of the 2000s, however, when the inflow of Russian-speaking migrants began decreasing and was gradually replaced by the growing influx of Central Asian and Caucasian migrants, FMS was reorganized to regulate external labor migration. Although FMS was dissolved, recreated, and reorganized several times between 2000 and 2016, oscillating between a law-enforcement agency and a civic structure, in reality it represented an autonomous, powerful bureaucratic structure with its own central management apparatus, hierarchies, and regional offices. As Abashin (2016) notes, despite its significant flaws, the concentration of resources and power to manage migration processes within one institution, FMS allowed for the consolidation of migration policy and created the conditions for reviewing migrant legalization issues from a more liberal point of view. The sudden decision to abolish FMS and the transfer of its migration regulation functions to the Ministry of Internal Affairs marked a significant shift in the Russian migration regime. As a result of this shift, migration service officials became de facto "police officers without uniforms." Consequently, migration policy lost its independent civic character and fell once again under the main law-enforcement agency, viewing migrants as potential illegal aliens posing a threat to the public order and security (Nikiforova and Brednikova 2018).

THE IMPACT OF IMMIGRATION LAWS AND POLICIES
ON THE FORMATION OF THE SHADOW ECONOMY

As shown in the previous section, the Russian migration regime is characterized by numerous legal inconsistencies and ambiguities. Because formal rules and requirements for the residence and employment of foreign citizens are complex, volatile, and constantly changing, most migrants can barely follow or understand the legislative changes. Migrants typically rely on their social networks as a source of information about such changes, but this information is often based on rumors and false knowledge. Even lawyers from human rights nongovernmental organizations find it difficult to fully understand Russia's immigration laws and bureaucratic procedures (Malakhov and Simon 2017). This also rings true for migration service officers, who begin their daily work by monitoring the FMS website to check the latest news and amendments to immigration laws (Nikiforova and Brednikova 2018). Given that the majority of migrants entering Russia are not well-educated, do not speak Russian, have poor knowledge of laws, and originate from the rural areas of Central Asia, it is highly unlikely that they can comply with the fluid immigration laws and operate legally within the labor market. Furthermore, migrants must deal with the arbitrary actions of police officers, migration officials, and border guards always seeking ways to exploit legal ambiguities and cumbersome bureaucratic procedures to generate informal benefits (Malakhov and Simon 2017). Consequently, the ambiguous and arbitrary nature of immigration laws and practices generates an immigration legal regime that pushes masses of migrant workers into domains of illegality, rendering shadow economy employment the only viable option.

Although the Russian authorities continually introduce draconian laws and develop the immigration control infrastructure, the Russian migration regime is plagued by corruption and a weak rule of law (Light 2010; Malakhov 2014; Schenk 2018). Thus, the implementation of such laws remains arbitrary and can be used by state officials to generate informal benefits. An extensive literature demonstrates the different dysfunctionalities of the Russian legal system (McAulley, Ledeneva, and Barnes 2006; Hendley 2012; Ledeneva 2013). Likewise, immigration laws are simply emblematic of the "unrule of law" culture in Russia (Gel'man 2004), characterized by the prevalence of informal rules and norms over formal institutions. Under these circumstances the more restrictive the immigration laws are, the higher the rate of informal payments migrants must make to Russian police officers, migration officials, and border guards to continue working in Russia. In other words corruption is the primary factor determining current immigration politics, given that the actions of a considerable number of Russian officials are driven not by legal-rational logic but by the logic of material interests (Malakhov 2014). In practice, then, even those migrants who possess all of the required paperwork cannot be certain that they are fully "legal" and that they will not experience problems when stopped by Russian police officers and migration officials (Reeves 2015; Round and Kuznetsova 2016). Thus, a "legal" or "illegal" status hinges on contextual factors, such as how, when, and where the interaction between migrants and Russian state officials takes place, as well as on individual factors, such as migrants' knowledge of informal rules and their ability to adapt to the legal environment (their street smarts and ability to find common ground [*obshchii iazyk*]) with state officials, bribery skills, and connections with street institutions, such as intermediaries and racketeers). Hence, the only path to becoming "legal" requires the use of various semilegal and outright illegal practices (Dave 2014a). These specifics of the Russian legal system give rise to a specific legal adaptation strategy, where migrants are required to master the informal rules and street laws. They must also develop the skills necessary to negotiate with informal channels to access employment, housing, social services, and other opportunities typically limited to those with legal status or hard to obtain in the current legal framework of the host country.

The informal practices surrounding residence registration provide an illustrative example. Despite the existence of a visa-free regime, Central Asian migrants are required to obtain residence registration within seven days of arrival in Russia. This procedure, referred to as *registratsiia* in migrants' everyday language, originates from the infamous Soviet practice of the *propiska* system, representing one of the main barriers to migrant legalization in contemporary Russia. Particularly problematic is that it is quite difficult for a typical migrant worker to find an apartment and a landlord willing to register him or her at that apartment address. It is especially difficult to obtain registration in big cities such as Moscow or Saint Petersburg, where the majority of migrants are concentrated. This process became more difficult following the adoption of the so-called law on rubber apartments in 2013, which made it illegal to register a large number of foreign citizens at the same address. As Malakhov and Simon (2017) note, the very design of this law was far removed from reality and open to corruption, given that migrants' average monthly salary is between 15,000 and 25,000 rubles (US$250–$400), whereas the average monthly rental costs range from 30,000 to 40,000 rubles (US$450–$650) for a modest two- to three-room apartment in the suburbs of Moscow. Because of their meager income, migrants usually buy a *koiko mesto* (mattress-sized sleeping space) for 4,000 to 5,000 rubles per month (US$60–$80) in an apartment shared by 15 to 20 people. The *koika-mesta* arrangements, while illegal, represent an inalienable part of migrants' daily lives in Russia. Given their illegal residence, migrants cannot obtain a registration at the address where they live. As a result, they are forced to buy a "clean fake" registration for a fee of 2,500 to 3,000 rubles for three months from private agencies and intermediaries well-connected to state officials. As Reeves (2013) describes, typically such "clean fake" registration addresses exist somewhere in the city and can be found in the official database when checked by the police, yet migrants never live there and have no connection to that building or its residents. This reality is an open secret among both migrants and state officials in Russia. Thus, when stopped by the police, migrants are vulnerable to being caught and fined for violating residence laws. Under these circumstances it is crucial that migrants act street smart and "perform" residence at their fictive address by knowing how to get there, which metro stations are located nearby, and the general details about the building. Having a "legal" residence depends largely on migrants' street smartness and their ability to play by the rules of the game.

Introduced in 2015 as a replacement for the work permit system, the new patent system became more problematic than the previous quota system. In practice, the new patent system primarily aimed to simplify the legalization of the work and residence registration status such that migrants could "come out of the shadows" and work legally. Despite its liberal nature, however, the patent system introduced complicated bureaucratic procedures and high legalization fees that further pushed migrants into the shadow economy (Heusala 2018). Within 30 days of arrival migrants are required to complete numerous procedures, such as pass language tests, obtain a medical examination, secure health insurance, acquire residence registration, and pay various fees. Thus, it is exceptionally difficult to complete all the procedures within the 30-day period, both from a bureaucratic and a financial standpoint. On average the cost of all these tests, the medical examination, the insurance plan, and the general fee for the patent reach approximately 25,000 rubles (about US$400), placing a heavy financial burden on migrants who have just arrived with little or no money (Nikiforova and Brednikova 2018). After obtaining a patent, migrants are required to pay a monthly fee for the patent, the amount of which depends on the region in which the migrant works (e.g., 5,000 rubles [US$80] for Moscow). Until 2014 the monthly patent fee was 1,000 to 1,200 rubles (US$15–$18), a reasonable and affordable sum. But the fee increased to 4,000 to 5,000 (US$60–$80) rubles after 2014. In addition to paying a monthly fee, migrants must renew their residence registration every three months, each time costing 3,000 rubles (US$30–$45). Until 2015 migrant's residence registration was automatically prolonged for the period during which the patent was valid. Beginning in January of 2015, however, migrants were required to renew their registration every three month via intermediaries. All of these legalization expenses fall well beyond the financial capacity of migrants, given their meager incomes. Even those migrants who received a patent find it hard to remain "legal" and eventually resort to the shadow economy. This is because a migrant's average monthly salary is 25,000 rubles, a sum significantly lower than the salary of Russian citizens. In addition to the monthly patent fee (5,000 rubles), migrants have food (3,000 rubles), accommodation (5,000 rubles), and transport (1,000 rubles) expenses. On top of these expenses they must send money home, which is the main motivation bringing them to Russia. If migrants pay the monthly fee and work legally, they can send about 10,000 to 11,000 rubles (US$150–$70) home. It is also possible to earn up to US$150 per month in Central Asia; the only reason drawing migrants to Russia is the motivation to earn more money than at home. Consequently, these expensive legalization procedures further push migrants into the shadow economy, where they can work without any documents (Kuznetsova and Round 2018; Schenk 2018).

These restrictive immigration laws and policies also led to the proliferation of a diverse set of legally fictitious spaces and illegal document schemes that generated informal benefits for the various state officials and intermediaries closely linked to the police and law-enforcement officials (see Reeves 2013; Dave 2014a). To cope with this restrictive legal environment, migrant workers normally approach numerous intermediaries (*posredniki*) who can provide various fake (*fal'shivka*), "clean fake" (*chistaya fal'shivka*), and "almost clean" (*pochti chistiy*) residence registrations, patents, and temporary and permanent residence permits, as well as fake Russian and Kyrgyz passports. One can easily spot numerous intermediaries (with a migrant background) in Moscow's Kazansky railway station and in air ticket offices (*aviakassi*) located near various metro stations. Given that the majority of these intermediaries are migrants from Central Asia, it is apparent that they operate under some sort of "protective roof" (*krysha*), often provided by law-enforcement officers. This trend is substantiated by Russian government statistics, which show that the most common crimes committed by migrants are those connected with document counterfeiting (Golunov 2014). Intermediaries can also consist of a broad range of people, such as lawyers, migrants' associations, diaspora activists, and legal and commercial firms offering documentation and "legalization services" closely connected to officials within the state administration, migration services, and police and security services (Dave 2014a). Illegal schemes even extend to the embassies of Central Asian countries, which informally provide various services to migrants.[4] The availability of such legally fictitious spaces and "legalization" schemes allows migrants to remain and work in Russia without authentic immigration papers. For example, many migrants initially obtain

FIGURE 4. A migrant's monthly income is divided into four different expenses: sending money home (уйга), accommodation (квартира), monthly work-permit fee (документ), and meals and daily transportation (узимга) expenses. As a result, this migrant has only 71 rubles (US$1) left for his monthly meals and transportation expenses. August 2016. Photo by author.

an authentic patent and work legally. But, after a few months and owing to the expensive monthly patent fee or delays in salary payment, migrants begin buying fake patent payment receipts from intermediaries at the Kazansky railway station. When stopped by police officers, migrants typically present these fake receipts. This strategy often works since police officers do not have the capacity to check the authenticity of various receipts. To discover whether receipts are authentic, police officers must send them to the tax department, a process that might take several days. Not wanting to engage in bureaucratic hassles, police officers usually let migrants go and, instead, target those "completely paperless" migrants not well-connected to Kazansky intermediaries. These examples indicate that the Russian policies of migration control have produced additional undocumented migrants for the shadow economy rather than simplifying the procedures for legalizing the foreign labor force.

In addition, the efficiency of entry bans as a migration management tool remains questionable. Following the legislative changes made on July 23, 2013, migrants who committed two or more administrative offenses began receiving a three-year entry ban. As a result, migrants banned from entry were prevented from extending or renewing their immigration papers and were required to leave the Russian territory as soon as possible (Kubal 2016a). In mid-2016 Olga Kirillova, head of the General Administration for Migration Issues of the Ministry of the Interior of Russia, reported that the total number of foreign citizens banned from entry approached 2 million people (Interfax 2016). The vast majority of these migrants were citizens of Tajikistan and Uzbekistan (Troitskii 2016). But no evidence showed that these measures produced the desired effect. A small decrease in the number of migrants resulted more from the recession in Russia in autumn of 2014, causing a drop in jobs and incomes, than from demonstrating the effectiveness of prohibitive measures (Abashin 2016). Thus, rather than reducing the number of undocumented migrants, these legal restrictions and punitive measures further contributed to the growth of the shadow economy. Migrants learned to sidestep restrictions by buying "new passports" or "clean fake" immigration papers from the numerous "legalizing firms" operating in Russia (Reeves 2013; Dave 2014a). They also limited their return trips home and concentrated instead on one long stay, during which they attempted to earn as much as possible, knowing that this might be the only opportunity they would have for a long time. Hence, the frequency of border crossings decreased, and many entry-banned migrants began overstaying in Russia without valid documents, thereby increasing the share of undocumented migrants in the labor market. This trend was apparently confirmed by official statistics, showing that nearly 3 million foreign nationals in Russia had already violated the legal terms of their stay (Pochuev 2015).

Another factor that pushed migrants toward "illegality" was the gap between legal decisions and deficiencies, as well as uncertainties in bureaucratic practices. The monthly patent payment serves as a relevant example. Migrants are required to pay a patent fee by the last day of each month; failure to do so leads to annulment of the patent. This requirement creates obstacles during holidays, especially during the New Year holidays, when Russians take a break until January 10. In Russia many legislative and administrative changes enter into force from January 1, including the budget classification code (KBK), which needs to be entered into an automatic payment terminal when paying in to the state budget. Simply put, migrants need to enter the correct KBK code when paying their monthly patent fee. Given that Russian state institutions are closed until January 10, migrants cannot access a new KBK code from the authorities and, hence, are unable to pay the patent fee on time, resulting in the annulment of their patent. Given these bureaucratic deficiencies, many migrants become "illegal" and are, therefore, forced to resort to the shadow economy. However, these bureaucratic deficiencies may also empower migrants. As mentioned earlier, entry-banned migrants remain within Russia since they are aware that they might not be allowed to reenter if they leave the country. Owing to the existence of extensive information channels among different migrant networks, many migrants have learned that they can actually remain and work in Russia illegally until their entry ban expires. After the expiration of their entry ban, migrants leave Russia and reenter with a new migration card, allowing them to begin another "migration adventure." Most migrants even receive a patent and residence registration. Yet these strategies remain short-term, and sooner or later Russian migration officials detect these infractions and issue new entry bans on migrants who overstayed during previous visits. Because of the massive number of such infractions, it may take several months or even a year for the Russian authorities to detect them. These assumptions are confirmed by the 2016 statistics, which show that, from the nearly 4 million foreign citizens listing their purpose of entry to Russia as "work" on their migration card, only 1.5 million received a patent, indicating that 2.5 million migrants remained in Russia illegally.[5] The above examples, thus, suggest that a close relationship between bureaucratic deficiencies and uncertainties exists, resulting in the growth of the shadow economy around labor migration.

At first glance, an analysis of Russian immigration laws and policies gives the impression of an inconsistent and chaotic process rather than a rational strategy aimed at combating illegal migration (see Mukomel 2012; Dave 2014a; Malakhov 2014; Abashin 2016). Abashin (2016) explains these inconsistencies by referring to the conflicting attitudes and ideological differences between various actors and lobby groups (liberals, conditional *siloviks*, nationalists, and neoimperialists) that struggle to push their own views regarding labor migration regulations. On the one hand, labor migration is viewed as inevitable and even necessary to address economic and demographic needs. On the other hand, migration represents a dangerous and undesirable phenomenon from a security and cultural perspective. In reality the driving logic behind constantly changing immigration laws relies on establishing a standard for distinguishing "us vs. alien" and "preferred vs. nonpreferred migrants." This logic is reflected both in antimigrant attitudes within society and official reactions and rhetoric within government circles. Given these conflicting views, it is unsurprising that liberal immigration rules existed alongside conservative measures (Malakhov 2014). In Abashin's (2016) view, the combination of these conflicting attitudes, discourse segmentation, and ideological polarization ultimately rendered Russian migration policy incoherent and volatile. But Reeves (2015) argues that these legal inconsistencies and ambiguities should not be viewed as a sign of state weakness or the failure of migration policies. In Russia, migration governance relies less on an integrated and purposive regime than on the proliferation of ambiguous spaces resulting from inconsistencies among the legal environment, administrative regulation, and the labor market. In addition, Schenk (2018) maintains that these legal ambiguities should be viewed as key features of migration governance since they produce low numbers of documented migrants that can be deployed as a powerful populist tool to satisfy antimigrant sentiments, as well as a source of *kormushka* (a Russian metaphor used to describe corrupt practices) by mid- and low-level state officials eager to generate informal benefits from a large army of undocumented migrants. Viewed in this way, the seeming inconsistency of the Russian migration policy provides a rational explanation and reflects the functioning of contemporary Russia's entire bureaucratic machine, which relies on Soviet-era governance techniques, as well as the material interests of state officials at all levels (Malakhov and Simon 2017).

Given the resistance of the *sistema* in Russian politics (Ledeneva 2013), it is unsurprising that efforts to liberalize it through, for instance, simplifying the legalization of foreign workers, have remained contradictory and incoherent (Malakhov and

Simon 2017). It has become quite common among migration experts to characterize the development trajectories of the Russian migration regime as a process of "one step forward, two steps backward" (Nikiforova and Brednikova 2018). The analysis of immigration laws and policies over the last two decades shows that whenever liberal laws appear in the migration legislation, they are immediately followed by restrictive amendments and bureaucratic obstacles that prevent migrants from legalizing their work and residence status (Abashin 2016; Malakhov and Simon 2017). Even the abolition of the quota system and the introduction of a single patent system for CIS migrants did not facilitate migrant legalization. Malakhov and Simon (2017) explain that the Russian migration regime functions through the persistence of a Soviet-era administrative culture. In this way governance is understood as imposing restrictions and prohibitions rather than encouraging and fostering society's self-organizing units. Thus, arbitrariness and restriction are embedded in the very logic of the legal system's functioning. The ramifications of this approach to migration governance mean that Russian officials understand immigration regulations not as a tool to facilitate migrants' general compliance with the law but rather as an instrument to discipline and punish migrants who fail to obey the law (Kubal 2016b). In addition, this approach provides an opportunity to generate material benefits for certain groups and officials (Malakhov 2014; Schenk 2018). Given these legal and bureaucratic uncertainties, informal practices and channels within the shadow economy become alternative means for migrant legal adaptation. In other words, the legal adaptation of migrants to the Russian context takes place through navigating the corrupt and inconsistent legal environment, adapting to "street laws" (*ko'cha qonunlari*), and mastering various semilegal or illegal practices within the shadow economy.

IMPLICATIONS FOR MIGRANT LEGAL ADAPTATION

As shown in the previous sections, the Russian migration regime is characterized by a large shadow economy predicated on a massive undocumented migrant labor force. In this sense lack of documentation is not the exception but rather a way of life for millions of migrants in Russia. The large-scale presence of Central Asian migrants on the streets of Russian cities provoked public discord and led to widespread antimigrant sentiments in Russian society (Abashin 2016). The ongoing demographic crisis further contributes to the growth of antimigrant attitudes. Because the Russian population has been declining since the 1990s, fear exists among Russians that non-Russians will become the majority of the population by 2050 (Marat 2009). Additionally, migrants experience racism across all social settings and everyday situations, in their interactions with migration officials, police officers, or border guards. A 2016 survey conducted by the Levada Center found that the majority of Russians (52 percent) agreed with the statement, "Russia for ethnic Russians," and nearly 70 percent of respondents thought that the government should restrict the influx of Central Asian migrants and that undocumented migrants should be expelled from Russia (Pipia 2016). Such negative attitudes toward Central Asian workers existed even during Soviet times despite the popular *druzhba narodov* (people's friendship) discourse. Central Asians working on construction sites (*limitchiki*) in Moscow and Leningrad were perceived as *chernye* (black) and faced discrimination (Sahadeo 2007). These antimigrant sentiments are used strategically by Russian politicians to gain popular support during elections. For example, the Moscow mayoral election in the summer of 2013 became the first political event in Russia during which migration represented one of the most intensely discussed topics during the preelection campaign (Abashin 2016). Despite their varying orientations and agendas, every candidate's campaign featured a strong antimigrant sentiment, proposing the introduction of more repressive migration controls. That campaign strategy was specifically dominated by the antimigrant speeches of the acting mayor, Sergey Sobyanin, who insisted that migrants should not attempt to settle in Moscow but rather should return home immediately after finishing their temporary work (Kingsbury 2017). These preelection campaigns further contributed to the spike in antimigrant sentiments in an already xenophobic Russian society.

The prevalence of such sentiments can also be explained by the biased portrayals of Central Asian migrants as "illegals" (*nelegaly*) or *gastarbaitery* (from the German word *Gastarbeiter*) used by the Russian mass media (Kuznetsova and Round 2018). Although the word *migrant* is not used at all in Russian immigration laws, the media and politicians gradually developed an informal definition of the term by referring to migrant workers from Central Asian countries that have a visa-free agreement with Russia (Abashin 2016). The legal categories introduced in the "Law on the Legal Status of Foreign Citizens in the Russian Federation" remain vague and do not explicitly mention the ethnicity of a foreign citizen: "A foreign citizen who arrived in the Russian Federation in accordance with the regulation who does not require a visa." Kondakov's (2017) analysis of Russian newspaper articles shows that following the introduction of new legal categories through the law, such categories then also appeared in newspapers, where they were reinterpreted in a more explicit manner. For example, Kondakov focused on *Rossiiskaya Gazeta*, which began using such categories as *bezvizoviki* (visa-free migrants) and "Central Asian migrants" interchangeably in 2006 and 2007. As Kondakov concludes, the legally designated "visa-free visitor" represents a racist definition of Central Asian migrants working in unprivileged and precarious jobs. This perspective is also reinforced by Demintseva (2019), who argued that in everyday life in Russia a migrant is defined as a person who does not look Russian, regardless of his or her legal status, citizenship, or period of residence. These racist media constructions shape public opinion and intensify xenophobic and pejorative attitudes toward migrants.

The rise of antimigrant attitudes also associates with the absence of formal migrant integration policies in Russia (Brednikova and Tkach 2010; Gorenburg 2014; Malakhov 2015). There is no educational infrastructure enabling migrants to acquire the skills necessary to adapt nor any state agency charged with the question of integrating and adapting migrants (Streltsova 2014). The Main Directorate for Migration Affairs (formerly FMS), part of the Ministry of Internal Affairs, primarily serves as a law-enforcement structure and is mainly concerned not with ensuring the rational regulation of labor migration but with issuing documents and taking punitive measures in relation to migrants who fail to obtain a patent. While Russia's Migration 2025 Concept highlights the need to integrate migrants, in reality it views migrants as cultural "others" requiring assimilation by erasing their cultural differences and norms of conduct (Kondakov 2017). Migrant adaptation problems, including the fact that many migrants are forced to work in the shadow economy, are explained as resulting from their premigratory cultural repertoires rather than as an outcome of structural barriers (Shnirel'man 2008). A strong belief within government circles argues against migrants bringing their legal cultures and ways of life to Russia and preparing them to face challenges.[6] In Russia migrant adaptation is thus understood as depriving migrants of their culture and traditions and forcing them to adopt the Russian culture.[7] Accordingly, in public discussions, as well as in policy documents, Russian authorities typically emphasize the cultural integration of migrants, while their economic, social, legal, and political adaptation is neglected (Aitamurto 2016). Consequently, alienation from Russian society is more common than adaptation or integration (Mukomel 2012; Yusupova and Ponarin 2016). Although migrants may live in an apartment building with local Russian citizens, the migrants barely enter into closer contact with the "native" inhabitants of their apartment building or their quarters (Demintseva 2017). Communication also remains limited in workplace settings. Many migrant workers work, live, and socialize in special industrial areas, bazaars, and ethnic cafés where few local Russian people enter. One study (though rather dated) conducted by Tyuryukanova (2008) found that only 8 percent of all Central Asian migrant laborers worked in jobs primarily consisting of Russian employees, whereas 60 percent of migrants worked in migrant environments, and about 30 percent worked in mixed environments.

The absence of a clearly thought-through migration policy can also be explained by the tendency to view Central Asian labor migration as a temporary phenomenon (Bisson 2016). As Nikiforova and Brednikova (2018) note, both the state and migrants are deluded by the illusion of temporariness. The state neglects the fact that Central Asian labor migration represents a permanent phenomenon, which deserves adequate attention in its migration policy. Migrants are also under the delusion that their stay in Russia is temporary and that they will eventually return to their home countries. This illusion of temporariness, shared by the state and migrants, sets the terms of existence for all those occupying the migration space and impedes any possibilities for integration (Nikiforova and Brednikova 2018). Because migrants are viewed as temporary cheap labor, they operate in a precarious position and are excluded from the state and social structures such as health care, education, and social support (Kuznetsova and Round 2018). Thus, Russian migration policy does not facilitate the legalization and adaptation of Central Asian migrants but rather orients them toward the creation of unbearable conditions so that fewer migrants enter Russia. This thinking is particularly visible in the words of the head of the Federation of Migrants of Russia: "If the person is coming to Russia for work, he must understand and be prepared that his life will be very difficult here. He must never think that he will live like a local here. He must understand that by making a decision to work in Russia he made a difficult choice in his life. If he wants to change his life, he must be ready to pay the price."[8]

Experiencing racism is thus a part of migrants' everyday life in Russia. Central Asian migrants serve as scapegoats, used by the Russian regime to divert the local population's attention away from domestic social problems, such as corruption, the lack of democratic freedoms, and economic stagnation (Kingsbury 2017). Migrants experience difficult living and working conditions and typically work informally, without a formal employment contract (Human Rights Watch 2009; Zabyelina 2016). Given that the majority of migrants remain undocumented and work in the shadow economy, Russian employers and intermediaries have a strong incentive to exploit migrants and withhold or delay their salaries. Employers understand that transactions completed in the shadow economy—in violation of labor regulations or tax codes—cannot be heard in state courts according to the Russian Civil Code (Urinboyev and Polese 2016). Moreover, migrants remain reluctant to approach state institutions, since doing so would reveal their undocumented status and invite punishment by the state. Even those migrants who possess all of the required papers and work legally cannot be certain that they will be paid for their work. A recent scandal connected with a subway construction project in Moscow serves as a good example. In this case the Tajik and Uzbek migrant workers who built the subway were not paid for five months. Migrants gathered near the office of the Ingeocom construction company demanding their unpaid salaries. But the company management said that the workers did not have the right to strike, since they were not citizens of the Russian Federation (*Moscow Times* 2017). Central Asian migrants also experience hardships in finding accommodation as a result of the anti-immigrant sentiment prevailing within society and the reluctance of property owners to let apartments to "non-Russians," even when migrants have the financial means to rent a separate room or apartment (Demintseva 2017). In addition, migrants must deal with corrupt police officers who regularly extort money from them (Light 2016; Round and Kuznetsova 2016). Today, anyone walking on the streets of large Russian cities (e.g., Moscow, Saint Petersburg, Yekaterinburg) will quickly notice police officers checking the documents of Central Asian and Caucasian migrants. This is particularly visible on the

Moscow metro, where police officers frequently stand at the top of escalators to stop migrants (Round and Kuznetsova 2016).

Accordingly, the general political situation in Russia does not allow migrants to approach formal institutions for redress, and they remain completely vulnerable to the whims of their employers (Laruelle 2007). Precious few civil society organizations and migrant rights activists in Russia are available for migrants to approach for protection (Korobkov 2007; Matusevich 2015). While diaspora groups in Russia are assumed to be the first port of call for migrants seeking assistance, the role and usefulness of such groups in migrants' lives is quite limited (Varshaver and Rocheva 2014; Berg-Nordlie and Tkach 2016). Media reports indicate that some members of Central Asian diaspora groups have actually facilitated the exploitation of migrant workers, at times acting as intermediaries between abusive employers and potential migrants (Fergananews.com 2016; Ozodlik Radiosi 2016). Furthermore, the capacity of civil society groups to provide support to migrants is quite limited given the continued persecution of nongovernmental organizations in Russia (Kuznetsova and Round 2018). A rare example of an effective civil society organization is "Tong Jahoni," a migrant rights organization led by prominent migrant rights lawyer and activist Valentina Chupik, who deals with several thousand cases involving Central Asian migrants. It is important to recognize, however, that resources and the reach of civil society institutions are rather limited given the "foreign agent" law. Therefore, the majority of migrants rely on their transnational networks, kinship groups, and informal social safety nets to organize their precarious livelihoods.

Thus, the everyday life of migrant workers in Russia is characterized by a constant sense of insecurity, threatened by exploitation, deportation, police corruption, racism, physical violence, and even death. The unrule-of-law environment dominates, and a legal or illegal status hinges on contextual factors and the individual's skills. Shadow economy employment remains the rule for many migrants, with little or no room for collectively mobilizing migrants. Despite these hardships, the possibility of working in Russia, from the perspective of migrants, provides a vital economic lifeline for their families back home, leading them to accept everyday injustices, exploitation, and racism (Matusevich 2015).

It is important to realize, however, that Central Asian migrants are not merely passive, agencyless subjects constrained by structural barriers but are capable of inventing various informal strategies to organize their precarious livelihoods. This complete lack of security compelled Central Asian migrants to create informal networks and migrant-concentrated areas and structures to cope with the risks and uncertainties of their ambiguous situations (Zabyelina 2016; Urinboyev 2017b). Such migrant-concentrated areas occupy a fixed spatial location, often situated in areas around bazaars and wholesale markets (Light 2010). The wholesale food bazaar "Food City" in Moscow's Kaluzhskoe shosse serves as one such "migrant enclave," where migrants created an informal infrastructure with its own informal "legal order" and governance structure. These migrant areas and the networks revolving around them serve as an alternative means to integrate and provide adaptation mechanisms for many migrants, granting access to basic public goods, such as jobs, housing, and physical and economic security. Such networks typically revolve around the bonds of kinship, region of origin, or ethnic affiliation, reproducing many "domestic" practices adapted to the conditions of migration and temporary residence (Abashin 2014; Urinboyev 2016). The existence of an informal infrastructure allows migrants to adapt in some ways to an otherwise restrictive legal environment, such as by devising specific survival strategies, creating intragroup solidarity, distributing information about jobs, and building up an informal social safety net to minimize risks to livelihoods and deal with emergency situations (e.g., medical treatment, repatriation of decedents to their home country, and so on). These networks, possessing their own infrastructure of trust, mutual aid, and social services (e.g., Kyrgyz clinic, Uzbek cafés, etc.), constitute an important social safety net for migrants (Matusevich 2015; Urinboyev and Polese 2016; Demintseva 2017). Some commentators refer to such migrant networks as *Uzbekskiy Peterburg* (Yakimov 2015), *Kyrgyztown* (Varshaver et al. 2014), and *Moskvaobod* (BBC Uzbek 2012). Hence, the distinctive feature of the Russian migration regime is the presence of a hidden world of migrants based on its own economy, a virtual platform, a legal order, and a welfare infrastructure. A "thick description" of these processes appears in the chapters that follow.

Uzbek Migrant Workers in Russia

A Case Study

Uzbekistan became an independent state in 1991 following the collapse of the Soviet Union. Like other newly independent post-Soviet states, Uzbekistan faced the complex task of building a new nation-state. Following on the heels of global (Western) good governance discourses, the political leadership of Uzbekistan made multiple bold claims about its strong commitment to the ideals of democracy, market economy, human rights, and the rule of law as well as its intention to dismantle Soviet-style governance (see Perlman and Gleason 2007). Simultaneously, Uzbek authorities made clear that the governance system, while adhering to global standards, would also employ Uzbekistan's ancient traditions, rich Islamic heritage, and centuries-old administrative traditions in its nation-building project (Karimov 1993). Many international organizations, such as the World Bank, the International Monetary Fund (IMF), and the United Nations Development Program (UNDP), promptly geared their development programs toward Uzbek authorities' reform agenda, thereby financing and initiating numerous good governance, market economy, and human rights projects.

But the complex and multidimensional nature of the challenges to political stability that Uzbekistan faced in the 1990s, for various reasons, rendered the government skeptical of genuine democratization and market reforms. The need to prioritize political stability over reforms was justified by the unstable political situation in Central Asia during that time. This included ethnic clashes between Uzbeks and Meskhetian Turks in 1989, ethnic conflicts between Uzbek and Kyrgyz people in southern Kyrgyzstan in 1990, and the civil war in neighboring Tajikistan between 1992 and 1997 (Warikoo and Norbu 1992; Fane 1996; Megoran 2017). Consequently, Uzbek authorities made it clear from the beginning that the "big bang" or shock therapy approach to transition would not suit Uzbekistan (Ruziev,

Ghosh, and Dow 2007). Instead, Uzbekistan adopted a gradualist approach, maintaining Soviet-era welfare policies and centralized control over the priority sectors of the economy (Spoor 1995). Thus, Uzbekistan continued to depend on imported consumer goods, currency controls, and the exploitation of rural labor. Authorities understood that a rapid transformation of the economy would affect the lives of millions, likely leading to social unrest. Hence, the Uzbek model of transition clearly reflected concerns regarding political stability and the peculiarities of the postplanned economy. In general, preserving economic stability and social and political order became the overarching rationale for rejecting all manner of economic and political reforms recommended by international institutions and for developing a strict border regime (Fumagalli 2007).

Notably, during the early years of its transition Uzbekistan achieved small yet positive and persistent economic growth because of its favorable economic conditions. These included the dominance of agricultural production, a low level of initial industrialization, and a rich natural resource base (Zettelmeyer 1998). Uzbekistan suffered less from the transition-associated depression than its Central Asian neighbor-states and was among the first to report positive output growth for the first time in 1996 (Spechler 2002). Interestingly, the cumulative decline in GDP between 1989 and 1996 remained lowest in Uzbekistan among all former Soviet republics. Uzbekistan did fairly well in terms of providing a social safety net, alleviating poverty, and limiting spending cuts in education and health care, particularly during the mid-1990s (Pomfret 2000; Johnson 2007). Soviet-style centralized economic management and strong social protection measures appeared successful during the transition period, since they prevented a large decline in outputs and served to maintain a reasonable standard of living. Furthermore, the agricultural sector prevented an increase in unemployment by providing job opportunities in rural areas. In this respect, during the early years of the transition, Uzbekistan maintained Soviet-era welfare policies and centralized control over the priority sectors of the economy, since these policies contributed considerably to its political stability and security.

But the gradual reform strategy appeared to serve as a short-term remedy. Although the gradualist approach to transition helped prevent a sharp loss to output and a consequential rise in unemployment and social unrest during the early years of the transition, by 2000 it had become clear that the economy had stagnated (Ruziev, Ghosh, and Dow 2007). This largely resulted from an active government intervention creating significant administrative barriers and a high tax burden, thereby causing high transaction costs for national businesses and fueling the informal economy (Ergashev et al. 2006). As Kandiyoti (2007, 44) maintains, the partial market reforms the government implemented in pursuit of stability resulted paradoxically in the inefficient allocation of resources and widespread corruption, requiring increased recourse to coercion. The centralized management methods negatively affected the agricultural sector in particular, evidenced by the government's intervention in the cotton sector by redistributing income from agriculture. This redistribution served to develop industries that produced substitutes to imports. Since agriculture traditionally formed the main shock-absorbing structure in rural areas, the reallocation of resources from agriculture to other industries negatively affected the rural population's standard of living (World Bank 1999; Ilkhamov 2004). Simultaneously, the government took a series of severe measures to liquidate—or formalize—informal economic activities (bazaars and petty cross-border trade), providing alternative means of survival for hundreds of thousands of people (Ilkhamov 2013). This left little room for informal income-earning strategies. While the Uzbek economy was categorized as experiencing above-average growth rates (about 7 to 8 percent) since 2004 (IMF 2012), these indicators hardly reflected everyday life in Uzbekistan, where many people, especially in rural areas, struggled to make ends meet (Ruziev, Ghosh, and Dow 2007; Ilkhamov 2013). Eventually, such developments compelled millions of Uzbek people to resort to labor migration as their primary livelihood strategy.

Russia stands as the primary destination for Uzbek migrant workers because of its visa-free regime, its relatively better wages, and the high demand for foreign labor (Laruelle 2007; Urinboyev 2016). Because the economies of Kyrgyzstan and Tajikistan have no extractive sectors, Kyrgyz and Tajik migrants arrived in Russia earlier (late 1990s and early 2000s) than the inhabitants of resource-rich Uzbekistan, where labor migration gained massive traction only in the middle of the first decade of the twenty-first century (Abashin 2014). Despite its relatively late arrival, Uzbekistan is normally ranked first among the post-Soviet countries in terms of remittances sent from Russia. According to statistics from June 2019, nearly 2.2 million Uzbek citizens were present within the territory of the Russian Federation (RANEPA 2019b). Currently, Uzbek migrants are dispersed across various regions of Russia, from Kaliningrad and Moscow to Vladivostok (Tolipov 2016). The great majority of Uzbek migrant workers are young, low-skilled men with a secondary school education. The majority of migrants originate from the densely populated and impoverished Fergana Valley, where the unemployment rate remains high (Laruelle 2007). As a result of this male-specific out-migration, many villages in Uzbekistan are nearly empty during the migration season (from April to November), inhabited primarily by women, elders, and children dependent on remittances sent from Russia (Urinboyev 2016). Uzbek migrants work primarily in the construction sector (23 percent), retail trade (18 percent), and service industry (19 percent), as well as in agriculture, industry, and transportation (Chikadze and Brednikova 2012). *Koiko mesto* (a mattress-sized sleeping space) in a shared apartment stands as the most common accommodation among migrants. Typically, migrants share an apartment with up to 20 people they only met after their arrival to Moscow (Demintseva 2017). Owing to high accommodation costs and precarious working conditions, migrants rarely bring their spouses to Russia;

instead, women remain alone with their children and in-laws and assume responsibility for many duties previously fulfilled by men (Reeves 2011). In turn, migrants send their earnings to their left-behind family on a monthly basis, typically covering their living expenses and securing other substantial needs, such as building a new house or buying a car, or to pay for life-cycle rituals, medical treatment, or education (Ilkhamov 2013).

Accordingly, these post-Soviet migratory trends reflect the social changes currently taking place in both Central Asia and Russia (Ruget and Usmanalieva 2008; Schmidt and Sagynbekova 2008; Hiwatari 2016; Urinboyev 2018a). Anyone walking along the streets of large Russian cities such as Moscow, Saint Petersburg, or Yekaterinburg quickly notices numerous Uzbek cafés and *choyxonas*. These cafés not only serve as eating places for Uzbek and other Central Asian migrants but also become meeting places for migrants during important social events and holidays. These migratory flows also carry important implications for migrant-sending communities in Uzbekistan as millions of Uzbeks (primarily men) move for the first time (i.e., becoming a "nomad") to Russia, leaving behind their families and community. Historically, Uzbeks have always been the most sedentary population in Central Asia, preferring to earn their livelihood in their home country (Levi 2007). Even during the Soviet era, ethnic Uzbeks exhibited the lowest mobility rate among Soviet ethnic populations (Ilkhamov 2013). In the 1980s, experts attributed Uzbeks' reluctance to voluntarily migrate to a presumed innate and incorrigible cultural attachment to their families and *mahalla* (Abashin 2014). Hence, because of their settled lifestyle, Uzbeks successfully preserved their traditional structures and social hierarchies despite the Soviet Union's coercive strategies. This contrasts to nomadic nations in the region, such as the Kazakh and Kyrgyz populations, which proved more receptive to Soviet modernization policies (Levi 2007). But we can no longer divide the Central Asian nations into settled and nomadic categories. Today, in both urban and rural areas of Uzbekistan labor migration has become rather normal—that is, it is a widely accepted livelihood strategy used by households to secure their basic needs and to generate resources for life-cycle events, construction, and entrepreneurial projects. Thus, the Uzbek lifestyle has become increasingly transnational since they live their lives across the border between two countries, simultaneously living everyday life and maintaining social relationships in both Russia and Uzbekistan.

The initial flow of Uzbek labor migration to Russia (in the late 1990s and early 2000s) was dominated by migrants with a good knowledge of the Russian language and a shared Soviet experience. By the late 2000s, however, migration flows became massive and changed in terms of the age composition and cultural background, bringing primarily a younger generation of migrants with no Soviet experience and a poor knowledge of both the Russian language and cultural norms (Nikiforova and Brednikova 2018). This new generation of migrants can be called the "children of the 1990s or post-Soviet era," since they have a considerably different mentality and ideas than earlier migrants who experienced Soviet times. This young migrant labor force sought primarily to earn as much money as possible in the short-term and then return home. Hence, the majority of Uzbek migrants did not seek to secure permanent residence nor to integrate into Russian society (see also Streltsova 2014). Even those migrants who received a permanent residence permit in Russia viewed their situation as "temporary" and maintained daily contact with their family and *mahalla* (local community) through smartphones and social media (Abashin 2014). Thus, "permanent temporariness" emerged as a lifestyle for Uzbek migrants and their left-behind families and communities.

Uzbek migrants do not have their own social infrastructure, such as special districts, shops, cafés, bazaars, or any other public places where they can meet and socialize in their free time. Naturally, hundreds of cafés offer Uzbek food in large Russian cities, and we can assume that these sites provide a platform by which Uzbek migrants may establish their own social infrastructure. But these cafés are scattered widely across cities and are not tied to specific areas, meaning migrants use these venues only for special occasions, such as to celebrate holidays, weddings, or birthdays (Demintseva 2017). Migrants usually work long hours without any days off in different parts of the city, which leaves little or no time for physical meetings with their village and *mahalla* networks. Another factor contributing to the absence of migrant social infrastructure is the corrupt policing practices that compel migrants to avoid public places. Given that the majority of Uzbek migrants remain undocumented or in a semilegal status and work in the shadow economy without formal employment contracts, Russian police officers can easily extort money from them. Even if migrants possess all of the documents required by the law, they are often asked for bribes when stopped by the police on the street or in the metro. Because of these experiences, Uzbek migrants do not organize in public places and try to make themselves as invisible as possible and avoid interactions with state institutions.

Despite the lack of social infrastructure and physical meetings, however, Uzbek migrants have their own virtual communities and engage in transnational activities using smartphone-based social media applications such as Telegram Messenger and IMO. Accordingly, owing to the rapid improvements in communication technologies, Uzbek migrants have created permanent, smartphone-based transnational communities in Russia, which typically include migrants originating from the same neighborhood, village, or town in Uzbekistan. This implies that Uzbek migrant communities do not arise based on their ethnicity but rather based on the area of origin, which may include both Uzbeks and Tajiks from the same city, district, or village in Uzbekistan (Varshaver and Rocheva 2014). That is, norms, lifestyles, and relationships embedded in the specific village or neighborhood community from where migrants originate are reproduced and maintained in the context of Russia. Hence, Uzbek migrant communities usually include migrants hailing from the same neighborhood, village, or town, which provides a fertile ground for establishing a high degree of social control, solidarity, and enforceable trust among migrants. Through these smartphone-mediated connections and networks migrants look for jobs and accommodations, receive assistance from their kinship and village networks, learn about the ways to maneuver around restrictions and corrupt police officers, and cope with the uncertainties of migrant life.

UNDERSTANDING UZBEK MIGRANTS' LEGAL CULTURE: PREMIGRATORY CULTURAL CODES AND EVERYDAY TRANSNATIONAL PRACTICES

Having existed under the Soviet planning system for more than 70 years, Uzbekistan embodies a peculiar blend of traditionalism and modernity. The ruling political elite remains quite secular and Westernized (in this case, Russified) given Uzbekistan's Soviet past, while a large portion of Uzbek society strongly adheres to religion, traditions, collectivism, and family and kinship norms (Poliakov 1992; Pashkun 2003). The everyday social order in traditional Uzbek society—including social positions, familial gender roles and hierarchies, kinship groups, and community—stems largely from patriarchal and collective values and norms, whereby an elder man decides the most important family and community affairs (Kandiyoti and Azimova 2004). The prevalence of traditionalism most likely results from the fact that Uzbekistan features a Muslim majority (nearly 90 percent of the population) and represented the "heartland" of three Sharia law–based independent states (Khiva and Kokand Khanates and the Emirate of Bukhara) until the late nineteenth century. As we shift focus from macro-level understandings of Uzbek legal culture toward ethnographic analyses of everyday life and social processes, it becomes more apparent that the behavioral imperatives, expectations, and social sanctions emanating from religious and traditional structures and values shape the basic parameters of everyday life and social relationships (Urinboyev and Svensson 2017). This implies that many features of the "collectivistic culture," such as the collective identity, emotional dependence, in-group solidarity, harmony, duties, and obligations (Triandis 2018), can also be found within Uzbek culture. These processes become particularly visible when observing daily social interactions in the realm of the *mahalla*—a centuries-old traditional self-governance institution in Uzbekistan deserving special attention when examining Uzbek migrants' legal culture.

The term *mahalla* enjoys common use in Uzbekistan, referring to a community built around common traditions, language, customs, moral values, and the reciprocal exchange of money, material goods, and services (Urinboyev 2013). Most Uzbeks identify themselves through their *mahalla*. For example, if a native is asked where s/he lives, that person typically responds, "I live in *mahalla* X" (Noori 2006). Thus, the *mahalla* includes all of the people living in the same neighborhood regardless of their familial or kinship ties. In other words, in Uzbek society, relationships stem not only from family and kinship norms, but they also rely on the informal norms and expectations generated by neighborhood proximity. In total, about 12,000 *mahallas* exist in Uzbekistan, and each *mahalla* contains 150 to 1,500 households (Urinboyev 2018b). *Mahallas* are led by an *oqsoqol* (leader) elected by residents. Because the state in contemporary Uzbekistan can no longer secure the basic needs of its population, *mahallas* now exist as informal welfare structures providing alternative access to public goods, services, and social protection measures (Urinboyev 2014). The cooperative behavior of *mahalla* residents relies on social norms that create order and increase group solidarity (Sievers 2002). Any failure to comply with *mahalla*-level norms might lead to informal sanctions, such as gossip, ridicule, humiliation, or even exclusion (Urinboyev and Polese 2016). Therefore, every resident attempts to conform to the social norms established within the *mahalla*.

Guzar (village meeting spaces), *masjid* (mosques), *choyxona* (teahouses), *gaps* (regular get-togethers), and life-cycle events serve as the key social and administrative spaces in the *mahalla*, where people meet on a daily basis and conduct the bulk of information exchanges (Rasanayagam 2002; Kandiyoti and Azimova 2004; Urinboyev and Svensson 2017). Typically, at least 12 to 15 residents can be found sitting in a *guzar*, regardless of the time of day. Since the *guzar* is a male-only place, women typically socialize either on the streets or inside households. Wedding ceremonies (*nikoh toi*) form another important social site at which all Uzbek people come together. In contemporary Uzbekistan most weddings share similar features: they are open to all *mahalla* residents, and 400 to 500 guests on average attend them. To turn down an invitation to a wedding is considered impolite. Each household in the *mahalla* is expected to take part in weddings and other ceremonies. The wedding ceremony in particular concerns the entire community, since it is arranged with the support of and resources from all *mahalla* residents. By arranging or attending a wedding, residents confirm their *mahalla* membership and engage in reciprocal transactions, since the wedding involves a great deal of exchange and reciprocity vis-à-vis money and material goods within kinship and friendship networks. Consequently, such a large number of transactions during weddings solidifies ties related to obligations and expectations within kinship and friendship networks, blending the moral aspects of social relationships with their material aspects. Therefore, weddings serve to illustrate key features of the social norms and hierarchies in Uzbek society: men and women sit separately at different guest tables, and the "best tables" are often reserved for people of influence, such as state officials, the police, highly educated people, successful businessmen, and wealthy relatives and friends. By carefully observing the placement and treatment of guests, we can easily compare one's social status and reputation to that of others.

Furthermore, life-cycle ceremonies not only constitute communal occasions but also activate networks of kin and neighbors enmeshed in ties of mutual obligation and reciprocity (Rasanayagam 2002; Urinboyev and Svensson 2013a).

These reciprocal relationships and obligations, activated and maintained through life-cycle ceremonies, ensure that neighbors and relatives can be relied on to help when *mahalla* residents experience hardships both "here" (in the village in Uzbekistan) and "there" (in Russia). Since *mahalla* residents regularly (typically daily) meet in these social spaces and attend most socializing events together, they have a mutually dependent relationship. These heavy social interactions produce a general expectation that each individual will help his/her family, kin, or *mahalla* members whenever necessary. Individuals who ignore or fail to comply with *mahalla* norms and collective expectations face social sanctions, such as gossip, ridicule, loss of respect and reputation, humiliation, and even exclusion from life-cycle rituals. Since people meet each other on a daily basis and interact regularly at social events, such interactions serve as a guarantee that social pressure and sanctions can be applied to an individual or his/her family or kinship group if they do not act fairly or do not help their neighbor or *mahalla* member. Thus, life-cycle ceremonies serve as key social arenas, where the "everyday legal order" is established, negotiated, and reshaped through reciprocal practices, social obligations, rumors, and gossip.

At the time of my fieldwork, from 2014 through 2018, in rural Fergana in Uzbekistan, I noticed that public confidence in the government had already evaporated owing to corruption, unemployment, and growing inequality. A widespread belief among Uzbek people held that the economy would improve in the post-Soviet period, as the wealth of the Uzbek people would no longer be sent to Moscow but would be retained locally and used for the welfare of the people. But very few Uzbeks reaped the rewards of independence. Because of a high unemployment rate and the absence of viable income-earning opportunities, millions of Uzbek families relied heavily on migrant remittances and felt compelled to send their male family members (husbands or sons) to Russia as migrant workers. Instead of continuing their education at the university, on graduation from secondary school or vocational college many young people choose to seek employment opportunities in Russia. Furthermore, the proportion of women migrating to Russia also increased. Daily conversations in Uzbekistan's rural areas revolved around the adventures of migrants in Russia, the amount of remittances, deportations, and entry bans. Most villagers use Telegram or IMO, enabling them to exchange daily news with village members working in Russia. In this way absent migrants remain "present" in their village through social media. While observing everyday life during my fieldwork, I also felt as though someone was always leaving for Russia, someone was waiting in Russia to receive them, and someone was returning home to attend a wedding or funeral. Hence, migration seemingly became a widespread livelihood strategy—that is, a norm for young and able-bodied men in Uzbek society.

Simultaneously, while I was observing daily social and economic relations in rural Fergana, it seemed as though state law remained nearly nonexistent. Rather, people's daily interactions and social behavior appeared regulated by informal *mahalla*-based norms promoting an alternative version of how they should behave. While the state in Uzbekistan appears omnipotent as a result of its infrastructural and coercive capacity, it carries very little meaning in everyday life at the *mahalla* level. When observing how people get things done and interact with the state officials, it is difficult to experience the state or its laws as a coherent entity. What we observe instead is an enormous degree of informal exchange and reciprocity involving money, material goods, and services all carried out through noncodified but socially reproduced informal rules. Hence, the normative values enshrined in the state legal system has not been internalized and remains external to the everyday legal culture in Uzbek society. Consequently, the state (and its legal system) rarely constitutes the only actor in society, while *mahalla*-based norms largely shape the basic parameters of everyday social behavior. This indicates that if we aim to better understand Uzbek legal culture, we must delve deeper into understanding the *mahalla* norms and practices that determine the rights and wrongs regarding everyday social behavior. These *mahalla*-level norms, identities, reciprocal relations, and social sanctions continue to shape Uzbek migrants' lives even when they move to Russia. This means village and *mahalla*-based trust and reciprocity networks remain crucial both locally (in Uzbekistan) and transnationally (in Russia). Thus, Uzbek migrants import and adapt their premigratory cultural and normative repertoires to Russia, especially when they work and live under the conditions of a shadow economy requiring alternative forms of law and order. I describe these processes in the next section.

UZBEK MIGRANTS' STRATEGIES TO ADAPT TO A NEW LEGAL ENVIRONMENT

The state remains "absent" not only in Uzbekistan, where people employ *mahalla*-driven solidarity to create alternative public goods and services, but also in Russia, where the media frequently portrays Uzbek migrants as potential criminals and carriers of alien sociocultural and religious identities leading to widespread antimigrant sentiments in Russian society. Owing to these ever-expanding antimigrant sentiments in Russian society, Uzbek migrants live largely isolated lives with few opportunities to interact with the host society. Migrants' poor command of Russian language further exacerbates this isolation. Thus, migrants interact in the Uzbek language even in their workplaces, given the existence of migrant mediators who facilitate daily communication between Russian employers and migrant workers. Therefore, rather than integrating into the host society, migrants rely on alternative paths to adaptation, employing networks based on kinship, shared village origins, ethnicity, or religion (Urinboyev and Polese 2016; Turaeva 2018).

Many of the Uzbek migrants with whom I spoke were completely unaware of the existence of Uzbek diasporic organizations. This is not surprising given the fact that Uzbek migrants are poorly organized and lack leadership. Some leaders of Uzbek diasporic organizations were suspected of being connected to organized crime or of being involved in preparing fake documents for migrants[1] (see also Fergananews.com 2016; Ozodlik Radiosi 2016). Uzbek migrants typically form a small social network, consisting of 50 to 100 people who all hail from the same district, village, or *mahalla*. Uzbek migrants often complained about the reluctance of Uzbekistan's embassy in Moscow to hear and address their grievances. Unlike the governments of neighboring Kyrgyzstan and Tajikistan, which have attempted to establish legal mechanisms to protect their citizens in Russia, Uzbek authorities typically provide little or no support to migrants who experience problems with dishonest employers or corrupt police officers. Consequently, the Uzbek state's unwillingness to fend for its citizens has further contributed to the "illegality" of Uzbek migrants in Russia, compelling them to look for alternative avenues of legal adaptation and navigation. Since most of the Uzbek migrants I encountered worked in the shadow economy, they could not approach Russian state institutions because of their undocumented status. Even the migrants' terminology clearly reflected their precarious livelihood in Russia. That is, Uzbek migrants rarely used the word *migrant* to refer to their noncitizen status in Russia; instead, they used the term *musofir*, which provides a more contextualized definition of what it means to be a migrant worker in Russia. Unlike the more neutral "migrant worker," *musofir* refers to a person who works in a foreign country and experiences risks, hardships, and challenges on a daily basis. As one Uzbek migrant I interviewed summarized, "We are not living in Moscow, but we are struggling to survive here (*Biz bu yerda yashamayapmiz, vizhivat qilishga harakat qilyapmiz*)." Hence, Uzbek migrants cannot rely on institutions in the host country, diasporic organizations, nor their home country's government.

The situation presented above should not, however, be understood as an attempt to depict Uzbek migrants as passive pawns constrained by structural conditions. Rather, Uzbek migrants have agency and can navigate around the restrictive legal environment in Russia. Owing to the complete lack of security, Uzbek migrants have created a diverse set of informal practices and structures that provide alternative (to state law) means to regulate their working lives, to cope with various risks and uncertainties associated with informal employment, and through which to seek redress for their grievances. As we will see in chapter 5, the emergence of informal, "street-based legal orders" serves as one relevant example.

The informal-document market provided another street-based informal channel enabling migrants to adapt to the restrictive legal environment through the production of "clean fake" Russian passports, residency documents, and work permits (see, e.g., Reeves 2013). Given the difficulties with obtaining authentic residence registration and work-permit documents, it has become quite normal for migrants to obtain various immigration and "legalization" documents from intermediaries operating in areas near railway and metro stations. Moscow's

Kazansky railway station stands as the most popular "legalization" site among migrants, where it is possible to buy numerous immigration documents, including a fake Russian passport. Consequently, the emergence of these "street-based informal adaptation channels" in the Russian migrant labor market results not simply from poorly implemented laws and dysfunctional institutions but also from the existence of a parallel world of migrants in Russia based on its own economy, legal order, and adaptation mechanisms (Urinboyev 2016; Urinboyev and Polese 2016). These examples allow me to argue that the legal adaptation of migrants in weak rule-of-law regimes such as Russia must be understood not only through migrants' knowledge of existing laws, legal status, and engagement with formal institutions but also in terms of their knowledge of the street law and informal rules, connections to street institutions, and their ability to adapt to a corrupt environment.

In addition to "street-based legal adaptation" channels, Uzbek migrants also rely heavily on their village and *mahalla*-based trust and reciprocity networks. Migration under the conditions of legal uncertainty and precarity requires the reproduction and maintenance of transnational identities and relationships that act as forms of social safety nets when migrants face hardships. Accordingly, Uzbek migrants reproduced most of their village-level mutual aid activities in Moscow to compensate for the absence of formal protective mechanisms. Thus, among prospective migrants, traveling to Russia equates with joining their *mahalla* and village acquaintances there. Many villagers who were considering a "migrant career" in Russia (whom I met during my fieldwork in rural Fergana) imagined their future migrant life as integrating with their *mahalla* networks, which already extended to various Russian cities. Halil (45, male), an Uzbek migrant who worked in Moscow at the time of my fieldwork (2015), clearly described this:

> Even if we move to Russia, a foreign country, and stay there for five to six years, we continue to follow our old *urf-odat* [social norms], habits, religion, and way of life. If one of us gets into trouble, we quickly inform our mahallas and village members both here (in Russia) and there (in Uzbekistan) via Telegram [a smartphone application] or through an ordinary phone call. We, migrants in Moscow, quickly collect money and try to help our mahalla members. If you turn away and do not help your mahalla members, information about your egoistic behavior will quickly spread among migrants and also travel to your mahalla via the internet.

Smartphones and social media serve as means of reproducing and maintaining village-level identities, obligations, social norms, and relationships across distances. Uzbek migrants, for example, quickly informed each other and mobilized resources when someone fell ill, was caught by the police, needed to send something home, or desperately needed money. These smartphone-based translocal interactions proved crucial to migrants' survival and served as an alternative social safety net. Abduvali (38, male), an Uzbek construction worker in Moscow, explained how this worked:

We usually avoid public places, because there are hundreds of police officers on the streets, seeking to "milk us" [extort money from migrants]. Instead, we use smartphones and social media to resolve problems and socialize with our co-villagers in Moscow as well as to maintain daily contact with our families, mahalla, and village friends in Uzbekistan. It is Moscow, and things are unpredictable here; we rely on our mahalla and village connections when we get into trouble. We are all migrants here, so we cannot turn our backs when our fellow mahalla members are in trouble. But, in order to reach your mahalla members, you must always have a mobile phone with you, and you must memorize their phone numbers. For example, let's assume that you are a migrant worker who is caught by a police officer and brought to the police station. Normally, police officers keep you in a cell for a few hours and check your documents very carefully, a tactic used to further scare migrants. After finishing the check, police officers give you two options: (1) you can pay a bribe immediately and go home, or (2) if you have no money, the police officers allow you to phone your friends so that they can bring money and secure your release. The second scenario is more common, and you need to call your mahalla members for help. Therefore, you must always have your mobile phone with you. In some cases a police officer might allow you to use their mobile phone to contact your networks, but not all police officers are nice. If you do not have a phone with you and are caught by the police, there is a high risk that the police officers will refer your case to court for deportation.

Islam, the religion of a great majority of Uzbek and Central Asian migrants, also serves as an alternative system of belonging and adaptation to the hostile and xenophobic Russian environment (Aitamurto 2016; Yusupova and Ponarin 2016; Eraliev 2018; Turaeva 2018). Turaeva, in her recent publication on "imagined mosque communities in Russia" (2018), argues that Muslims in Russia view themselves as all belonging to one community since they identify themselves as Muslims, attend services at mosques, eat halal food, celebrate Eid, and share the same values. A large diversity of Islamic infrastructures can be found, such as mosques, alternative medical care, halal cafés, and networks of trust, assistance, and solidarity; here, migrants can also find refuge from daily racism and police abuse, and they can network to find employment and opportunities for education, health care, and other forms of social support (Turaeva 2018). Moreover, religion also offers consolation and comfort when migrants experience racism, as illustrated in the words of Muhammadsoli (33, male), an Uzbek mechanic in Moscow:

I was not religious before and regularly drank vodka. You know here in Russia vodka is cheaper than bread. Vodka offered me some kind of relief when I faced daily discrimination on the streets and in my workplace. But, after I started reading *namaz* (i.e., praying and becoming religious), my approach to life changed. I usually ignore when Russians call me "churka" [dumb] or "cherniy" [black] because I know that Allah is with me and I feel morally superior to these racist people.

Turning to the role of civil society, we see that the unionization rate among Uzbek migrants remains exceptionally low. This low rate most likely stems either from a lack of knowledge among migrants about the existence of trade unions or from the low level of trust among migrant workers regarding the effectiveness of trade unions. Only 2 percent to 3 percent of Central Asian migrants are aware of the existence of the Trade Union of Migrant Workers (*Profsoyuz Migrantov*).[2] Another contributing factor lies in the absence of a trade union culture in the migrants' home countries, which affects their legal adaptation strategies in Russia. Interestingly, Uzbek migrants can more easily adapt to the corrupt environment in Russia and negotiate the bribe rate with police officers than make legal claims through trade unions and migrant-rights organizations. This legal behavior is unsurprising given that Uzbek migrants are socialized into the Uzbek legal environment, in which police corruption is commonplace (Urinboyev and Svensson 2013b). Hence, Uzbek migrants' premigratory cultural codes and experiences play a crucial role in their legal adaptation strategies once in Russia. Many of the Uzbek migrants with whom I spoke have experienced corrupt policing practices in Uzbekistan, meaning that they arrived in Russia with similar "legal baggage" given what they must deal with vis-à-vis corrupt Russian police officers. In other words Uzbek migrants already possessed the "street skills" necessary to negotiate the "rules of the game" when they come into contact with Russian police officers. Markovska, Serdyuk, and Sokurenko (2019) reported a similar observation in their study of Ukrainian migrant workers in Russia.

Being undocumented represents a way of life for many Uzbek migrants. Because Russian immigration laws are complex and constantly changing, it is nearly impossible for migrants to remain documented and follow the latest legal developments. This problem is further exacerbated by the arbitrary actions of Russian police officers, immigration officials, and border guards who view migrants as a source of *kormushka* (feeding troughs). Police officers understand that migrants carry fake or "clean fake" residence registrations given that they do not live at the address where they are registered. Police officers, then, use this as a means to extort bribes from migrants they stop by demanding to see their residence registrations and work permits. Even those migrants who possess all of the required documents are afraid of or reluctant to demand their rights (*kachat' prava*) when stopped by the police. Whereas Kyrgyz and Tajik migrants frequently challenge Russian police officers, Uzbek migrants tend to offer bribes to police rather than make legal claims. To some extent, these behavioral patterns are connected with the widespread police corruption in Uzbekistan where paying bribes to police for minor infractions has become something of a norm. Instead of demanding their rights, people in Uzbekistan solve their problems with the police by offering them informal payments (Urinboyev and Svensson 2013b). Subsequently, Uzbek migrants have drawn from their premigratory experiences and cultural repertoires when interacting with corrupt Russian police officers, who always look for reasons to extort money from migrants. Commenting on Uzbek migrants' legal culture,

Dima (32, male, police officer in Moscow), sarcastically explained how much easier it is to find a "common language" with Uzbek migrants:

> It is not so easy to extort money from Kyrgyz migrants, even if their documents are not clean. They demand their rights and resist until the end. Tajik migrants are also tough. If I stop them and then take them to the local police department [*otdel politsii*] for an additional check, at least 10 Tajik migrants come to the department to secure the release of their fellow countryman. They do so even when their countrymen are undocumented. But things are a lot easier with Uzbek migrants. I catch Uzbek migrants and their documents are in order. But, interestingly, Uzbeks immediately get 500 rubles from their pocket and give it to me. Therefore, an Uzbek passport is a joy for many police officers.

Thus, informality remains part and parcel of Uzbek migrants' daily life in Russia. On the one hand, Uzbek migrants carry their premigratory cultural and normative repertoires to Russia and draw on them as an adaptation strategy when dealing with the uncertainties and precarity of shadow economy employment. On the other hand, the Russian governance system, including the institutions and actors charged with enforcing immigration laws and policies, is corrupt and arbitrary, creating a space for various informal and illegal strategies. The combination of these two features—that is, migrants' legal culture and the host country's legal environment—produces a peculiar legal adaptation strategy that empowers and grants agency among migrants to navigate the system. Thus, I argue that in weak rule-of-law migration regimes such as Russia, migrants are not passive entities but have agency and display capacity to negotiate the "rules of the game." In turn, migrants use that agency, as well as the opportunities provided by the weak rule of law and the corrupt political system, to negotiate with informal channels to gain employment and other opportunities that are limited (to those with a legal status) or hard to obtain in the current legal framework of the host country. The "thick" description of these processes will be provided in the next chapters.

4

Uzbek Migrants' Everyday Encounters with Employers and Middlemen

Drawing from the ethnographic study of Uzbek migrant construction workers' everyday encounters with Russian employers and middlemen, this chapter examines how migrants in Russia organize their daily lives and navigate labor market uncertainties under the conditions of an extensive shadow economy. As discussed in previous chapters, shadow economy employment is a way of life for many migrants in Russia. This pattern is common not only among Central Asian migrants but also among migrants from Azerbaijan, Armenia, Moldova, and Ukraine who predominate in informal employment. This reality led to a widespread assumption in both the Russian political and media discourses that migrants choose to work in the shadow economy for tax avoidance purposes (Kuznetsova 2017). But informal work is not a choice made freely by migrant workers; instead, it is primarily driven by the employers' motivations to reduce labor costs. Even if migrants possess all of the required immigration papers, employers often refuse to formally employ them, not wanting to pay the necessary taxes and contribute to social security.[1] As a result, migrants are forced to work without any employment contract. As Williams, Round, and Rodgers (2013) have demonstrated, this also stands true for many ethnic Russians unable to operate in full compliance with the formal labor market owing to employers' practices. Therefore, informal employment remains unavoidable for both Russian citizens and migrants. Given these realities, it is no surprise that Gimpelson and Kapeliushnikov (2014) concluded that the proportion of the informal labor market in Russia in 2013 stood at between one-fifth and one-third of all employment.

Another contributing factor lies in the complicated and expensive legalization procedures that compel many migrants to reside and work without residence registration and work-permit papers (Reeves 2015; Kuznetsova and Round 2018). According to Russian legislation, the employment of foreign citizens must take

62

place on the basis of a work permit and a written contract, implying that the absence of these documents violates immigration and labor laws. Such an absence may lead to the issuance of an entry ban or deportation. Since the majority of migrants remain undocumented and work without any employment contract, Russian employers and middlemen have a strong incentive to exploit migrants and withhold or delay their salaries. Ultimately, Russian employers remain confident that migrants will not seek redress from state institutions given their undocumented status. In addition to bureaucratic barriers, the fact that many Central Asian migrants, particularly those from rural regions, do not have a sufficient command of the Russian language and laws pushes them toward informal employment (Laruelle 2007; Marat 2009). The construction sector has a proven capacity to absorb undocumented migrants with few language skills, low salary expectations, and high insecurity (Urinboyev and Polese 2016). The role of various intermediaries (*posredniks*) is pivotal to negotiating and channeling migrants' access to shadow economy employment. These intermediaries possess a wide range of networks and information about employment, accommodation, and immigration documents.

Accordingly, the everyday lives of migrants in Russia are characterized by a constant sense of insecurity and precarity. Reporters and human rights activists have extensively documented the difficult living and working conditions of labor migrants in Russia (Human Rights Watch 2009; Súilleabháin 2013; Umidbek 2015). With the exception of a few ethnographic studies (Reeves 2013, 2015; Urinboyev 2018a), the prevailing research also describes migrant workers in Russia as helpless victims subject to numerous human rights abuses, such as exploitation, discrimination, unsafe working conditions, wage theft, physical violence, police corruption, arbitrary detention, and deportation (Alexseev 2015; Kubal 2016a; Round and Kuznetsova 2016; Zabyelina 2016; Kondakov 2017; Malakhov and Simon 2017; Kuznetsova and Round 2018; Schenk 2018).

This chapter situates itself within these scholarly debates, demonstrating how migrants navigate the labor market risks and uncertainties through informal rules and transnational practices. More specifically, it will show how Uzbek migrants, as an antidote to the risks and uncertainties of the shadow economy, have created an informal adaptation infrastructure, based on its own economy, legal order, trust, and mutual aid networks. The existence of such an informal infrastructure allows migrants to devise specific integration and "legalization" strategies, create an informal job market, and establish informal social safety nets to share the livelihood risks and deal with precarious conditions. These processes are particularly visible in the construction sector in Moscow, where the informal employment of migrant workers is widespread and carried out through so-called *po rukam* (handshake-based) labor contracts. Such contracts involve multiple formal and informal actors with different kinds and loci of power: construction companies, middlemen, migrant workers, Russian police officers, Chechen racketeers, and migrants' left-behind families and communities. This chapter, through a transnational ethnographic study of Uzbek migrant workers in Russia and their home village in Uzbekistan, aims to show how the interaction between the aforementioned actors across borders (via smartphones and social media) produces "informal legal orders" that regulate and enforce the "rules of the game" in the informal migrant labor market in Moscow. In doing so, I show how the informally produced legal order serves as an alternative (to the state law) to organizing migrants' daily lives and adapting under the conditions of an extensive shadow economy. Furthermore, I demonstrate how the informally produced legal order impacts the outcomes of many practices that Uzbek migrants (and other actors) adopt in Moscow. Thus, I use this case as a lens to pursue broader questions—that is, to offer a legally pluralistic framework for the study of migrant legal adaptation in a weak rule-of-law context.

The data for this chapter were gathered during the first period of my fieldwork in Moscow and the Fergana Valley (Uzbekistan) in 2014 over eight months. In addition to participant observation with migrants in Moscow, interviews and observations were conducted in the migrants' home village in Uzbekistan. Observations took place at "gossip hotspots," such as the *guzar* (village meeting space), *choyxona* (teahouse), *gaps* (regular get-togethers), and at life-cycle events (e.g., weddings and funerals). Informal interviews with village residents were, in this respect, as useful as the Moscow fieldwork in allowing me to better understand the evolution of the dynamics between actors.

THE (INFORMAL) CONSTRUCTION
SECTOR IN MOSCOW

The use of undocumented migrant labor remains quite common in the construction sector, particularly in residential and road construction projects (Malakhov 2014). The overconcentration of undocumented migrants in this sector is not accidental, since many construction companies and large wholesale markets are informally owned by the *siloviky*—that is, high-level (retired) officials of the Russian Federal Security Service (FSB). Even those construction companies not owned by *siloviky* cooperate closely with them by regularly paying a "protection fee" (*dan' za kryshovanie*).[2] This renders the construction sector one of the most corrupt sectors in the Russian economy, where the interests of large businesses and high-level state officials overlap and where the use of undocumented migrants is commonplace and tolerated.

The construction sector resembles a flat pyramid. Clients (*zakazchik*), general contractors (*genpodryadchik*), and subcontractors (*subpodryadchik*) occupy the top tier, while a huge army of migrant workers lies at the bottom.[3] Migrants tend to carry out all of the (strenuous, yet low-value) physical work. *Posredniks* (middlemen) mediate between migrants and the client, who seeks to minimize expenses and pay as little as possible.

The client at the top is typically an organization receiving state or private funding for various construction projects. The client typically hires a general contractor for construction, installation, and design. The general contractor is completely responsible for the implementation of construction, installation, and design work. The contractor is not directly involved, however, since he primarily acts as coordinator and intermediary agent, using several subcontractors for the actual construction work. A subcontractor is typically a construction company responsible for constructing, installing, and designing work by finding and employing skilled laborers.

The construction companies aim to complete projects with minimal possible expenditures. If they employ Russian citizens, their profits will fall. Migrants do not expect a high salary and are easy to manipulate and blackmail. Even so, if a company is found to hire migrants illegally, it faces a fine of 800,000 rubles (US$12,000) per illegally hired migrant worker. The usual solution involves identifying a Russian citizen to act as a middleman between the company and the migrant workers. All transactions are conducted by a handshake (*po rukam*), thus liberating the company from any contractual obligations. But, regardless, the construction company regularly pays a protection fee to a high-level FSB official as insurance in case something happens.

The Russian middleman finds skilled migrant construction workers. It is difficult, however, for him to establish trustworthy relations with migrants given various language barriers and cultural differences. To minimize the risks, the Russian middleman strikes a deal with an Uzbek or Tajik migrant *posrednik*.

A migrant *posrednik* can fulfill three possible functions: *posrednik*, *brigadir*, and *prorab*. A *posrednik* supplies skilled migrant workers to contractors and retains a *dolya* (share) of between 10 percent and 15 percent of each worker's salary. A *prorab* supervises groups of migrants on a daily basis and is responsible for the quality of their work. A *brigadir* leads a work group (brigade or *brigada*) and contributes to the physical work, claiming a higher salary for his dual roles and more extensive experience.

Given the absence of formal mechanisms for control, coercion, and conflict resolution, trust is crucial. The Russian company responsible for construction will have the capital and contacts with the producers of construction materials but not with the workers. This is entrusted to a middleman, normally a Russian. The middleman has contacts with the street world of construction and knows some migrant middlemen who enjoy authority among workers, know their language, and can manage a *brigada*. Of course, it is not possible to trust everyone, and each person must establish his reputation such that personal connections and social capital are crucial to most agreements in the construction sector.

Apart from the construction materials, other transactions go unrecorded. Migrants often occupy an irregular position and are not paid directly. Migrant middlemen receive payment from Russian middlemen and then distribute the money to the migrant workers, taking a percentage (*dolya*). Middlemen can try to increase their income by decreasing their workers' salaries or the number of people they hire, possibly decreasing the quality or slowing down the construction work. Migrants need someone they can trust, and they agree to pay a portion of their salary to the middleman; however, they need to be certain that they will be looked after and that the percentage they pay is fair. They also need to trust that they will be paid, which is why they tend to work only with people whom they already know.

FIRST FIELDWORK VISIT TO MOSCOW:
LEARNING THE VOCABULARY OF THE
LEGALLY PLURALISTIC MIGRANT LABOR MARKET

In search of empirical clues, on January 23, 2014, I traveled to Moscow, Russia, to conduct ethnographic field research. The afternoon flight from Copenhagen to Moscow on Aeroflot took just under three hours, and I arrived at Moscow's Sheremetyevo International Airport in the evening. After passing through customs and passport control, I walked toward the airport forecourt, where Misha, an Uzbek migrant worker, was waiting for me in his car.[4] Because Misha and I hail from the same district in Fergana, Uzbekistan, I was excited to meet my *zemlyak* (fellow countryman) for both personal and academic reasons. Misha welcomed me with a smile; we shook hands and hugged each other, since we had not seen each other for seven years. I then placed my belongings in the boot of his car, and we quickly headed to the northeast of Moscow city, where my hotel was located.

Sheremetyevo International Airport is not far from the Moscow city center; it takes 25 to 30 minutes to drive to the center during off-peak hours. But because I arrived in the evening, when traffic congestion on the Moscow Ring Road (MKAD), is at its highest, our trip lasted more than two hours. Nonetheless, the traffic jam provided a good opportunity for us to catch up on what had happened since we had last seen one another. I briefly explained to Misha my migration research and asked him if he could help me collect data about Uzbek migrant workers' everyday lives and experiences in Moscow. Misha seemed interested in my work and promised that he would put me in touch with migrant workers. Misha is one of the pioneer migrants, having brought many of his covillagers and acquaintances (roughly 200 migrants) to Moscow. He arrived in Moscow in 2002, when labor migration was still a new phenomenon in Uzbekistan. At the time of my fieldwork he worked as a *posrednik* in the construction sector, acting as an intermediary between migrant workers and Russian construction firms. As a non-Russian, it would be difficult for him to deal directly with Russian construction companies. He was well-trusted by Russian middlemen, however, who preferred not to deal directly with migrant workers. Before taking up this challenge, Misha worked as a taxi driver, earning US$500 to US$600 per month. It was as a taxi driver that Misha made Russian acquaintances and developed an extensive network that later paved the way for him to become a *posrednik* in the construction sector, the highest rung on the career ladder many migrant workers strive to reach. He apparently enjoyed his work greatly and believed that his role as a *posrednik* was pivotal in the migrant labor market.

I was truly intrigued by Misha's success story and, subsequently, wanted to learn more about his work. Misha is one of the few middlemen who successfully combine the three roles of *posrednik, prorab,* and *brigadir.* This results from his fluency in Russian and Uzbek, and his ability to build and lead a construction *brigada.* His vast network of contacts secures him many *zakaz* (jobs) per year. The work of a middleman in the Russian construction sector remains largely informal, meaning that Misha's work lies well beyond state law and bureaucracy; hence, no written (formal) contracts regulate his working relationships with different parties. Rather, Misha concludes *po rukam* (handshake) style agreements with migrant workers, Russian *posredniks,* and construction firms. An amount is agreed on and paid periodically as the construction progresses. As a *posrednik,* Misha's primary role focuses on finding well-skilled migrant construction workers, taking full responsibility for the quality of the construction work, and addressing migrants' daily concerns (e.g., accommodation and food) and legal problems (e.g., police problems). For his service as a *posrednik,* he typically takes a *dolya* (share), whereby each migrant laborer gives 10 percent to 15 percent of his salary to Misha.

Finding skilled and reliable migrant construction workers who can be trusted not to steal construction materials and to perform their tasks in accordance with state standards is difficult. Kinship and a common village origin are quite important in this regard. Given this social proximity, Misha's *erkakcha gap* (literally, "man's word") is sufficient for his workers. When Misha approaches someone not from his village—or at least his district—they rarely agree to work under him. Fraud cases are common in Moscow, whereby *posredniks* cheat migrants and do not pay their salaries. Coming from the same village establishes not only a social bond but also a social responsibility in the workers' minds. Both the family of the *posrednik* and the workers share a territory and interact daily to such a degree that noncompliance with the agreed-on obligations from either side would trigger a chain reaction with the workers' families. This would put direct pressure on the *posrednik*'s family in the village, pressure that might not happen if the two men's families lived far from one another.

Because of this, all those involved understand that a failure to comply with an agreement not only brings immediate consequences but also results in consequences in their home village, given the involvement of entire families in these transactions. An important feature lies in how a conflict may be resolved, which depends on the different standpoints. Because no formal institution or rule exists, each party is likely to endorse a set of rules more convenient to them, thereby indicating the existence of "parallel legal orders" in the Russian migrant labor market. Here, parties may refer to *ko'cha qonunlari* (laws of the street), *erkakchilik* (literally, "manliness") rules, Uzbek village rules, Sharia law, state law, or anything in between. I discuss these in further detail below.

This spontaneous conversation with Misha provided an excellent introduction to the migrant labor market in Moscow, enabling me to obtain my first insights into how Uzbek migrants cope with and gain access to the labor market in the restrictive Russian legal environment. By referring to *po rukam*, Misha was actually talking about the highly informal nature of the migrant labor market. This marked the first time I learned about the informal contracts between migrant workers, migrant middlemen, and Russian construction firms, whereby migrants could gain access to the labor market without any work permits or Russian-language skills. Hence, *po rukam*–style construction work appeared sophisticated, representing a highly efficient system benefiting all parties involved. But Misha's story was not complete, since he did not discuss those cases in which one of the parties (the migrant, the Russian *posrednik*, or the construction firm) fails to comply with the *po rukam* contract. Given the highly informal nature of the migrant labor market in Moscow, I wondered how the *po rukam* contract worked in practice and whether any extant regulatory structures were capable of resolving disputes when one of the parties does not fulfill its contractual obligations.

Misha, recognizing my interest in his work, invited me to visit his workplace in Solnechnogorsk (Moscow province) so that I could acquaint myself with his construction team (hereafter, *brigada*). This invitation offered an ideal opportunity for me to see and experience migrant workers' everyday lives. Thus, I accepted the invitation with great enthusiasm. Before leaving me at the hotel, Misha told me that he would pick me up from my hotel the next morning at 8 a.m. I thanked him, and we parted.

MISHA AND HIS *BRIGADA*: COMMON VILLAGE ORIGIN AND ENFORCEABLE TRUST

As planned, on the following day, Misha picked me up from my hotel, and we headed to Solnechnogorsk. For Misha it was just a typical workday, although this trip was a very special experience for me. We arrived at the construction site at about 10 a.m., at which time all of the *brigada* members were working on the 17th floor despite the freezing cold weather (the outdoor temperature was −25 degrees Celsius). Since the *brigada* was busy working, I tried to carry out some observations on the construction site and gathered information about *brigada* members and their living and working conditions. Misha's *brigada* consisted of 12 migrant workers, and their main job was to install new windows in mid- and high-rise buildings. On average the *brigada* works 10 to 12 hours each day, without any days off. They are allowed to take a day off only in exceptional circumstances, for example, if there is a lack of materials (e.g., silicone caulking or nails) needed to complete the window installations. Misha purchases the necessary food items (bread, vegetables, rice, pasta, cooking oil, etc.), and members of the *brigada* make meals for themselves. This means that each day one migrant, on a rotating basis, is assigned the task of preparing lunch and dinner for everyone. There is no clear boundary between work and nonwork activities in the *brigada*'s everyday operations. The same construction site serves as both workplace and accommodation. The *brigada*'s accommodation during my fieldwork was located on the fourth floor of the building and consisted of two rooms: one narrow, cramped room full of rudimentary bunk beds with old mattresses, blankets, and old clothes used as pillows; and one slightly bigger room for handwashing, cooking, and eating that fell short of even basic hygiene standards. The indoor temperature was around 20 degrees Celsius thanks to two electric heaters. The *brigada* could access an outdoor toilet, but no indoor or proper bathroom facility was available for their use.

The *brigada* returned to their room at about 1 p.m. to have lunch. Almost all members have smartphones with internet access. They regularly used Odnoklassniki (a popular social media site in the post-Soviet space) to check the latest news, view photos, and send instant messages to their families and friends in Uzbekistan. Some migrants made phone calls to their family, telling them that they were fine and would send money home as soon as they received their salary. Mansur, today's "chef on duty," prepared *osh* (a festive Uzbek rice dish), and all members of the *brigada* looked satisfied and happy. The *osh* was served in a large bowl and shared by everyone sitting at the table. While eating *osh*, they primarily discussed how to avoid errors in installing windows and perform tasks in accordance with state standards. As the *brigada* leader, Misha gave instructions, distributed tasks, and told members to be more industrious. The *brigada* members attentively and obediently listened to his instructions and orders, treating him as a boss. Those migrants who smoked asked Misha to bring Winston cigarettes the following day, while others requested that he top up their mobile phones. One of the migrants asked Misha to send money to his family, since his father needed money for urgent medical treatment. Although Misha had not yet received payment from Stas (the Russian *posrednik*), he tried to fulfill all of the requests from his *brigada* using his personal savings to do so. Misha also tried to meet the bathing needs of the *brigada*. He explained that on that day he would take three *brigada* members to his apartment in Moscow city so that they could take a shower and get some rest. As an observer, I thought that Misha not only acted as a *posrednik* but also exhibited paternalistic leadership characteristics by treating his *brigada* in a fatherly manner and providing for their needs on a rotating basis. The roles and relationships between Misha and his *brigada* seemed well-organized and balanced, giving me the impression that a *po rukam*–style contract does indeed work.

Accordingly, Misha and his *brigada* members lay at the center of a complex net of intertwining relationships. In Moscow, *brigada* members operated under Misha, respected his authority, and called him "elder brother," regardless of their age difference. On the one hand, *brigada* members had little choice but to trust him to deliver

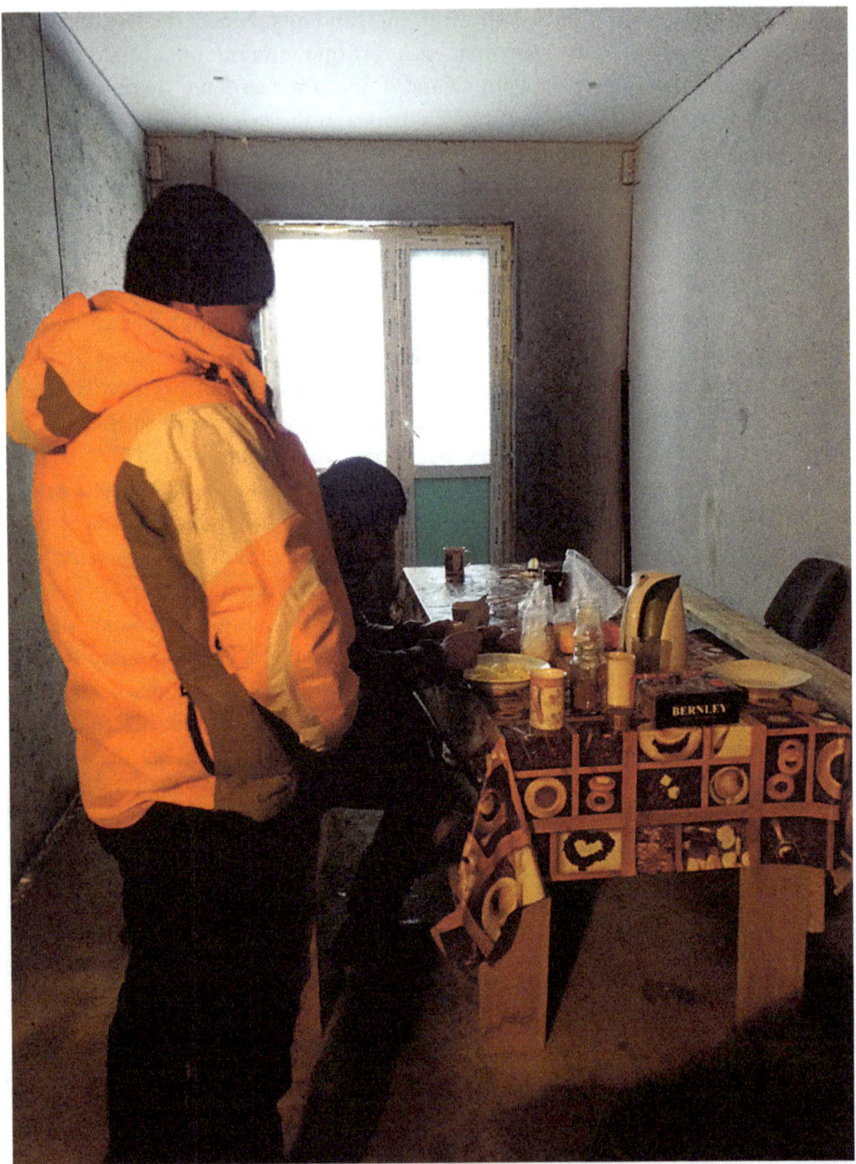

FIGURE 5. Misha and his worker prepare lunch for brigada members. January 2014, Solnechnogorsk, Moscow province, Russia. Photo by author.

their salaries, to take care of them if they faced difficulties, and to help them with documents. On the other hand, this trust relied on the understanding that, because they came from the same place and their families were in touch with one another, it would be too costly for Misha to cheat them. Any monetary advantage would bring only short-term benefits and would be matched by retaliation at the village level. Ultimately, money is not everything; in the village and other small communities, reputation, prestige, and trust account for much more. Misha's capacity to provide for his countrymen also placed him and his family in a higher social position in Shabboda. As noted in a number of other empirical studies (Pardo 1996; Zanca 2003), reputation and status actually matter. Money may play a major role but only in the short-term. In the long-term and in a dependence-based network, the capacity to generate money in a sustainable way is more important. This ability relies on trust and the capacity to not let others down (White 1994). Despite his high social status and solid reputation, however, Misha's position rested on a weak premise. As long as he is perceived as bringing more benefits than troubles, he will be supported and praised by his workers and their families. But when this perception is questioned or the benefits become intangible, any allegations might be used to attack him and negotiate a better deal (or break the current one).

After visiting the construction site on a daily basis, I was able to develop a close relationship with all of the members of the *brigada*. Because the workers and I hail from the same district, almost all of them knew or had heard about me, which led to my being accepted as *svoi* (our own)—that is, an "insider" with whom both work and nonwork issues can be discussed. In turn, I also tried to remain open-minded and briefly explained my research to them, introducing myself as a migration researcher writing about Uzbek migrant workers in Russia. Accordingly, my first fieldwork visit (January 23–29, 2014) allowed me to establish a close relationship with migrant communities and enhanced my understanding of Uzbek migrants' everyday working lives and experiences in Moscow.

FIELDWORK VISIT TO FERGANA (UZBEKISTAN): TRANSNATIONAL DEPENDENCY PATTERNS

A second research aim that spontaneously emerged during the course of my fieldwork related to exploring the processes of everyday material, emotional, social, and symbolic exchanges between Misha's *brigada* members and their left-behind families and communities in Uzbekistan. I assumed that technological developments would produce a simultaneousness of events and instantaneous interactions between migrant-sending and -receiving societies, possibly leading to the emergence of transnational ties and networks. Since all *brigada* members used smartphones and social media, I inferred that there must be a daily exchange of information between the *brigada* and their sending community. I was particularly interested in investigating whether it was possible to glean the patterns of transnationalism among Misha's *brigada* and their left-behind families and communities. Furthermore, if this was possible, I wanted to examine how these transnational interactions impact the outcomes of practices that Misha and his *brigada* (and other actors) adopt in Moscow.

Armed with these research questions, I traveled to the Fergana region of Uzbekistan for two weeks of fieldwork between January 31 and February 15, 2014. Shabboda, where the families of Misha and his *brigada* live, is a village in the Fergana region, consisting of 28 *mahalla*, with a population of more than 18,000 individuals. Likewise, migration is a widespread livelihood strategy, simply a "norm" for young and able-bodied men in Shabboda. As I expected, villagers were well-informed about the living and working conditions of Misha and his *brigada* members. This resulted largely from technological developments that reduced the importance of distance and created an everyday information exchange between Shabboda and Moscow. Wherever I went and with whomever I spoke, the central topics of conversation were migration and remittances. Misha and his *brigada*'s Moscow adventures lay at the center of "village talk." Given that Misha provided many village residents with jobs in Moscow, his family members enjoyed a high social status and much prestige in the village. Therefore, when invited to weddings, Misha's father was always offered the "best table" and was served more quickly than others. Misha was specifically praised by the parents of his *brigada* members for employing and taking care of their sons. But not all villagers shared this view. Some residents I encountered argued that Misha's *posrednik* work was incompatible with the principles of Islam and Sharia law since he took *dolya* from migrants' salaries without doing any physical work. Some even believed that Misha "eats a lot" and covertly steals from his covillagers. But even if some villagers questioned the correctness of Misha's work from a religious perspective, many refrained from applying religious labels and made a small exception for a greater gain—that is, each *brigada* member's ability to make a living and send money home. In her study of the role of *posredniks* in the market for accommodation in Moscow, Madeleine Reeves (2016) also found that *posredniks* held ambiguous reputations within the migrant community. On the one hand, they were praised as "diplomats" who provided access to accommodation, work, and documents; on the other hand, they were vilified as "con-artists" who made money from other migrants' economic vulnerability and unfamiliarity with the city.

TENSIONS WITHIN THE *BRIGADA*

Following a two-month break, I returned to Moscow for a follow-up fieldwork visit, from April 5 through 15, 2014. Like my previous trip, I visited Misha's *brigada* in Solnechnogorsk on a regular basis. But this time things were different. Although the *brigada* had already completed half of the window installation work, they had not been paid for their work since January. I also learned that two migrants had already quit the *brigada* in response to payment delays, and other members were also considering leaving. In general, the *brigada*'s daily conversations revolved primarily around questions regarding why they were experiencing payment problems and what measures they could take to receive payment for their work. Simultaneously, they were under heavy pressure to send money home, since their left-behind families depended on such remittances to meet their basic needs. Misha's situation was particularly delicate, because he had actually failed to secure the migrants' salaries. But he insisted that he was also a *musofir* (alien) in Russia, just like everyone else, and blamed Stas (the Russian *posrednik*) and the construction company for the payment problems. The *brigada* seemed empathetic toward Misha and did not hold him responsible for the payment delays.

Despite being present on the construction site on a daily basis, Stas continued avoiding any possible contact with *brigada* members, completely refusing to discuss financial issues with them. He often stated that his agreement was with Misha, not with the *brigada*, so he discussed all matters only with Misha. This situation eventually led to hostility and frustration, since *brigada* members felt ignored and voiceless even though they had completed all of the hard work. As a result, the *brigada* questioned Stas's honesty and discussed several options for how to retaliate if they did not receive the promised salary. Several migrants suggested that they should either break all of the installed windows or steal construction materials. Others suggested that they should physically or materially harm Stas, by, for instance, burning his car or physically beating him. But given his personal responsibility for the *brigada*'s actions, Misha asked the *brigada* to remain patient and refrain from taking any collective measures; otherwise, they would risk their salary and safety further. In Misha's view the only realistic solution was to continue working with Stas, given that the *brigada* members were working without any legal work permits. Even if they worked legally and filed a complaint with the Russian Federal Migration Service or courts, the migrants' chances of success were near zero, since Stas and the construction company could easily win the case by bribing state officials. Misha argued that migrants are nobodies in Russia, and thus warned the *brigada* that they might easily end up in prison if they harmed Stas materially or physically. Fearing the consequences of their plans, the *brigada* obeyed Misha and decided not to take any retaliatory measures against Stas. They were reluctant, however, to complete any further work, demanding that Stas pay at least one-third of their salary. As a *brigada* leader, Misha had to keep things going and convinced the *brigada* that he would secure their salary by the end of April if they completed the window installation work. The *brigada* continued to work in April, believing that Misha would keep his word.

Thus, the situation within the *brigada* was developing in completely different ways from that which I observed during my first fieldwork visit. Feelings of help-lessness and anger were clearly visible in the *brigada*'s daily conversations. Despite the payment delays, most *brigada* members appeared to trust and accept Misha's leadership. Two members, however, did not trust Misha and decided to quit the *brigada*. These events signaled that something serious was developing or taking place within the *brigada* of which I was probably unaware given my "outsider" status. In this regard I looked to the left-behind families and communities of the *brigada* as an alternative source of information.

To further understand the situation, I traveled to Fergana for additional field research between April 27 and May 21, 2014. After arriving in Shabboda, I visited Misha's and the *brigada's* families in order to determine what was actually happening in the *brigada's* life. The first thing I noticed was that the *brigada's* Moscow disputes and problems were gradually emerging in the village. Family members were well-informed about the latest developments in Moscow. From my conversations I learned that Misha had failed to live up to his promises and did not secure the *brigada's* salary by the end of April. These developments eventually led to the *brigada* disbanding, and, subsequently, a dispute arose between Misha and the *brigada* over money. Simultaneously, the *brigada's* families began pressuring Misha's family and demanded that either Misha or his parents must take responsibility for their sons' salaries. Misha's parents refused to take any responsibility, however, arguing that the dispute should be discussed and resolved in Moscow, where it was taking place, not in the village. In mid-May I learned that Misha had made a new promise, stating that he would get the money from the Russians by the end of June. Thereafter, all of the *brigada* members would be paid for their work. Their family members decided to wait one more month, hoping that Misha would keep his word this time. Subsequently, the dispute ceased and remained muted in the village. Most people I met at the village's "gossip hotspots" such as the *guzar* (village meeting space), *choyxona* (teahouse), and at weddings remained unaware of these developments.

"STREET LAW," CHECHENS, AND THE POLICE IN MIGRANT MOSCOW

When I returned to Moscow in the summer of 2014 (July 29–August 6, 2014), I learned that the *brigada* had completely disbanded and the migrants were working in different places. Most had found new jobs at a construction site in Balashikha, a city in the Moscow province, while others were working at a bazaar or meat warehouse. Misha no longer had employees and was working alone, carrying out *haltura* (daily labor) for individual (private) persons. Misha and the *brigada* members were in open confrontation, since Misha had again failed to fulfill his promise. Since the *brigada* worked informally, they knew that they could not resort to legal measures to address their grievances. Not wanting to lose their money, however, the *brigada* instead approached a group of Chechen protection racketeers, asking them to recover their money from Misha and offered 20 percent of the total sum of money owed to them as payment for their protection services. I learned that Chechen racketeers were known as *qozi* (judges) among Central Asian migrants, providing an alternative (to the state) justice system and means of settling disputes through threats and violence. However, the *brigada*'s appeal to the racketeers was futile, since Misha had stronger connections with the Russian paramilitary police (OMON). When I asked Misha about the details of the incident, he talked excitedly about his triumph over the Chechens:

I tried to explain to the *brigada* why the payment was delayed, but they didn't want to hear me. Things are simply beyond my control. Although we are all covillagers, they didn't show any mercy and shamelessly used Chechen racketeers against me. I was willing to pay them, but after what they did to me, they wouldn't get anything from me. This incident happened in mid-July. They called me, demanding that I must pay their salary immediately. I told the *brigada* that I would give them money as soon as I received payment from Stas. Afterwards, the tone of the conversation suddenly changed and they started to threaten me, saying that they would give me to the Chechen racketeers. Many migrants get terrified when they hear the word Chechen, because Chechens are violent and rule street life in Moscow. So, the *brigada* thought that I would also be scared to death and surrender immediately.

Seemingly, the *brigada* underestimated me. I have been living in Moscow since 2002, so I have also lots of powerful connections on the street. I told the *brigada* that they can give me to any Chechen racketeer. At the same time, I informed them that if they used racketeers against me, we—all sides—must abide by the "laws of the street." According to street laws, if the *brigada* decide to use Chechen racketeers as the *qozi*, they must fully waive their claims against me, because they are transferring the case to the racketeers. In other words, they quit the game automatically. In that case, I owe money to the Chechen racketeers, not to the *brigada*. This means that the *brigada* demands money from the Chechens, since they take full responsibility for recovering the money from me. If the Chechens don't succeed, the *brigada* loses all the money, and I no longer owe anything to the *brigada*. Hence, I told the *brigada* that they must be men and abide by the street rules if they use racketeers. They accepted these conditions, and we agreed that our relationship would end there.

Within a few days I received a phone call from the Chechen racketeers asking to meet for a *razborka* (violent showdown) in Moscow's Bibirevo district on July 17, 2014, at around 10 p.m. Before the meeting, I was warned that I owed them 800,000 Russian rubles (US$12,000) and that I must bring this amount to the *razborka;* otherwise, my life would be in danger. But I told them that they wouldn't get a single ruble from me and that they could do with me whatever they wanted. I knew that the *razborka* would be violent since I refused to pay. Therefore, I contacted my friends who work at OMON, asking them to protect me during the *razborka*. They are always eager to protect me, because I regularly pay them with *ko'ki* [Uzbek metaphor for US dollars].

At the agreed-upon time and day, I, together with five of my "friends" in plain clothes, arrived. The Chechens were late, usually a tactic intended to scare their victim further. But they eventually arrived. They got out of the car, saw the five suspicious Russians, got back into the car without uttering a word, and drove away. They never attempted to contact me again.

This unexpected turn (for the *brigada*) generated a further conflict. Misha and his *brigada* now had diametrically opposing views of the outcome. Misha's understanding was that he was indebted to his fellow villagers and would honor it, even if he had to pay with his own money. But the fact that his *brigada* employed Chechen racketeers as *qozi* had changed their relationship. They were no longer brothers in the same pan, but were now *brigadir* and *brigada*. The *brigada* had transferred their credit to a third party (the Chechens), such that Misha was no longer in debt to them but to the Chechens, with whom everything had now been settled. Referring to street laws, Misha believed that he was no longer obliged to pay the *brigada*. Thus, for Misha, this marked the end of the dispute.

The members of the *brigada* held a different view. They were creditors, and they wanted to be paid regardless of how. Once the Chechens failed to recover their money, there were two possible interpretations. One was that the debt was lost, since Misha had had to spend some resources to face the Chechens. Even if he did not pay his Russian friends directly, he now owed them an extra favor. He would have to pay them more next time or might not be able to ask for a further favor when a need arose. The *brigada* was possibly unable to see it this way. For them, the initial situation and the final situation were identical. They still had a credit with a given person. From their side, the Chechens agreed to attempt to recover their money, but there was no discussion of what would happen if they failed. The Chechens decided that facing Misha with his OMON friends was too costly and preferred to give up, losing only the few hours they had spent organizing the meeting and attempting to scare Misha.

During this fieldwork visit I invited all 12 *brigada* members for dinner at an Uzbek café in order to understand "the other side of the coin." From my conversation with them I learned that they were still determined to continue "the battle." While acknowledging Misha's victory "on the street," they still insisted that Misha must pay the *brigada*'s members' salaries, regardless of the circumstances. One member in particular, Baha, openly expressed his views:

> True, we lost the game according to the laws of the street. But, this doesn't absolve Misha from his responsibilities. His actions go against the religious norms. According to Sharia law, it is *haram* [sinful] to steal someone's money. It is also *haram* to take *dolya* from someone's salary. We worked hard even during the cold winter months and fulfilled our work duties, while Misha gave us orders and did not do any physical work. We agreed that he would take at least 15 percent *dolya* from our salaries, so his main task was to guarantee that we received our money on time. So if he can't get the money from Stas or the construction company, this is his personal problem, not ours. We shook hands with him, not with the Russians. We don't care whether he pays our salary from his own pocket or gets it from the Russians. He is constantly blaming the Russians, but we don't want to hear anything about his private deals with the Russians. The only thing we care [about] is our *po rukam* agreement with Misha.

Bek, the youngest member of the *brigada*, argued that "almost all Russian people are honest and never cheat migrants [*O'ris aldamaydi*]." He believed that Misha was just using Stas as an excuse to steal their money. In contrast, Nodir, another migrant, held the opinion that Misha and Stas were accomplices and were "staging the show together" to fool the *brigada*. While listening to their conversation, I noticed that they were considering various options to recover their money from Misha. When I asked what measures they were most likely to take, they replied that they would spread gossip about Misha in the village, hoping that would force him and his family to pay their salary.

THE QUIET POWER OF GOSSIP

Accordingly, the dispute again moved to Shabboda, so I immediately booked my flight and traveled to Fergana on August 6, 2014, to follow the latest developments in the village. As expected, *brigada* members were constantly calling their families in the village, asking them to put additional pressure on Misha's family by spreading gossip at the *guzar, choyxona*, and at weddings, places where people gather and conduct the bulk of village information exchanges. When I visited these social spaces, I observed that most village residents already knew about how "Misha exploited and 'ate' his fellow villagers' money." Most residents held the opinion that Misha was responsible for securing the *brigada*'s salary irrespective of the circumstances, since the *brigada* trusted him and worked hard during the cold winter months. They argued that a person must never assume this role if he cannot keep his word. Some villagers even accused Misha of human trafficking and exploitation, criminal acts according to Uzbek legislation. Moreover, the villagers held Misha responsible for the *brigada*'s legal problems, since the migrants did not have the money to obtain work permits because of the payment delays. Thus, they were banned from reentering Russia for five years. The villagers also invoked religion to interpret Misha's actions, arguing that according to Sharia law, it is unacceptable to take *dolya* from someone's salary. In this way Misha was viewed as a bad Muslim who earns money through *haram* means.

The relationship between Misha's family and the families of the *brigada* was especially problematic. The *brigada*'s families regularly visited Misha's house and created scandals on the street, telling all of the neighbors about the money conflict. They also spread gossip at wedding ceremonies, where the majority of villagers gathered. Moreover, the *oqsoqol* (community leader) and *imam* (leader of the mosque) intervened, warning Misha's parents that the details of the dispute would be made public during the Friday prayers at the mosque if Misha refused to pay his fellow villagers' salaries. The *brigada*'s families were also considering using legal measures as a last resort if the situation persisted:

FIGURE 6. Villagers conducting daily information exchanges. August 2014. Photo by author.

We are currently spreading gossip about Misha in the village. We hope this shaming strategy will yield some sort of result. If Misha's parents continue to ignore us, we will contact Uzbek law-enforcement bodies, for example, *uchastkovoy* (local police), *prokuratura* (a public prosecutor), or SNB (National Security Service). But, we won't rush to resort to these measures. Misha is our neighbor, and we don't want to ruin his life. So, we want to give him one more chance before officially reporting him to the law-enforcement bodies.

Misha's family was thus under huge village pressure. Most villagers began to look at them as bad Muslims who did not hesitate to eat *haram* food. From my observations I noticed that life was no longer bearable for Misha's family, since they had to face daily taunts and sarcastic remarks on the village streets. Misha's father's situation was particularly bad. Because of the widespread gossip and rumors about his son, he could no longer attend the village *guzar* and weddings where most people socialize. When I asked Misha's father how he would solve this problem, he explained that he would call Misha in the coming days and ask him to pay his debts immediately. Thus, that village pressure was slowly changing the course of developments.

Immediately following my Fergana fieldwork visit, I headed to Moscow (September 2–30, 2014) to determine if village events had any impact on Misha and the *brigada*'s actions in Moscow. As I expected, Misha was well-informed about the latest village news. He was quite frustrated and angry at the *brigada*, but at the same he was pragmatic and knew that he needed to do something to settle the dispute once and for all. Otherwise, his family would continue to suffer from village pressure. When I asked him how he would settle the matter, he said that he had already borrowed money from his friends and that he would pay the *brigada*'s salary within a few days. After a few days I invited all of the *brigada* members for lunch at an Uzbek café located in Moscow's Babushkinskaya district. From our conversation I learned that Misha had indeed paid them, so all of them appeared satisfied. Hence, the extension of village-level social norms and sanctions across borders proved effective as an enforcement mechanism, ultimately determining the outcome of this specific dispute. While Misha was able to stand up to Chechen racketeers, village pressure eventually forced him to prioritize his family's reputation and harmony within his family over money.

PLURALISTIC LEGAL ORDERS, THE SHADOW ECONOMY, AND MIGRANT'S LEGAL ADAPTATION

This chapter demonstrates that the use of a large-scale migrant labor force under shadow economic conditions led to the emergence of a "parallel world of migrants," a world in which it is possible to observe the patterns of informal governance and plural legal orders. The lack of formal rules does not necessarily mean that no rules exist. The dispute that arose between Misha and his *brigada* sheds some light on the nature of the informal labor market in Moscow, which remains informal, to a large extent, but consists of well-functioning regulatory mechanisms. In the (informal) construction sector in Moscow, as the case study of Misha and his *brigada* illustrates, multiple legal orders are negotiated and serve to regulate the "rules of the game." Negotiators range from local (Moscow-based) actors such as construction companies, Russian *posrednik*, migrant *posrednik*, migrant workers, moonlighting Russian police officers, and Chechen racketeers, to transnational (Uzbekistan-based) actors such as migrants' left-behind families, village residents, and community religious leaders (the *imam* and *oqsoqol*). Informality, as this case study shows, thus, may represent a "parallel legal order" that regulates the "rules of the game" in the shadow economy.

Based on the empirical material presented in this chapter, I believe that we need to go beyond "law-first" perspectives emphasizing the legal environment and migrant legalization strategies as key factors to understanding migrant legal adaptation. We must broaden our analytical lens to include "informal legal orders" that provide alternatives (to the state law) regulations and adaptations within migration regimes where the rule of law remains weak and informal governance prevails. As empirical data show, owing to the inability or unwillingness of the Russian legal system to regulate the migrant labor market, another parallel legal order has emerged as a governance tool. The existence of such an informal infrastructure allows migrants to devise specific adaptation and "legalization" strategies, create an informal job market, and establish informal social safety nets and rules to share the livelihood risks and deal with uncertainties. At first glance these informal practices come across as spontaneous responses; however, considering their magnitude and intensity through smartphones, they emerge as a more or less institutionalized custom in migrants' daily lives. Thus, the study of migrants' legal adaptation in weak rule-of-law contexts should look beyond the facade of the formal system and immigration laws and instead retrain the focus on migrants' agency and actual coping strategies under the conditions of informal employment.

Uzbek Migrants' Everyday Encounters with Street-Level Institutions

Between January and May of 2019 I conducted five months of intensive ethnographic fieldwork in Kumkapi, probably the most ethnically and culturally diverse quarter of the Fatih district in Istanbul, Turkey. Until recently, Kumkapi was known as the center of the Armenian community, home to the seat of the Armenian Patriarchate. But, recently, Kumkapi became a predominantly Uzbek quarter, where thousands of Uzbek migrant workers reside and work. Kumkapi, in the words of many Uzbek migrants I encountered there, is an "Uzbek *mahalla*," where almost everyone, even local Turks and Kurds, speak and understand the Uzbek language. Walking through the streets of Kumkapi, one can find dozens of cafés and restaurants serving Uzbek food, numerous cargo companies that ship clothes to Uzbekistan, many clothing stores and stalls selling fashions suitable to Uzbek culture, and even *nos* (Uzbek snuff) sold by a local Uzbek-speaking Turk. This recent transformation of (predominantly Armenian) Kumkapi into an Uzbek *mahalla* can be explained by the introduction of the draconian entry-ban legislation enacted in Russia in 2013 and 2014, which compelled many entry-banned Uzbek migrants to reorient their migration destination from Russia to Turkey. Uzbeks can travel visa-free, and they can work and reside informally in Turkey without any immigration papers. As such, more than 90 percent of the migrants I met during my fieldwork possessed neither a residence permit (*oturma izni*) nor a work permit (*çalışma izni*), meaning informal residence and employment was a way of life for many Uzbek migrants in Istanbul. Unlike in Russia, where (undocumented) migrants frequently pay bribes to Russian police officers, Uzbek migrants in Istanbul suffered less from police corruption and enjoyed relatively unimpeded mobility in the city given Turkish authorities' tacit acceptance of cheap and legally unprotected migrant labor. Thus, the Turkish migrant labor market seemed like a good alternative to the ever-tightening Russian migration regime, allowing many entry-banned Uzbek migrants to continue supporting their families.

Despite this relatively liberal migration regime, however, many of the Uzbek migrants I interviewed in Istanbul were nostalgic for their Russian migration experiences and planned to return to Russia as soon as their entry ban expired. When I asked migrants to explain why they preferred the Russian migrant labor market to Turkey's, they stated that in Russia they had more control over their working conditions and could take some action when faced with the uncertainties and risks of informal employment. In particular, one of my interviewees, Sherzod, commented that in Moscow one may turn to the "street world" to recover money if s/he experiences problems getting paid for work. In Istanbul, however, such street-based mechanisms do not exist, leaving migrants vulnerable to the whims of dishonest Turkish employers and intermediaries. When referring to the "street world," Sherzod actually referred to protection racketeers in Moscow, individuals such as those we met in the previous chapter, whom migrants approached when they experienced problems related to enforcing contractual obligations related to informal employment.

I suspect these Istanbul experiences confirmed many of my earlier observations about the role of "street-level institutions" in the Russian migration regime. During my fieldwork in Moscow (January 2014–August 2018), I noticed that many Uzbek migrants approached protection racketeers, asking them to "solve questions" (*reshat voprosy*). Migrants interchangeably utilized the terms *reket* and *razborshik* to refer to protection racketeering groups who provided an alternative (to the state) justice, contract enforcement, and dispute settlement through threats and violence. The demand for protection racketeers' services was particularly high in sectors such as bazaars, construction, agriculture, and the informal document markets (e.g., Moscow's Kazansky railway station). Quite often, migrants asked Chechen racketeers to recover their money (typically their salary) from employers and middlemen, offering 20 percent of the total sum of money collected as payment for such services. Chechen racketeers were known as the informal street judges among migrants. In addition, I learned about several instances in which Russian police officers acted on an informal basis as protection racketeers in the migrant labor market, offering salary recovery and physical protection (from other extortion rackets and bandits) for a fee.

As part of my fieldwork in Moscow, I approached 100 Central Asian migrant workers in July and August of 2015, asking the following question (among 90 other questions): "What measures would you take to recover payment if you had not been paid for your work?" In total, 42 percent of respondents stated that they would seek redress from protection racketeers if they experienced problems getting paid for their work. Another 15 percent said that they might seek redress via formal legal institutions, although they were not confident that this strategy would solve their problem given their noncitizen status. Another 43 percent believed that migrants cannot do anything to claim payment for their work since many of them are without documents and work illegally without a written employment contract. Accordingly, the level of trust in formal legal institutions remained quite low among the migrants I interviewed. Thus, nearly half believed that protection racketeers were useful for addressing their problems, as shown in the following explanation proffered by one respondent:

> The laws of the state are unjust and often punish innocent people. If you have money, you can easily bend state laws. But things are well-regulated on the street. Street law is fairer and more just than state law. The main aim of state law is to punish people, but street law is fair and makes a distinction between innocent and guilty people. Money cannot buy everything on the street, but you also need to comply with *erkak-chilik* [manliness] rules and keep your word. Therefore, you find more justice and order on the streets than in state institutions. If you are honest and keep your word, the laws of the street will protect you, but if you swindle and exploit people, you cannot escape punishment, even if you have money. (Botir, 36, male, Uzbek migrant worker)

This example may be interpreted as not only a consequence of poorly implemented policies and a weak rule of law but also as a reflection of the existence of plural legal orders in the Russian migrant labor market. An extensive literature demonstrates the various dysfunctionalities of the Russian legal system (Humphrey and Sneath 2004; Ledeneva 2009; Gans-Morse 2012; Hendley 2012). In this respect migration laws are simply part and parcel of the weak rule-of-law environment in Russia (Gel'man 2004; Ledeneva 2013), which is characterized by the prevalence of informal rules and norms governing formal institutions. Under these circumstances we can assume that migrants do not deal with the rule of law but rather invent various tactics and strategies to organize their working lives and to seek redress for their problems. Since many migrants work informally and violate Russian labor laws, employers and intermediaries understand that no state body will enforce contracts and, therefore, have a penchant for swindling migrants. According to Russian legislation, transactions completed in the shadow economy—that is, beyond labor regulations and tax codes—cannot be heard in state courts. Moreover, migrants working in the informal sector are reluctant to seek legal protection from state institutions because they might be further punished by the state for working without an employment contract. Because of their inability to access formal institutions, migrants increasingly rely on street-level institutions such as protection racketeers to enforce contractual obligations in the (informal) migrant labor market.

This chapter explores the interconnections of the migrant labor market, the shadow economy, and street-level institutions and their implications for migrants' everyday working lives and legal adaptation strategies. I investigate these issues through the ethnographic study of the everyday lives and experiences of Uzbek migrant workers in Moscow, carried out between January 2014 and August 2018. Before proceeding to the empirical data, in the next section I review the literature on protection racketeering in post-Soviet Russia. This review provides the contextual information and defines key terms necessary for understanding the empirical material.

PROTECTION RACKETEERS AND THE STREET WORLD IN POST-SOVIET RUSSIA

An extensive literature exists on private protections (Buchanan 1980; Gambetta 1993; Fiorentini and Peltzman 1995; Asmundo and Lisciandra 2008). Gambetta's study on private protection in southern Italy has been particularly influential, a study in which he defined the Mafia as a "specific economic enterprise, an industry which produces, promotes, and sells private protection" (1993, 3). Russia has also received much attention through a wide array of research on private protections (Handelman 1995; Aslund 1997; Frisby 1998; Humphrey 1999; Frye and Zhuravskaya 2000; Skoblikov 2001; Frye 2002; Volkov 2002). The emergence of private protection in Russia coincides largely with the demise of the Soviet Union in 1991 and the ensuing chaos and institutional vacuum of the early 1990s, which compelled many Russian businesses to rely on criminal protection racketeering groups to provide alternative means of contract enforcement and dispute settlement (Gans-Morse 2012). Therefore, much of the scholarly literature on private protection in Russia tends to focus on developments in the 1990s, when under Yeltsin's leadership the Russian state weakened and lost its ability to ensure law and order. This, in turn, led to the emergence of protection racketeering groups that provided security, contract enforcement, debt recovery, and dispute settlement through threats and violence. In post-Soviet Russia, as Volkov (2002) describes, the transition from a state-controlled economy to a free market (e.g., the liberalization of prices and the privatization of assets) was quickly accomplished without adequate effort to establish efficient state institutions aimed at protecting private property. State institutions were simply inefficient in debt recovery and contract enforcement, subsequently producing a high demand from private businesses seeking alternative structures for enforcement and protection.

Another factor contributing to the proliferation of protection racketeering lies in the reforms of the state security and law-enforcement structures in the 1990s. These reforms aimed to diminish the power of law-enforcement structures by decentralizing and reducing their number of personnel (Volkov 2000). Such changes led many discharged security and law-enforcement officers to seek alternative employment in the "protection racket industry," where they discovered a way to convert their skills into a marketable asset. Volkov (2002) refers to such private protection structures as "violent entrepreneurs" or individuals who offered an "enforcement partnership," what became known in colloquial Russian as a *krysha* (literally, the Russian word for "roof" in relation to the protection racketeers provide to businesses). The types of protection racketeering groups consisted of the following:

(a) units of discharged police and security officers acting as protection racketeers, (b) nonstate and legal private protection companies, and (c) organized criminal and bandit groups. As Volkov (2000) notes, in the 1990s up to 70 percent of all business contracts were enforced by protection racketeers, without involving formal state institutions. Thus, protection racketeering groups were viewed as more efficient than state law-enforcement bodies in solving the day-to-day problems faced by Russian businesses (Frisby 1998, Volkov 1999, Frye and Zhuravskaya 2000).

A review of the literature indicates that "the era of racketeering" ended with the 1990s in most Russian regions (Hendley, Murrell, and Ryterman 2000, 2001; Gel'man 2004; Volkov 2004; Gans-Morse 2012). The bulk of these studies showed a dramatic decline in the use of protection racketeers, and firms began to rely extensively on formal legal institutions and lawyers to resolve problems. In Skocpol's words, "the state was being brought back in" with the onset of Vladimir Putin's regime in Russia. Hence, the restoration of a strong state has become the distinctive feature of the post-2000 period in Russian politics and a major slogan of Putin's presidency (quoted in Gel'man 2004). As Gel'man (2004) notes, soon after Putin became president, agents of "state capture" were peripheralized, "oligarchs" lost their control over the political agenda, regional governors were subordinated to the center, and criminal protection racketeers were marginalized. Yet studies illustrate how that return to a strong state did not lead to the emergence of a rule-of-law environment in Russia; rather, state institutions turned into powerful tools of manipulation, and attacks and threats by high- and low-level state officials directed at property rights have become the dominant feature of everyday business life in Russia (Volkov 2004; Gans-Morse 2012). Understandably, issues such as corruption, kleptocracy, informal institutions, the unrule of law, and authoritarianism have become fashionable topics of research for scholars studying Putin's Russia (see, e.g., Gel'man 2004; Ledeneva 2009; Humphrey 2012; Morris and Polese 2015a). Research focusing on protection racketeers has significantly declined in the last decade.

Based on my ethnographic study of Uzbek migrants' daily experiences in Moscow, I argue that protection racketeers remain a salient feature of the Russian sociolegal environment. Protection racketeers are particularly visible in the informal migrant labor market, providing alternative means to enforce contracts, recover debt, and settle disputes for migrants, whose access to the formal legal system is constrained by multiple structural barriers. Two types of protection racketeers are quite common in the migrant labor market: Chechen and Dagestani protection racketeering groups and (former) police and security service officers acting as protection racketeers. Even though the Chechens and Dagestani are more visible, other ethnic groups such as Armenians, Azerbaijanis, and emerging Uzbek, Kyrgyz, and Tajik groups are also active in the street world. Despite these differences, the main functions of these groups consist of security, risk control, debt recovery, and dispute settlement. A review of existing scholarly literature indicates that there is a lack of research on the relationships among protection racketeers, migrant workers, employers, and intermediaries in the Russian migrant labor market. Existing research on the Russian migration regime focuses on push-and-pull factors of migration (Denisenko 2017); difficult living and working conditions among migrants (Round and Kuznetsova 2016); immigration laws and practices (Kubal 2016b); racism, xenophobia, and the exclusion of migrants (Agadjanian, Menjívar, and Zotova 2017); corruption and migration governance (Schenk 2018); the health status of migrants (Weine et al. 2013); the political economy of housing and migrants' everyday lives (Reeves 2016); female migrants' experiences (Tyuryukanova 2011); migrant illegality and the shadow economy (Heusala and Aitamurto 2016); the social and cultural adaptation of migrants (Mukomel 2013); migrant religiosity and the role of Islam in migrants' everyday lives (Aitamurto 2016); the Eurasian Economic Union and its impact on labor migration (Schenk 2017); the radicalization of migrants (Tucker 2015); transnational practices and the livelihoods of migrants (Urinboyev 2018a); and family migration (Nikiforova and Brednikova 2018). In this chapter I move beyond the existing research by reorienting the focus from "traditional migration research topics" to more hidden and difficult-to-access arenas, thereby providing a "thick description" (Geertz 1973) of the Russian migrant labor market "in action." That is, I provide an in-depth investigation of interpretations, experiences, and behaviors among migrants when they try to seek "law and justice" through street-level institutions.

MIGRANT LABOR MARKET AND THE STREET WORLD

The Russian migrant labor market can be viewed as a small "state within a state" or a parallel legal order with its own informal networks of power, hierarchies, division of labor, and enforcement mechanisms. The role of ethnic cleavages remains crucial in these informal power relationships. Migrants from Azerbaijan and Armenia are well-established and occupy managerial positions in the migrant labor market. This stems from the fact that Armenian and Azerbaijani migrants came to Russia during Soviet times and established a strong position in the Russian migrant labor market. Bazaars in large Russian cities such as Moscow and Saint Petersburg are controlled by Azerbaijani migrants, while the construction sector is largely dominated by Armenian migrants. Central Asian migrants, who arrived in Russia relatively late in the 1990s and early 2000s, occupy a weaker position and are often employed by Armenian or Azerbaijani employers. Because many of these employment relationships occur informally (that is, outside labor and tax regulations), Azerbaijani and Armenian employers often withhold or delay Central Asian migrants' salaries. Even if migrants possess the required work documents, finding employers willing to employ them legally and pay the required employment taxes remains quite difficult. Given the absence of formal employment relationships, it is already common knowledge that many migrants are cheated and do not get paid for their work.

Under these circumstances Central Asian migrants frequently approached Chechens and Dagestanis, who act as *qozi* (a *qadi* or a judge) in the street world, providing contract enforcement and dispute resolution services for a fee. Chechens and Dagestanis (both citizens of the Russian Federation) enjoy a reputation as violent *bespredely* (limitless or lawless individuals) in the street world and act as a *reket/razborshik* (racketeer) in the migrant labor market. They are physically fit, skilled in the use of weapons, and some have a criminal record given their past violent behavior. The need for protection racketeers is particularly high in the construction sector, an industry with a high concentration of undocumented migrants and where salaries are frequently left unpaid. A prominent migrant rights activist in Moscow reported that at least 20 percent of Central Asian migrants have had some relationship with protection racketeers.[1] While protection racketeers are viewed as an element of the criminal world, for Central Asian migrants in Russia who operate outside the formal legal system, seeking redress through protection racketeers represents a rational strategy. As Malakhov (2014) noted, the criminal world sometimes acts in positive ways, "covering" migrants in cases when they experience problems with contract enforcement or getting paid for their work. A recent video report by Ozodlik/Radio Free Europe Uzbek Service highlights the role of protection racketeers in the recovery of salaries, where one manager of a cleaning company, who owed Uzbek migrants 150,000 rubles (US$2,250), was forced to pay 75 percent of the migrants' salaries after interference from *turmadagi zeklar*—that is, racketeers serving prison sentences (Ozodlik Radiosi 2018).

We must note, however, that protection racketeering groups may also act as extortionists. As reported by Ozodlik Radiosi/Radio Free Europe Uzbek Service (2015), in Ulan Ude, the capital city of the Republic of Buryatia (Russia), a group of Uzbek migrants declared themselves the *smotriashiy* (criminal authority) and demanded a monthly protection fee from Uzbek migrants working in Ulan Ude. This group regularly visited Uzbek migrants' workplaces, mediated in conflicts between migrants even if not requested to do so, and imposed *razborka* (showdown or final settlement) fees on migrants. Migrants who did not pay were beaten or blackmailed with threats of deportation since many migrants worked illegally. When demanding a fee from migrants, an Uzbek criminal group stated that a large portion of the money generated from migrants was distributed to the *obshak* (a mutual assistance fund among the criminal community) in prison, where their fellow Uzbek criminal authorities were serving prison sentences. This criminal group was eliminated following a special operation carried out by the Russian Federal Security Service (FSB).

Russian *siloviky* (security service officers) also constitute a key collective in the migrant labor market. Until recently, many bazaars and construction sites were controlled primarily by Azerbaijani and Armenian businessmen. In the last 10 years, however, 14 markets or bazaars were closed in Moscow by the *siloviky*. The closure of markets resulted from a "fight against contraband, crime, and drug dealing" (O'Flynn 2009). In reality, the main aim of these closures was to seize properties owned by Azerbaijani, Armenian, or Chechen groups. As a result, the *siloviky*, particularly officers of the FSB, gained control over some markets and construction companies in Moscow. For example, Moscow's largest wholesale food market, Food City (*Fudsiti*), where thousands of Central Asians work, is informally controlled by a high-level FSB officer.[2] Many Uzbek migrants I encountered there worked without work documents since they fell under the protection (*kryshovanie*) of a high-level FSB officer who ensured that no raid by immigration officials would occur on the market's territory. Chechen and Dagestani protection racketeers were also absent from the Food City area, since it was an open secret that the market fell under the protection of a top FSB official. In that sense Food City provides an example of the growing role of Russian *siloviky* in the migrant labor market, as illustrated in the following extract:

> Food City is a separate republic. It is safe here, and you can work without any documents. FMS [immigration officials] and police don't check us [migrants] here. Even Chechens cannot play a role here. As long as you stay inside the territory of Food City, you can be sure that you are safe from danger. We just pay a *dolya* [share or protection fee] to our *kuratori* [curators] and they make sure that we can work here without problems. One of our curators said that this market belongs to a very influential FSB official. (Arabboy, 34, male, Uzbek migrant)

Some Russian police officers also act as protection racketeers in the migrant labor market. They usually serve as an *advokat* (defense lawyer) during the *razborka*, defending the *posrednik* (middleman) and Russian employers vis-à-vis Chechen and Dagestani racketeers. This was clearly illustrated in the previous chapter when Misha, an Uzbek *posrednik*, described his reliance on the assistance of Russian police officers when his covillagers used Chechen racketeers against him. It should be noted that when police officers operate on the street, they use *pogonyalo* (nickname) and do not reveal their police identity. They also use an ordinary, basic Nokia phone and refrain from using smartphones, fearing that smartphones—particularly iPhones—are tracked by FSB. Such police-based protection racketeering groups are called *krug*, a circle that operates covertly in the migrant labor market and represents an ally to *posredniks* and Russian employers needing protection from other street-level institutions. Not all *posredniks* can become an acquaintance of members of a police-related *krug*. Individuals must work in the construction sector and bazaars for many years in order to build networks and establish relationships with hidden street-level institutions.

My fieldwork indicates that the role and influence of Tajik migrants in the street world is growing. When walking through the streets and metros of Moscow, one can spot many Tajik migrants whose appearance resembles Chechens. Like Chechens, they grow a beard and wear sports clothes, white socks, and running shoes. Even their haircuts resemble those of Chechens. Tajiks imitate Chechens not only in their mannerisms but also in terms of racketeering. It is possible to find

FIGURE 7. Everyday life in Food City, Moscow: Shadow Economy Hotspot. August 2018. Photo by author.

many Tajik protection racketeers at construction sites and bazaars. In addition, some cases exist whereby a Tajik diaspora leader regularly recruits Chechen protection racketeers to settle salary-recovery disputes.[3] One important explanation for the growing role of Tajiks on the street lies in their characteristically tight-knit community and their unity around their ethnic identity. This feature serves as a safety net when someone from the Tajik migrant community gets into trouble or needs help when there is a fight on the street.

A massive brawl between Tajik migrants and Chechens in Moscow's Khovanskoye cemetery on May 14, 2016, illustrates the growing role of Tajik migrants in the street world. Tajik migrants traditionally worked in Moscow's cemeteries by providing services such as grave digging, repairing enclosures around burial plots, or refreshing flowers. According to the *Moscow Times* (2016), the funeral business represents a lucrative sector in Moscow, generating 1 billion rubles (roughly US$16 million) in profit annually. Officially, Moscow's funeral services are managed by the state-owned burial company Ritual, which enjoys a monopoly over the provision of funeral services. But, as the *Moscow Times* reported, up to 80 percent of the sector operates in the shadow economy, and Tajik migrants form only a small portion of that lucrative shadow business. The conflict between Tajiks and Chechens resulted from the fact that Tajik migrants refused to share 50 percent to 90 percent of their earnings with the newly appointed director of the cemetery, Yuri Chabuev. As a result Chabuev, with support from Chechen racketeers, decided to push Tajik migrants from the funeral services sector. Chechens arrived at the cemetery with guns and threatened to bury the Tajiks in the cemetery if they refused to pay a *dolya* (share). But the Tajik migrants, supported by a racketeer from Tajikistan's Gorno-Badakhshan (Pamir) region, strongly resisted the Chechens and threw them out of the cemetery. These events indicate that the Tajik migrants' sphere of influence is growing, whereby they now compete with Chechens and Dagestanis at the street level.

Many similar cases emerged in the construction sector. For local Russians these incidents simply resemble a fight between migrants, but for migrants it represents a means of survival. Different migrant groups often engage in massive brawls and try to divide territories and spheres of work. These processes are often coordinated by so-called *chernie brigadiri* (black brigadiers) or *kuratori*—that is, various intermediaries and racketeers who divide the territories and sectors into spheres of influence and distribute jobs to migrant workers. For example, minibus (*marshrutka*) drivers in Moscow are primarily Pamiris, an Iranian ethnic group from Tajikistan's Gorno-Badakhshan region. Thus, a Pamiri *kurator* serves as a gatekeeper and does not allow migrants from other ethnicities (even ethnic Tajiks) to enter this sector. In turn, Pamiri migrants pay a monthly share to their *kurator* for protecting their interests. Similar situations exist in bazaars and construction sites, where migrants must pay a share (*dan'* or *dolya*) to the *chernie brigadiri* and *kuratori* on a monthly basis. This illustrates how things work in the Russian migrant labor market. These processes are regulated by street law and enforced via street-level institutions such as racketeers and various intermediaries.

Unlike the Tajik migrant community, however, no strong ethnic identity or solidarity exists among Uzbek migrants. Rather than organizing around their ethnic identity, Uzbek migrants form small communities that include migrants originating from the same region, district, village, or *mahalla*. Thus, place-based identity is stronger than ethnic identity among Uzbek migrants. For instance, migrants from Uzbekistan's Bukhara region do not mix with migrants from other regions such as Fergana or Kashkadarya. Because of the absence of a strong ethnic identity and solidarity, Uzbek migrants remain poorly organized, rendering them vulnerable to the whims of dishonest employers and middlemen. As a result, many cases of salary nonpayment plague the Uzbek migrant community. As a way to cope with the uncertainties and risks of informal employment, Uzbek migrants frequently approach Chechen and Dagestani racketeers in cases of the nonpayment of salaries. I describe these processes in the next section.

BAHA AND HIS TEAM:
SEEKING JUSTICE ON THE STREET

Baha is a 28-year-old male migrant construction worker from Uzbekistan's Fergana Valley. Between March and May of 2016, Baha, together with three of his covillagers, completed an *Evroremont* (an apartment renovation according to Western standards and design) in a midrise building located near Moscow's Tsaritsino metro station. Baha and his team members did not possess any work documents and were informally employed by Nuriddin, an Uzbek *posrednik* from Bukhara, an ancient city in Uzbekistan. In turn, this Uzbek *posrednik* worked for a small construction firm that belonged to a Russian woman, Anna Gennadiyevna. Baha and his team worked three months, but they received salary only for two months, while the third month's salary remained unpaid. Each worker should have received 35,000 rubles (roughly US$550), 140,000 rubles (US$2,200) for all four men. When Bana asked the Uzbek *posrednik* to pay their salary, the Uzbek *posrednik* said that he had not received payment and blamed the construction company for the payment delays. Then, Baha and his team contacted Anna Gennadiyevna, asking her to speed up the payment. But Anna Gennadiyevna refused to pay them, insisting that she had already paid their salary to the Uzbek *posrednik*. Thus, neither the Uzbek *posrednik* nor the construction firm showed any serious intention to pay their salary, bouncing Baha's team back and forth for two weeks.

Baha and his team did not even consider seeking legal aid from the Russian state institutions given that they all lacked immigration documents and worked without any formal employment contract. They believed that the Russian legal system was dysfunctional and would not protect them even if they possessed all of the required documents and worked legally. Given these circumstances, the most realistic option available to them to recover their salary was to approach a *razborshik*. Because Baha came to Moscow in 2011 and had worked on various construction sites, he had many friends and acquaintances. Frustrated with being ping-ponged between the Uzbek *posrednik* and the construction firm, Baha contacted his friend Tesha, a migrant from Uzbekistan's Kashkadarya region who was well-connected to the street world, asking him for a contact to a Chechen protection racketeer. This was not the first time Tesha was asked to serve as a bridge between migrants and Chechens; he had handled many similar requests in the past. But, before connecting anyone to the Chechens, Tesha carefully explained the basic principles of street law to Baha:

> You need to be a real man (*haqiqiy erkak*) when you deal with street people. If you claim that you are a real man, you have to stay manly until the end (*raz muzhik do kontsa muzhik*). This is the law of Moscow. Honesty and decency are very important traits on the street. Before you tell your story to a Chechen *razborshik*, you must be 100 percent confident that all of the facts and details of your story are true. The main role of the *razborshik* is to establish justice and punish guilty people. If you provide false information and accuse the honest employer (*ish beruvchi*) of not paying your salary, you will pay a heavy price. As a punishment, they will first beat you and then force you to pay the amount you stated in your claim in relation to the employer. Also, you must pay monetary compensation for the time and effort Chechens spent handling your case. They can demand any amount they want for compensation, and you have to pay it. In some cases you will also be ordered to pay moral damage to the employer for tarnishing his name. Therefore, when you contact a *razborshik*, they ask you three times whether the information you have provided is correct. When you transfer your claim to a *razborshik*, you should stop your communication with the employer and follow the *razborshik*'s instructions. It is exclusively the *razborshik*'s call to investigate the case. The *razborshik* will invite both the claimant and defendant to the *razborka*. If the *razborshik* succeeds in recovering your money, you must pay him a fee. There is no fixed rate. Some *razborshiks* ask for 20 percent, while some others work at a rate of 50–50. On the whole, the average price currently is typically 20 percent to 30 percent of what they collect. Often, *razborshiks* also charge the employer as punishment for his dishonest behavior. But in cases when the *razborshik* cannot recover your money, he is expected to pay your money from his own pocket. So, the *razborshik* also has certain rights and obligations. You find more order on the street than inside state institutions.

Events unfolded exactly as Tesha described. After being connected to Chechens via phone, Baha and his team members were asked to provide all of the facts and details of their case. The Chechens repeatedly asked Baha whether he was providing a true story and warned him that he himself would have to pay the price if any of the details were inaccurate. After finishing this initial "manliness ritual," the Chechens asked Baha to provide them with the address and phone number of the Uzbek *posrednik*. Baha and his team were advised not to take any further action and to wait for the next steps. The migrants agreed to pay 30 percent of the total amount collected (i.e., 42,000 rubles, approximately US$650) to the Chechens as payment for their work.

Two days later, the Chechens contacted Baha and asked him to come immediately to a designated place on the north of Moscow where the *razborka* would take place. The aim of the *razborka* was to determine the validity of Baha and his team's claim. When Baha arrived at the *razborka* site, he found that four Chechens and the Uzbek *posrednik* were already there. First, Baha and his team were given a chance to present their complaint. Then, the Uzbek *posrednik* was asked to comment on the situation and defend himself if he felt he was innocent. Rather than denying Baha's story, the Uzbek *posrednik* admitted that what was described was true, but he insisted that he too was a victim, blaming Anna Gennadiyevna and her construction firm for payment problems.

The Chechens did not accept the Uzbek *posrednik*'s justification as a valid excuse. In the Chechens' view Baha and his team entered into a "manly agreement" (*erkakcha kelishuv*) with the Uzbek *posrednik*, not with the Russian woman, implying that the Uzbek *posrednik* was responsible for payment to Baha and his team regardless of any other circumstances. The verdict was thus made by the Chechens that the Uzbek *posrednik* would pay Baha and his team's salary within a maximum of three days. In addition, the Uzbek *posrednik* was also ordered to pay 25,000 rubles (US$400) to the Chechens for the time they had spent to *reshat voprosy* (solve the issue). The Chechens warned the Uzbek *posrednik* that his "throat would be slashed" if he failed to pay the stated amount by the deadline. The Chechens' confident voice relied on the firm belief that Uzbek migrants, like many other migrants in Russia, were rightless *chernie* (blacks), and no serious police investigation would follow should some Uzbek migrant be killed. The Chechens were even aware that the Uzbek embassy in Moscow would do nothing to protect the rights of its citizens in Russia. Not wanting to risk his life, the Uzbek *posrednik* eventually paid both Baha and his team as well as the Chechens, an outcome that would not have occurred if Baha and his team had not resorted to street-level institutions.

TIMUR: SEEKING JUSTICE THROUGH PRISON

Timur is a 26-year-old male migrant construction worker from the Fergana region of Uzbekistan. He arrived in Moscow in June of 2012, shortly after finishing vocational college. Unlike his fellow villagers in Moscow who shared common accommodations and pursued intertwined lives, Timur stayed in a communal, shared apartment where the majority of tenants (*kvartiranti*) were ethnic Tajiks from Samarkand (Uzbekistan) and Khujand (Tajikistan). His decision to stay away from his covillagers stemmed from his efforts to diversify his social network and connections (*tanish-bilish*) in Moscow, crucial for finding a decent job. This was where Timur made Tajik acquaintances and established an extensive network that later proved helpful when he experienced problems getting paid for his own work.

At the time of my fieldwork in 2015, Timur worked on a construction site in Shchyolkovo City, Moscow province. His main job was to install CCTV cameras in newly constructed midrise buildings. Timur's boss was a *posrednik* from

Kyrgyzstan who, in turn, worked for the Russian construction firm. The employment relationship between all parties—Timur, the Kyrgyz *posrednik*, and the Russian construction firm—was based on a *po-rukam* (handshake-based) agreement, implying that these transactions were informal and took place beyond labor and tax regulations. Timur worked for the Kyrgyz *posrednik* for five months, but he was not paid for his last two months of work, an amount totaling 60,000 rubles (about US$950). When Timur asked the Kyrgyz *posrednik* whether he was willing to pay his two-month salary, the *posrednik* stated that the Russian construction firm was delaying payment, not him. Timur waited for more than two months, hoping that the *posrednik* would pay his salary. But he continued telling the same story. It was thus apparent that the Kyrgyz *posrednik* was unwilling to pay the remaining salary, which led Timur to look for alternative ways of recovering it.

Because Timur shared an apartment with Tajik migrants, he became a part of the wider Tajik community. On a daily basis he ate food with them, slept in a shared bedroom, played cards with them during their leisure time, and even shared sex workers with them when they went to various brothels. Owing to his close relationship with Tajiks, Timur knew that he could rely on them to help recover his salary from the Kyrgyz *posrednik*. When Timur asked his Tajik roommates if they could do anything to help him, they gave him the phone number of their Tajik friend Farkhod, who was serving a prison sentence in one of the correctional colonies (prisons) in the Moscow province.

Farkhod was one of the most influential protection racketeers in Moscow. In 2013 he was sentenced to seven years in prison for racketeering and extortion-related crimes. The fact that he did not reveal the names of his partners in crime, taking individual responsibility for all of the charges, further increased his sphere of influence on the street. Despite being physically situated inside the prison, he was very much present in Moscow's migrant labor market and continued acting as the head of the Tajik racketeering group in Moscow. This was possible as a result of widespread corruption within the prison system. Farkhod and many other inmates had access to smartphones (with an internet connection), as well as to vodka, drugs, and sex workers. All of these "luxuries" were organized by *menty* (low-level prison officials), always looking for ways to supplement their meager incomes. Since a smartphone was considered a sensitive object that could reveal the secrets of the prison, its use and dissemination inside the prison was heavily controlled. Therefore, *menty* secretly carried it to the prison, hiding it in their anuses. Given these difficulties, smartphones were very expensive inside the prison. For example, if the cheapest Chinese Huawei smartphone cost 8,000 rubles (US$125) in a store, *menty* sold it to inmates for 24,000 rubles (US$375). Given the difficulty of getting and keeping a smartphone in prison, Farkhod's phone was only on and available for conversations at three times each day: early morning (between 5:00 and 6:30), after lunch (between 2 p.m. and 3 p.m.), and in the evening (between 8:00 and 10:30). Thanks to the availability of a smartphone, Farkhod continued his racketeering activities and regularly received "warm-up money" (*grev*) both from his partners and migrants. Farkhod regularly used a smartphone-based mobile payment application and updated his social media accounts on a daily basis, posting his own photos and pressing the "like" button on pictures of Russian and Tajik girls.

In accordance with the instructions of his Tajik friends, Timur placed a call to Farkhod in the evening, a time when he was better able to solve street-level issues. After introducing himself and explaining how he found Farkhod's contact details, Timur recounted all of the problems he had experienced to Farkhod and politely asked whether he could help him recover his salary from the Kyrgyz *posrednik*. In turn, before taking on this challenge, Farkhod asked Timur whether he would be able to stand by his story during the *razborka* and whether he was ready to pay 20 percent of the disputed money recovered. Farkhod also explained the basic rules of street law, emphasizing that Timur must remain honest, behave like a man (*erkakchilik*), and avoid any contact with the police. After Timur accepted these conditions, Farkhod moved to the next stage, wherein Timur was asked to provide the *posrednik*'s ethnicity, full name and phone number, the name of the construction firm, the exact amount of the salary in question, and, most important, the name of the district in which Timur worked. Knowing the name of the district was crucial, since each district had its own *smotriashiy*, meaning Farkhod needed to be sure that he was not stepping on someone's toes. Finally, after checking all of the details, Farkhod accepted the challenge and asked Timur to await further instructions without taking any independent action.

The next day, Timur received a phone call from Farkhod. It was a conference call where Timur, Farkhod, and the Kyrgyz *posrednik* were on the line simultaneously. Before starting the investigation, Farkhod warned both Timur and the Kyrgyz *posrednik* to be honest and that they would be severely punished if they attempted to bend the truth. First, Farkhod asked Timur to describe what had happened and what claim he had in relation to the Kyrgyz *posrednik*. Then, the Kyrgyz *posrednik* was given the chance to respond to Timur's complaint. Unsurprisingly, the Kyrgyz *posrednik* blamed the construction firm, stating that he also did not receive his own salary from the Russians. Farkhod immediately interrupted the Kyrgyz *posrednik*, stating that Timur made an agreement with him, not with the Russians, so he was responsible for securing Timur's salary regardless of other circumstances. Farkhod did not continue the conversation any further and quickly moved to the final settlement and ended the *razborka*.

As a result of the *razborka*, the Kyrgyz *posrednik* was given a maximum of three days to pay Timur's salary. In addition, the *posrednik* was also ordered to top-up or deposit 15,000 rubles (US$240) to Farkhod's phone number. Farkhod made clear to the *posrednik* that his life would be in danger if these two payments were not made by the deadline. Timur was also reminded that once he received his salary from the *posrednik* he must also deposit 20 percent of the salary recovered—that is, 12,000 rubles (US$190)—to Farkhod's phone number so that he could continue using his mobile payment application. Not wanting to tangle with the *zek* (a Soviet term used in relation to persons serving a sentence in corrections facilities or prisons), the Kyrgyz *posrednik* quickly paid Timur's salary and deposited the stated amount to Farkhod's phone number. Timur also deposited money to Farkhod's number the same day.

STREET LAW AND MIGRANT LEGAL ADAPTATIONS

As we have seen in this chapter, many migrants work without written employment contracts, which often results in the nonpayment of salaries. Given the complete lack of formal legal protections, many migrants seek redress from street-level actors who provide alternative (to the state) forms of contract enforcement, debt recovery, and dispute settlement through threats, violence, and street law. When observing everyday interactions in the migrant labor market, it becomes difficult to view the Russian state and its legal infrastructure as a coherent entity. Instead, what we see is an informal, parallel world of migrants based on its own noncodified but socially reproduced and legitimate forms of governance and legal order. From this perspective the apparent reinvigoration of street-level institutions in Russia may be viewed as a reaction to the Russian state's inability or unwillingness to provide decent working conditions for migrant workers. Hence, street-level institutions should not only be viewed as an element of the criminal world; they may very well constitute an alternative legal order when the state and its legal system fail to enforce the rules of the game of society.

Accordingly, one possible inference is that the Russian migrant labor market resembles a "state within a state," with its own informal networks of power, hierarchies, divisions of labor, and legal order. The street-level institutions act as enforcement mechanisms for informal employment relationships. Despite its almost mythical coercive power, the Russian state and its legal infrastructure remain "formally" absent in the street world of the migrant labor market. This argument, however, does not necessarily imply that street-level institutions are completely separate from the state. Rather, the Russian state actors are informally present in the migrant labor market, as numerous racketeers, "street networks," "intermediaries"' have varying levels of informal connections with officials and organs of power. The street-level institutions can thus be regarded as parallel legal orders, functioning in a close symbiosis with the state actors, which regulate the rules of the game in the migrant labor market. The intrinsic message of this chapter is that the legal adaptation of migrants in Russia must be understood not only through migrants' capacity to comply with immigration and labor laws but also in terms of their interactions with street-based legal orders that offer alternative forms of redress, legal adaptation, and economic security.

Uzbek Migrants' Everyday Encounters with Police Officers and Immigration Officials

During my ethnographic fieldwork in Moscow (January 2014–August 2018), I frequently visited a construction site in Balashikha, a small city in Moscow province where dozens of Uzbek migrant construction teams performed various types of construction work in high-rise residential buildings. Because the construction of the residential buildings had already been completed, the primary task performed by these Uzbek construction teams entailed the final finishing and design work, such as window fitting, painting, flooring, wallpaper installation, plumbing, or electrical installation. Like many construction projects in Moscow, this Balashikha-based project was coordinated by a Russian intermediary who worked for a large construction company responsible for the overall project implementation. Because of language barriers and cultural differences, however, the Russian intermediary coordinated the construction project through several Uzbek migrant middlemen who were well-connected to migrant construction workers, enjoyed authority among them, knew their language, and could manage construction brigades. In turn, the migrant middlemen struck deals with various Uzbek construction teams (each consisting of 5–10 migrants), acting as an intermediary between different parties.

Nearly all of the Uzbek migrants I encountered there worked without any written employment contract and did not have an authentic residence registration or work permit. Migrants working there said that it was impossible to go "legal" (*qonuniy yurish*) in Balashikha, since they all, regardless of whether they were documented or not, had to pay a bribe to police officers. In the words of the migrants, Balashikha used to be a forbidden military zone during the Soviet times, where foreigners were not allowed to live or work, and this Soviet legacy was strategically used by police officers who always sought reasons to extort money from migrants.

When stopped by the police, migrants were often warned that they were working in a forbidden zone and that they needed special permission from the Russian state—permission created to justify the police demands for bribes from migrants. The police typically demanded 2,000 rubles (US$30) to ignore this "infraction," but migrants often managed to get away with paying 500 rubles (US$8). When police officers approached the construction site, everyone hid. Migrants typically spent most of their time inside the apartments where they simultaneously worked and lived. Unless a Russian complained or a letter arrived from a prosecutor, the police did not enter and check the apartments.

Given their daily experiences with corruption, migrants developed multiple strategies to avoid the police. If they needed something from the market, they usually checked the area thoroughly to make sure no police officers were around. When they saw the police on the street, they quickly informed one another. But it was not always possible to avoid hungry police officers, who frequently wander around markets and bus stops. If a migrant was caught when buying food stuff for the construction brigade, all of the migrants shared the cost of the bribe paid to police, viewing it as part of their food expenses. Whenever I visited my key informants (migrant brigades) in Balashikha, they quickly brought up the subject of police corruption and talked openly about situations in which they had paid bribes to Russian police officers. Migrants often told different stories and anecdotes about police corruption. During my visit to Balashikha in April of 2014, I organized a small *pilaf* (a festive Uzbek rice) party for several migrant brigades as a way to socialize and establish a close relationship with them. We sat at a nicely decorated table, eating *pilaf* and talking about the migrants' daily lives and adventures in Russia. Spontaneously, one of the migrants provided an anecdote about police corruption:

There was one Russian police officer who made his fortune extorting money from Uzbek migrants. He worked near construction sites, where many migrants lived and worked. Due to the existence of thousands of migrants in his territory, he generated lots of income and became very rich, to the extent that he managed to buy a villa in Rublevka, an elite residential area in the western suburbs of Moscow where many Russian billionaires live. This was an unexpected turn for the police officer, who was not actually a Muscovite, but from Siberia. He was very proud of his achievement and continued to extort money from migrants on a daily basis. However, one day his 12-year-old son, his only child, died in a car accident. This tragic event left the police officer deeply saddened. Because the police officer shared his revenues with many people in the government, many state officials showed up to his son's funeral. Even Sergey Sobyanin, the mayor of Moscow, attended his son's funeral to express his condolences. When the funeral was about to end, suddenly more than 100 Uzbek migrants arrived at the funeral, all of whom were sad and crying as if they had lost their own child. The police officer recognized many of the migrants as individuals from whom he had regularly extorted money. But, still, the policeman could not understand why so many migrants felt sorry for him and cried even though he had terrorized them on a daily basis. When the police officer asked the migrants why they had come to the funeral despite their bad experiences with him, one migrant replied, "Of course, we must be here. True, he is your son, not ours. But do not forget the fact that we raised him for many years, paying for his food, clothes, toys, and all of the other expenses related to his childhood. We invested more money in your son than you."

That last phrase was accompanied by loud laughter and nodding, showing the migrants' awareness of the widespread police corruption slyly hinted at in the anecdote. This anecdote indicates that police corruption has become something of a norm, whereby finding migrants who have not paid a bribe to Russian police officers remains difficult. The anecdote also clearly provides a clue regarding the existence of a plethora of interests and networks within the Russian government that benefit from informal transactions involving police officers and migrant workers. This anecdote thus begs the question of how migrant legal adaptation takes place within a legal environment characterized by corruption and lacking a rule of law. In this chapter I provide illustrations of this process by presenting substantial ethnographic data on migrants' everyday interactions with police officers and immigration officials.

BECOMING "LEGAL" IN A CORRUPT AND WEAK RULE-OF-LAW ENVIRONMENT

As discussed in previous chapters, Russian immigration laws determining the conditions for the legal status of foreign citizens remain inconsistent, poorly enforced, and often contradictory (Kubal 2016a). This is unsurprising given that much of the academic literature describes the Russian legal environment as corrupt, arbitrary, and repressive (Sakwa 1995; Gel'man 2004; Solomon 2004; Ledeneva 2006). Thus, even those migrants who possess all of the required documents cannot be sure that they will not encounter problems when they come into contact with Russian police officers and immigration officials (Reeves 2015; Kubal 2016b). Given the weak rule of law, widespread corruption, and arbitrary law enforcement, being "legal" or "illegal" hinges on contextual factors and individual skills. These factors and skills include how, when, and where the interaction between migrants and Russian state officials takes place as well as migrants' knowledge of informal rules, street smarts, bribery skills, and ability to negotiate and find common ground (*obshiy yazik*) with state officials. These legal uncertainties imply the near impossibility of a migrant being fully documented, while the only path to asserting one's "legality" requires using various informal and illegal practices and procedures (Dave 2014a).

Much of the prevailing research tends to portray Central Asian migrants in Russia as passive, agencyless subjects. As such, they are constrained by the punitive legal environment, pointing out how being undocumented incapacitates migrants and invades their lifeworlds, leading to ever-present threats of exploitation, deportation, police corruption, racism, physical violence, and even death (Light 2010; Ruget and Usmanalieva 2010; Reeves 2015; Abashin 2016; Kubal 2016a; Round and Kuznetsova 2016; Agadjanian, Menjívar, and Zotova 2017; Nikiforova and Brednikova 2018; Schenk 2018). A similar perspective also commonly pervades the broader "migrant illegality" literature (based on research conducted in North America and Western Europe), where immigrants' legal status represents a key factor determining various paths, as well as the quality and timescale of migrant integration (Massey, Durand, and Malone 2002; Coutin 2003b; Calavita 2005; Menjívar 2006, Gleeson 2010). In other words documented and undocumented migrants have such varying experiences that they constitute two different social classes.

The treatment of migrants as passive, agencyless subjects, however, may preclude us from looking at their actual coping strategies and navigational skills. Take the example of Malaysia, as Garcés-Mascareñas (2010) shows, where undocumented migrants, unlike documented migrants, enjoy more opportunities to change jobs, can negotiate their salary and working conditions, can avoid extra fees to enter or remain in the country, and can extend their stay in the country regardless of their economic situation or health status. Garcés-Mascareñas (2010) suggests that illegality can be viewed as a form of everyday, hidden resistance to state migration control policies. In Russia, by comparison, migrants also face similar constraints where they must deal with the arbitrary and repressive legal environment that does not allow migrants to legalize their work and residence status. Even those migrants with perfectly "clean" documents cannot be certain that they are "legal" when stopped by police officers. In the Russian context, however, "illegality" does not automatically incapacitate migrants, confining them to the space of vulnerability and legal nonexistence. Rather, it becomes a way of life, something of a norm for millions of migrants in Russia. Consequently, when the state forbids things or makes it nearly impossible to follow official procedures, it creates the need for informal and illegal means of getting things done (Morris and Polese 2015b). This means that migrants are forced into informal relations with the state in their everyday life (Kuznetsova and Round 2018). As we have seen, these constraints force many migrants to operate in the shadow economy (Heusala and Aitamurto 2016), where they can survive with false immigration documents and follow informal adaptation paths. This is confirmed by the Russian government's 2015 statistics showing that nearly 3 million foreigners in Russia violated the legal terms of their stays (Pochuev 2015). In fact, some experts estimate that there are around 5 million undocumented migrants in Russia (Chikadze and Brednikova 2012).

Given the magnitude of the shadow economy, the migrant labor market in Russia and the multiple informal and illegal practices revolving around it should not be viewed as abnormal behaviors but rather as institutionalized practices, a parallel legal order emerging out of the corruption and weak rule of law that characterizes much of the Russian bureaucracy. Thus, a distinctive feature of the Russian migration regime is the large shadow economy based on its own economy, legal order, and welfare infrastructure (Urinboyev and Polese 2016).

The above considerations have informed my approach in this chapter, which aims to examine not the limitations of the legal system but rather the unintended consequences that empower the agency of migrants to navigate the system. More specifically, in this chapter I aim to show that in hybrid regime contexts such as Russia, migrants are resilient and active agents and creatively use the opportunities provided by the weak rule of law and the corrupt political system to navigate the structural constraints and negotiate and assert their legal status. These processes can be explained by the vested interests of relevant Russian state actors (e.g., the police and immigration officials), where each of these actors view the (informal) migrant labor market as a source of *kormushka* (a feeding trough) and attempt to "take their own piece" of it. These patterns become particularly discernible when we attend to migrant workers' everyday experiences, tactics, and coping strategies when they attempt to negotiate the "rules of the game" with Russian migration officials and police officers. Although these processes and strategies may come across as manifestation of corruption and a weak rule of law, they actually constitute a real mode of migration governance and, thus, reveal the broader sociolegal context in which migrants' legal adaptations occur. In this chapter, then, I suggest that the study of migrants' legal adaptation should move beyond the structuralist (Western-centric) perspectives that emphasize the importance of one's legal status and the enduring power of the legal environment. That is, in order to better understand migrants' relationships to the host state's law and institutions in hybrid regime contexts, we should introduce a new analytical lens encompassing not only the legal centralistic approaches but also a legally pluralistic perspective accounting for informal norms and practices.

To illustrate these processes, the next sections focus on migrants' everyday encounters with the two aforementioned Russian state actors. As I mentioned earlier, I collected the empirical data presented in this chapter while conducting my ethnographic fieldwork in Moscow between January of 2014 and August of 2018. In the sections that follow, I first present the informal interviews and observations, which focus on migrants' everyday encounters with police officers and immigration officials, two key social arenas through which migrants experience the legal environment in Russia. Throughout what follows, I use pseudonyms for all of the names that appear here. I also present some relevant empirical examples from in-depth (semistructured) interviews with 100 Central Asian migrants (Kyrgyz, Tajik, and Uzbek) I conducted between July and August of 2015. The interview questionnaire consisted of 91 open-ended questions and covered 15 different topics. For this specific chapter, however, I chose to present the results specifically focusing on police-migrant interactions. Thus, the chapter focuses on a small portion of the empirical data I collected within the larger project. A more comprehensive description of the interview details appears in chapter 1.

MIGRANTS' EVERYDAY ENCOUNTERS WITH POLICE OFFICERS

In today's Moscow any visitor will quickly notice the large number of police officers visible on all major streets and in all public places. A more attentive observer will notice police officers frequently stopping and checking the identity documents of non-Russian-looking passersby. This is particularly visible on the Moscow metro, where police officers typically stand at the top of the escalator and enthusiastically carry out document checks. Many of these stopped passersby are citizens of Central Asian republics (Kyrgyzstan, Tajikistan, or Uzbekistan) who left their home country given the lack of viable income-earning opportunities.

It is through these street-level massive document checks that the (informal) implementation of Russian immigration policies and laws takes place. In Russia, where the rule of law remains weak and corruption prevails, it is actually police officers who claim the prerogative of defining who is *zakonno* (legally) residing and working within the territory of the Russian Federation, even though they are not legally entrusted with enforcing immigration laws (Reeves 2013; Dave 2014; Kubal 2016b).[1] For many police officers, who receive a meager salary from the state, migrants represent the most lucrative source of *kormushka* (feeding trough), compensating for their low salaries.[2] As Round and Kuznetsova (2016) observed, when stopped by the police, migrants must show their work patent and labor contract. Police officers understand that the majority of migrants remain undocumented, and even legally employed migrants often experience problems with their residence registration documents since they do not actually live at the address where they are registered. Yet, even if migrants present all of the required documents, police may simply claim that those documents are fakes in order to extort money.

Although these massive document checks by the police clearly contradict Russian legislation, the authorities tacitly endorse them. In *Policing Migration in Soviet and Post-Soviet Moscow*, Light (2010) explains Russian police's extortionist behavior, referring specifically to the Moscow city government's attempts to keep Central Asian migrants in a constant state of fear and insecurity, thereby discouraging them from settling down permanently in Moscow. This resulted from the Moscow city government viewing migrants as a burden to its budget since migrants use public services without paying for them. Under Russian legislation, however, only the federal government has the authority to regulate immigration. Thus, the Moscow city government and the country's regions do not have the legal right to restrict the entry of foreign nationals. Unable to limit migratory flows, as Light (2010) maintains, the Moscow city government deployed three methods to deter migrants: (a) random checks of migrants' identity documents in public places, (b) raids on workplaces (e.g., construction sites) targeting undocumented migrants, and (c) deploying police officers at points of entry and transit areas, such as railway stations and the city's metro system. All three of these methods are implemented by police officers, whose main task is to keep migrants in a constant state of fear and vulnerability so that they do not feel welcome and only seek temporary stays. In return, the Moscow city government tacitly tolerates abusive and corrupt behavior among its police officers.

The system of police performance assessment and reporting serves as another factor driving massive document checks. According to the system of assessment from the Russian Ministry of the Interior, each police officer must disclose a certain number of criminal cases and report them to higher authorities so as to collect the required points and demonstrate that s/he is indeed "working" (Dubova and Kosal's 2013). This assessment method, commonly known as a *palochnaya sistema* or *plan* (quota system), was developed during Soviet times and continues to enjoy wide practice in the post-Soviet era as a key method of performance assessment of police officers on a monthly basis. This requirement forces them to invent various schemes and tactics. For instance, each month police officers must disclose a certain number of robbery and prostitution cases. Instead of doing real work, they stop two Uzbek female migrants in the street, bring them to the police station, and ask them to sign a sheet of paper indicating that they were involved in prostitution. Quite often, migrants do not read the paper but sign it so that they are quickly released. After getting their signature, the police let them go. In turn, police officers report to their superiors that they caught two sex workers and fined them. This is how they fulfill the "prostitution quota." The same logic applies to document checks and bribes. On a daily basis police officers stop and check the identity documents of a certain number of migrants in order to generate revenues for their superiors and themselves. But getting caught by police officers is particularly risky during the last part of month, since police officers must catch undocumented migrants and transfer their cases to court. Therefore, migrants commonly use the expression *planga tushib qolish* (fall within the quota/plan) to apply to migrants whose cases are transferred to court for possible deportation. Aware of these possible risks, many migrants avoid public places at the end of each month.

Given these realities, migrants understand the near impossibility of being "completely legal." As one migrant rights' activist ironically described it, "the primary aim of Russian migration laws is to fight against legal migrants, not illegal migrants."[3] As a result, migrants have developed various informal strategies and tactics to navigate the system, a parallel world based on its own rules. Rather than trying to be "legal," an unrealistic and unattainable status in contemporary Moscow, many migrants simply buy fake work permits and residence registration documents produced at underground printing houses at Moscow's Kazansky railway station. Echoing these views, Salim explains why many migrants are reluctant to legalize their work and residence status in Russia:

> It is almost impossible to go legal [*qonuniy*]. Even if you try to follow all of the laws and have proper documents, *melisa* [police officers] can always find a way to "milk you" [extort money]. Therefore, instead of paying the patent [work permit] fee each month, it is easier and cheaper to buy fake documents at *Kazansky vokzal* [railway station]. The rate of the bribe is almost the same, regardless of whether your documents are clean or fake. (Salim, 35, male, Uzbek janitor in Moscow)

In reality, Salim's observations are not unfounded. Many migrants I interviewed stated that if a migrant is caught by the police without any documents, s/he must pay a bribe of 5,000 rubles (US$80) to be released. But, if a migrant shows at least fake documents to the police officer, the rate of the bribe decreases and s/he can get away with paying approximately 2,000 to 3,000 rubles (US$30–$45). Indeed, when stopping migrants on the street, police officers cannot verify whether migrants have authentic documents. This is because immigration law lies clearly under the prerogative of the General Administration for Migration Issues of the Ministry of Internal Affairs (GUVM). Thus, district-level police officers do not have direct access to the GUVM database and must submit an inquiry to GUVM if they want to determine the authenticity of immigration documents (Kubal 2016b). Many police officers are overburdened with various tasks and uninterested in transferring each migrant's case to the courts. Instead, they endeavor to release migrants as soon as possible after they pay a bribe. This represents an optimal outcome for both parties: the police officer generates additional income, and the migrant continues to work in Russia using fake immigration documents.

To further investigate this, during the last period of my fieldwork in August 2018, I conducted daily observations in Moscow's metro stations, streets, and public areas such as parks, shopping malls, and supermarkets in order to gain insight into how migrants organize their daily lives and routines. Interestingly, wherever I went, whether in metro stations, bus stations, or parks, I observed many instances of police officers checking the documents and bags of several migrants. Through careful observation, it is possible to witness those migrants pulling money from their pockets to bribe the police. I also conducted observations at the Kazansky railway station, a primary migration hub in Moscow where migrants acquire fake and clean fake immigration documents. When leaving the Komsomolskaya metro station, I came across Bakhtiyor, an Uzbek middleman selling *registratsiya* (a residence registration document). Some passerby migrants approached him, asking about the price of the registration and whether it works when shown to the police. Accordingly, he provided a price list and told them about three different types of registrations. Bakhtiyor explained that they can buy a "handwritten registration" for 300 rubles (US$5), a "printed registration" for 500 rubles (US$8), or a "clean fake registration" for 1,500 rubles (US$25). When the migrants asked him which worked best, Bakhtiyor responded that the "clean fake registration" was the best since it can be found in the official database. Furthermore, Bakhtiyor described the other two types—handwritten and printed registrations—as fakes not existing in the official database, which may cause problems if the migrants were caught by immigration officials during raids. He made clear, however, that the printed registration would be sufficient to convince police officers on the street, who often lack the time and energy to check the authenticity of documents. It is noteworthy here that Bakhtiyor honestly informed his potential clients in advance of the pros and cons regarding when and where his products work. This example illustrates that what identifies a document as fake or real is not simply its quality as authentic; contextual and situational factors also matter.

In addition to contextual and situational factors, migrant's individual navigational skills are also important. The case of Hoshim (33, male) and his brother Nodirbek (25, male) provides a relevant example. On April 14, 2015, Hoshim and Nodirbek visited Moscow's Red Square for sightseeing. Hoshim was planning to return to Uzbekistan the next day, so he wanted to do some sightseeing before leaving Moscow. In fact, Hoshim had a fake work permit and residence registration, but his brother Nodirbek had an authentic patent and "clean fake" residence registration that would appear in the database if checked. If these two brothers were stopped and checked, one may quickly assume that Hoshim would experience trouble with the police since his documents were fake, while Nodirbek would be allowed to go free. As anticipated, when exiting the Okhotny Ryad metro station, the police stopped both Hoshim and Nodirbek for a document check, and the two brothers were taken to a small room inside the metro station where the police usually check migrants' documents. Ironically, Nodirbek ended up paying a bribe to the police officer, whereas Hoshim was allowed to go without losing any money. While taking the bribe, the police officer praised Hoshim for going "legal" and warned Nodirbek that he would not forgive him the next time if he was caught with fake documents. The police officer also added that Nodirbek should follow his brother's example and go "legal" in Moscow. When I asked Hoshim to comment on this situation, he replied that his brother was a young, inexperienced migrant and did not know how to behave when stopped by the police. Unlike his brother, Hoshim was street smart and knew how to appear "legal" when talking with the police. Hoshim explained that one's legal status does not entirely depend on the existence of authentic documents. Instead, and more importantly, one must master the street rules and learn how to perform "legality." This anecdotal evidence illustrates the importance of informal rules and street life in migrant legal adaptation processes and reveals the peculiarities of Russia's immigration legal regime, wherein migrant's legal status remains fluid and depends on contextual factors and individual artistic skills.

The case of these two brothers is far from unique. I observed many similar incidents during my fieldwork, where street smartness, knowledge of the informal rules, and bribe-negotiation skills played a decisive role in migrant-police interactions. Aziz's experience with a police officer illustrates this:

Two weeks ago, my friend Olim and I were returning to our accommodation from work. Suddenly, a police officer popped up in our way and asked both of us to show our documents. My friend Olim had documents (although fake), but I forgot my documents in the apartment. After checking us, the police officer said that Olim can go, but he asked me to follow him to the police station. Olim did not want to leave me alone and tried to negotiate with the police officer. But I immediately stopped Olim and asked him to leave me alone with the police. Because Olim came to Moscow recently, he did not know that police officers were psychologists and their expectation of the bribe rate largely depends on the migrant's behavior. By trying to help me, Olim was actually increasing my value, which in turn results in a higher bribe expectation. In an everyday situation, for example, where the normal bribe rate is 500 to 1,000 rubles (US$8–$15), I might have ended up paying 2,000 rubles (US$30) if Olim continued to negotiate further with the policeman. If your friend walks away and leaves you alone, the police understand that there is no one who will get you out of trouble, so he will release you for 500 rubles. Because I had many similar experiences, I was not afraid of the police, and this time I decided not to pay even a single ruble to him. The police officer locked me up in a temporary cell and offered to release me if I gave him 1,000 rubles. I knew that he would not keep me long, and I told him that he can keep me in the cell forever, if he wanted. As anticipated, the police officer kept me in the cell for three hours and, finally, after seeing that I was determined not to give him any money, he became frustrated and threw me out of the police station, swearing loudly "*poshel na khuy churka*" [fuck off, dumb ass]. Due to my patience, I was able to save 1,000 rubles. The only bad thing was that I was hungry and could not eat until I was released. (Aziz, 32, male, Uzbek construction worker in Moscow)

Sardor's story is even more intriguing, illustrating migrants' resiliency and resourcefulness. On January 20, 2016, Sardor finished work quite late and missed the last train to his accommodation, situated in a Moscow province district. He only had 200 rubles in his pocket, and it was freezing outside, with an air temperature of around −18°C. Thus, he needed to find alternative accommodations urgently. Suddenly, he saw two police officers on a night patrol at the station. Because Sardor needed a place to stay, he started screaming and pretended to be drunk, hoping that the police officers would notice him and then take him to a police station where he could spend the night. As expected, the two police officers quickly approached Sardor, and one of them kicked him in the ass, a method typically applied to show that Central Asian migrants are nobodies in Russia. Sardor needed a place to stay, so he did not react to the police officer's action and obediently followed their orders. When they reached the station, Sardor was placed in a cell where migrants are temporarily kept. But Sardor was aware that the police would not keep him long, so he needed to do something in order to extend his stay in the cell until the morning. Luckily, Sardor had a Huawei tablet with him, which had lots of pornographic movies on it. He quickly began playing one of the finest movies, hoping that the police officers would be interested. This strategy

FIGURE 8. Russian police officers work hard and hunt for money (i.e., migrants) during cold winter days. Moscow, January 2015. Photo by author.

worked well and grabbed the police officers' attention, since they were bored with their daily routines and eager to do something fun to kill time. Sardor also had cigarettes with him, and he gave the entire pack to them. Given these strategies, Sardor managed to please the police officers and quickly befriended them. As a result, Sardor was allowed to sleep in the cell until morning.

These examples suggest that Uzbek migrants are not merely passive pawns constrained by a repressive and corrupt legal environment but are resourceful, displaying the capacity to adapt to the situation in their host country. Street smartness, knowledge of the informal rules, and mastering bribery skills remain crucial to migrants' survival. Migrants understand that police officers are more interested in generating additional income from migrants than transferring their cases to court for deportation, as exemplified in the following:

> Police officers also have a conscience. For example, you agree to a 500-ruble bribe, but you only have a 1,000-ruble banknote. You give them 1,000 rubles and they return 500 rubles to you. As Russians say, "*dogovor dorozhe deneg*" [an agreement is more valuable than money]. You can negotiate the bribe rate with the police, just like you negotiate the price of potatoes in a bazaar. You state your offer, he asks you to add a little, and you agree. Police officers are also people, and they have children. They have no interest in transferring our cases to the courts or to the immigration office. If they send our cases to court, they will not make any money. Secondly, it will be extra work for them, like going to the court and so on. It is easier for them to take our

money and release us. They transfer our cases to court only when they have a special order or "plan" from their boss, which directs them to find a certain number of
migrants for deportation on that day. (Soli, 41, male, Uzbek taxi driver in Moscow)

During my fieldwork I also conducted in-depth (semistructured) interviews with
100 Central Asian migrants in Moscow (July–August 2015), asking about their
daily experiences with Russian police officers (among 14 other topics). Briefly, the
basic characteristics of my informants were as follows: 92 percent were male, given
the reality of the gendered constitution of Central Asian migrants (approximately
80 percent of all Central Asian migrants are male). In addition, the majority of
the interviewees were young, ranging in age from 21 to 45 years old (92 percent),
married (62 percent), and had completed upper secondary school or a vocational
education (84 percent). In terms of employment they worked in construction
(55 percent), at a supermarket (10 percent), as a cleaner and in housing maintenance (8 percent), in a warehouse (5 percent), as a domestic worker (4 percent), as
a taxi driver (4 percent), in a bakery (3 percent), and in other sectors (11 percent).
Only one-third of the informants (31 percent) could easily communicate in the
Russian language.

In the next section I present some relevant empirical examples focused on
migrant-police interactions. These include (a) relationships between migrant
workers and the police, (b) corruption and bribes, and (c) migrants' navigational
strategies and informal practices. Police corruption remains widespread: 85 percent
of the migrants I interviewed indicated that they had paid a bribe to Russian
police officers. The process of negotiating a bribe also seems well-established.
Both police officers and migrants actively engage in negotiating the rules of the game.
Usually (in 55 percent of my cases), police officers initiate bribery and openly state
the amount they want. Then, migrants negotiate and try to lower the amount of the
bribe. In almost as many instances, though (45 percent), the police officer does
not directly ask for a bribe but drops a hint, saying something like, "What do you
think? What shall I do with you?" Then, the migrant is expected to take the initia-
tive and state the amount he or she can pay. But police officers usually increase the
amount and demand more money. My interviews showed that police corruption
has become a norm within the migrant labor market to the extent that 96 percent
of the migrants I interviewed provided the same amount for the average bribe (500
to 1,000 rubles).

Of the migrants I interviewed, 76 percent stated that Russian police officers
now commonly ask for a bribe in migrants' native languages. One of the Uzbek
interviewees explained: "Look, we need money and we came to Russia and we are
all trying to learn Russian. The same logic applies to police officers. Migrants
are feeding their kids. So, police officers are also trying to learn Uzbek. We all need
to learn the languages that feed us."

The majority of my interviewees (89 percent) believed that police officers' primary motivation for stopping migrants on the street was not aimed at

maintaining law and order but to find problems in migrants' documents and subsequently pressure them to pay a bribe. And because it is almost impossible for a migrant to be "fully legal" in the Russian context, more than three-quarters (78 percent) said that possessing real, authentic documents is not associated with a significantly lower likelihood of paying a bribe to a police officer. Despite widespread police corruption, however, only 4 percent of the migrants I interviewed referred to corrupt policemen as their primary problem. More crippling were the high work-permit (patent) fees (43 percent) and homesickness (25 percent).

MIGRANTS' EVERYDAY ENCOUNTERS WITH IMMIGRATION OFFICIALS

In this section I focus on the everyday interactions between Russian immigration officials and migrant workers. When examining these daily interactions, I present empirical examples encompassing two different periods: (1) empirical data covering developments between January of 2014 and April of 2016, when the Federal Migration Service (FMS) was responsible for migration management in Russia and (2) empirical data focusing on the post-FMS or GUVM period (April of 2016 through August of 2018), when FMS was dissolved by Presidential Decree on April 5, 2016, after which its functions were transferred to the General Administration for Migration Issues (GUVM) of the Russian Ministry of the Interior. The presentation of empirical data reflects this chronological order.

In 2014, during my first year of fieldwork, I conducted observations at several FMS offices in the north of Moscow. On January 24 I visited a local FMS office in Moscow's Bibirevo district. When I approached the FMS office, I found hundreds of Central Asian migrants standing in line to submit their documents for work permits. Despite the freezing temperature, around −25°C, all migrants were forced to wait outside, queuing in an area consisting of an iron-bar fenced-in space. The area resembled a shed in which sheep are kept within a tiny enclosure complete with iron-bar fencing. This scene left me with the impression that Russian authorities treat migrants as subpar humans. Since there were hundreds of migrants queuing, I did not wait long and asked the person in charge of the queue to add my name to his registration book. He registered my name and told me to return in three days.

As planned, I returned to the Bibirevo FMS office on January 27 early in the morning. After waiting approximately 45 minutes, I was finally allowed to enter the FMS building, where migrants were submitting their documents and biometric data. Inside the office, and together with migrants, I again waited in a queue among those waiting to speak to an FMS official. When standing in the queue, I saw three migrants approach the FMS official managing the queue and ask him if he could expedite the processing of their work permit application if they "thanked him" properly. The FMS official smiled and positively welcomed this gesture but

FIGURE 9. Reception facility at an FMS Office in Moscow's Bibirevo district. January 2014. Photo by author.

pointed to one Uzbek man standing near the reception area, assuring them that he could fix everything. The three migrants then approached the Uzbek intermediary, asking him if he could help them with their documents. The Uzbek intermediary explained, "If you give me 35,000 rubles (US$560), I will create a clean work permit for you. I always work *halol* (honestly), and people who get their documents through me experience no legal problems. As I said, I always work *halol*." Afterward, he gave the migrants his phone number and instructed them to call him after 6 p.m. Interestingly, this Uzbek man was not an official employee of FMS but rather a *posrednik* (intermediary) whose main function was to act as a bridge between migrants and FMS officials by facilitating the informal transactions between the two parties. From my observations I concluded that the FMS employee never directly accepted the bribe; instead, they use the *posrednik*'s services to keep themselves free of reproach from corruption charges. That is, the FMS employees used well-organized, institutionalized, and well-established informal practices to accept bribes. Migrants were familiar with this practice and, therefore, primarily used this informal system to obtain work permits.

On April 7, 2014, I visited another FMS office in the north of Moscow. It was a typical workday at FMS, with about 500 to 600 migrants waiting in line. Dozens of buses were situated near the FMS building, bringing many migrants from the Moscow region. I spotted migrants from almost all of the post-Soviet republics, including Armenians, Azerbaijanis, Kyrgyz, Moldovans, Tajik, Ukrainians, and Uzbeks. There were only a few female migrants; approximately 80 percent of all visitors were men. There were no public toilets on the FMS premises. Owing to the large number of migrants, some were pushing the line forward, and the FMS officers screamed and cursed at the migrants to maintain order. The FMS employees did not show any respect toward the migrants and openly used the racial slur *churka* (dumb ass) toward those migrants who attempted to jump the queue. Since I was viewed as a part of the crowd, I also experienced the "privileges" of being a migrant worker.

FIGURE 10. Russian Federal Migration Service Office in the north of Moscow. Migrants line up to apply for work permits. Photo by author.

In fact, FMS was blamed for the chaos, since there was no area for those migrants who had to wait, even in freezing temperatures. But FMS created those queues intentionally, because the queues served as a *kormushka* (feeding trough).

A small "bistro" café situated at the FMS office's gate sold coffee, tea, and snacks to migrants, although the main function of this café was not to sell food and drinks; rather, it served as a place for migrants and middlemen to negotiate the price of two main services: (1) fast-track access to the FMS building for a fee and (2) facilitating a bribe for applying for and receiving a work permit. In truth, this café, owned by Armenian migrants, did not exist the previous year. Before opening the café, the Armenian migrants "settled" in the FMS office by selling coffee, tea, and hotdogs from a car's trunk to migrants submitting their documents for work permits during the cold winter months. In addition to selling drinks and fast food, they also offered the opportunity for migrants to warm themselves up in their car for 500 rubles (US$8). In addition, they charged 1,000 rubles (US$15) if a migrant wanted to enter the FMS building ahead of others. Previously, they worked as follows: a migrant arriving at FMS at midnight paid 1,000 rubles. As a rule, if the migrant wanted to enter first, s/he had to register her/his name first. Thus, migrants arrived at midnight, slept in the car until the next morning, and then registered their name first when the FMS employee opened registration. This business became quite profitable, and the Armenian migrants became rich, subsequently opening their bistro. Because of their daily presence in the FMS area, the Armenians established a close relationship with the FMS employees, allowing them to create an informal, fee-based fast-track system that they offered to migrants. The standard rate for fast-track access was 2,000 rubles (US$30). If the line was too long, the price may increase to 3,000 rubles (US$45). Migrants who did not pay for fast-track access were forced to wait at the FMS premises for many hours, in some cases, up to three days. The profit generated from this informal business was shared equally between the Armenians and the FMS employees. For example, each day they sold about 70 to 80 fast-track access "passes," collecting approximately 150,000 rubles (US$2,400).

These observations indicate that the bureaucratic process of applying for a work permit was intentionally designed to be complicated, such that migrants would be compelled to approach informal actors (such as the Armenians mentioned above). The harder the process of obtaining a work permit was, the more willing migrants would be to informally pay intermediaries. As one immigration lawyer in Moscow explained, FMS employees are not well-paid; thus, they intentionally extend the document processing times in order to create queues. These queues then generate an additional source of income for them.[4]

Another area where immigration officials and migrants come into daily contact lies in the system of residence registration. In Russia all foreign citizens and stateless persons must register within seven working days after their arrival at the address where they reside. The FMS/GUVM, responsible for immigration control and management, also manages the registration service. But migrants cannot independently register their address. If migrants attempt to register, they must appear with their landlord. But few landlords in Moscow agree to register Central Asian migrants at their address, given fears originating from Soviet times that a person registered at their apartment might obtain co-ownership rights following residence for a certain period of time. Landlords, thus, are also reluctant to legally rent apartments to migrants, since they think that the apartment will turn into a "rubber apartment," a location where a tenant might bring another 20 migrants to the apartment, an illegal practice. Migrants cannot afford to rent apartments alone, given their low salaries. Typically, 15 to 20 migrants share an apartment and the cost of the monthly rent. These constraints create an informal market for residence registrations, whereby intermediaries, typically well-connected with immigration officials, offer a fictitious registration service.

The residence registration rules were further tightened following adoption of a new Federal Law (N 163-FZ), "On Amendments to the Federal Law on the Migration Registration of Foreign Citizens and Stateless Persons in the Russian Federation." Until June of 2018, migrants could register at the legal address of the company employing them. Following legislative changes, however, migrants were no longer allowed to register at the juridical address, meaning that registration was possible only at an individual's actual residential address. Clearly, many migrants could not comply with these new rules, which created further demand for the services of informal document intermediaries. The Russian police were also granted an additional opportunity to extort money from migrants since they understand that no migrant actually lives at the address linked to their registration. In other words, the residence registration serves as another source of *kormushka* for many Russian state actors, as illustrated in the words of one immigration lawyer I interviewed during my fieldwork:

> If there was a desire to have more legal migrants, they [the Russian authorities] could easily restore order by eliminating the residence registration requirement. Apparently, many forces do not have such a desire. One of our former deputies sent a proposal to FMS/GUVM suggesting the complete abolishment of the residence registration rules. He justified his proposal by referring to the large number of illegal migrants as well as to the extensive bureaucracy and extra paperwork immigration officials must deal with in their daily work. But, he received a negative response from a high-level immigration official. It is quite obvious that they do not want to abolish the registration system because they generate large revenues from it.[5]

Nasiba's case serves as a relevant example here. On August 5, 2014, I went to an air ticket office situated next to a metro station in northern Moscow. This ticket office was managed by Nasiba, a 40-year-old female migrant from Osh, southern Kyrgyzstan. Officially, she sold air tickets to migrants; in reality, however, her primary job was to act as an intermediary between migrants and immigration officials with regard to residence registration, work permits, and other immigration documents. Profits linked to selling tickets remained quite small, since Nasiba sold tickets quite cheaply without adding to the original ticket price. Instead, she generated most of her revenues from facilitating migrants' immigration documents. Nasiba was fluent in the Russian language and had a solid command of Russian immigration laws.

In addition to immigration documents, Nasiba also provided various types of services. For a fee of 1,000 rubles (US$15), Nasiba checked whether migrants had any administrative offenses registered in different government databases, possibly leading to the issuance of an entry ban. Given that an individual could receive an entry ban even for minor administrative law violations, many migrants were eager to check whether any offenses might prevent them from reentering Russia. Nasiba also provided information regarding any pending fines applied to migrants, when and where they were issued, and, in cases of an entry ban, when, where, and why it was issued. These types of information were available only through the FMS and border service databases, since they shared a combined database. The database for traffic police was also linked to the FMS database, since traffic code violations were also linked to the entry-ban system.

All of these means of access were possible given Nasiba's connections within the FMS. Since many migrants were not in a position to independently secure immigration documents, the role of document intermediaries like Nasiba remained crucial in facilitating migrants' legal adaptations. Nasiba typically took photocopies of migrants' paperwork and sorted various other issues and procedures herself (e.g., completing and submitting applications). When the documents were ready, she sent the migrants to the FMS office and secured fast-track access for them so that they could leave their fingerprints and pick up their documents. When I asked Nasiba whether immigration documents produced at Moscow's Kazansky railways station were reliable, she said that she viewed most documents issued through sources there as fake. As she explained, at Kazansky station they provide nicely designed residence registrations and work permits, but each of these are typically fake and do not appear in the FMS database. Nasiba frequently boasted that the residence registrations and work permits "issued" by her office carried a 100 percent guarantee, thanks to her connections at FMS:

> I had a colleague who worked with me here. Currently, she works part-time at FMS. She cooperates with us in exchange for kickbacks. Therefore, all of the registrations we issue are clean since we get them directly from FMS. If I created fake documents, I could not continue to work here, because migrants would come and shoot me. I am just a *posrednik;* migrants come and submit their passport copies and migration cards. I scan those documents and send them to our contact at FMS. After that, they complete the registration form, stamp it, and send the completed document.

One could argue that the setting up of Multifunction Migration centers in Moscow, Moscow region, and other major cities has made it easier for migrants to acquire legal documents. One of the first and largest multifunctional migration centers was opened in 2015 at Sakharovo, a small village located in the Troitsk administrative district, which lies 64 km from Moscow city. Unlike in the past, when migrants obtained their work permit documents through intermediaries and waited in long queues, as of 2015 migrants could obtain the required documents and apply for a work permit (patent) independently, without making an informal payment to an intermediary for services and fast-track access. The only disadvantage to this system was that the multifunctional migration center lies quite far from Moscow, meaning migrants must travel long distances and lose one full day of work.

Indeed, when we read the "law in books," the procedures for obtaining immigration documents might seem somewhat simplified. But, in reality, it has become even more difficult to legalize one's migration status. This is due to high legalization fees and bureaucratic uncertainties and inefficiencies that push many migrants into illegality. Another reason is that immigration officials have limited ability to generate informal benefits that were closely connected with the system of queues and work permits. Following the opening of multifunctional migration centers, immigration officials lost a rather substantial portion of their revenues. The only source of *kormushka* they now have at their disposal lies in the residence registration business. An immigration official who previously earned an additional 50,000 to 100,000 rubles (US$800–$1,600) monthly today must rely on her/his salary, hardly enough to meet her/his living expenses. Since nearly all processes and services are highly digitalized at the multifunctional centers, no intermediaries are needed, and it is impossible for immigration officials to take bribes.

Given these changes, immigration officials now appear to sabotage the changes, making it hard for migrants to obtain work permits and related documents. Many of the migrants I interviewed stated that immigration officials are excessively strict and refuse to accept migrants' applications for various illogical reasons not stipulated in official procedures. They require migrants to present various documents not mentioned in the list of mandatory documents, such as translating passports into Russian. But, when migrants present these additional documents, immigration officials continue to find issues with them. For example, one Uzbek migrant presented a translated version of his birth certificate, in which the original stated that the certificate was issued by the Uzbekistan SSR; accordingly, the translator also used Uzbekistan SSR. But the immigration official did not accept the translated document, arguing that "SSR" must be spelled out. One case involved the refusal of a migrant's application from further processing given the absence of a comma in the application. An immigration lawyer I interviewed provided this explanation of the flip side of these processes:

> Immigration officials are simply sabotaging the process. They intentionally make migrants' lives difficult, hoping that they make noise and complain that the multifunctional migration center cannot serve migrants. They want migration services to be returned to individual districts, so that they can again calmly take money. Most likely, such logic explains their actions. Therefore, where corruption existed before, implementing changes would be difficult.[6]

. . .

As the empirical material presented in this chapter demonstrates, both police officers and immigration officials are more interested in having more undocumented migrants than managing labor migration in a more rational and formalized way. This stems from the vested interested of Russian police officers and immigration officials, who regard migrants as a source of *kormushka*, whereby these actors attempt to "take their own piece" from it. The empirical material also shows that migrants remain active agents in these processes since they develop various strategies and tactics to negotiate the "rules of the game" with Russian migration officials and police officers.

The empirical data presented here should not be understood as an attempt to portray corruption, extortions by police, and other informal practices as arbitrary and unregulated. Although these processes and strategies may come across as a manifestation of corruption and a weak rule of law, they should also be viewed as an informal yet real mode of migration governance in Russia. Thus, these processes reveal the broader sociolegal context in which migrants' legal adaptations occur. From this perspective migrant legal adaptation processes in the context of a hybrid regime such as Russia should not be understood merely through the legal centralistic lens that emphasizes the importance of one's legal status and immigration laws. Instead, we must also focus on alternative avenues that account for the role of informal rules and practices in migrant legal adaptation processes. Thus, I conclude that the study of migrants' legal adaptation should move beyond legal centralistic perspectives that emphasize the merciless application of immigration laws (e.g., "legal violence," "legal nonexistence," and "deportability"). To better understand migrants' relationships to the host state's laws and institutions in hybrid regime contexts, a new analytical lens encompassing not only the legal centralistic approaches but also the legally pluralistic perspective accounting for informal norms and practices should be adopted.

The Life Histories of Three Uzbek Migrant Workers in Russia

This chapter presents the life histories of three male Uzbek migrants in Moscow, which I label the "three heroes of the book." These men experienced many challenges during their initial migrant periods and then successfully adapted into the labor market and host society given their knowledge of the informal rules of survival and street life and their ability to adapt to changing circumstances. These three life histories resulted from my extensive ethnographic fieldwork carried out between 2014 and 2018 in Moscow and the Fergana Valley (Uzbekistan). Throughout that period I maintained regular contact with these three heroes and closely observed the developments in their life through intensive fieldwork site visits and smartphone-based communication. This difficult endeavor was possible given that the three heroes and I all hail from the same region in Uzbekistan, which enabled me to build a trustworthy relationship with my heroes and gain access to their daily lives and mundane activities in Moscow. Observing their lives afforded me the opportunity to collect their narratives related to informal adaptation and the street world and to observe situations where they maneuvered around immigration and labor laws and solved problems through informal rules and channels. I present these life histories in a separate chapter primarily to explore—ethnographically and biographically—the interconnections between various structural and individual factors described in the previous chapters. This presentation allows me construct how migrants maneuver through the Russian legal system and among the police, immigration officials, and border guards, and how they produce various forms of informal governance and legal order to organize their daily lives. Throughout what follows, I use pseudonyms for all three of these heroes and all of the other individuals that appear in the life histories.

The first case focuses on Zaur, an undocumented migrant who works in a supermarket and receives a proper salary (comparable to a Russian citizen's salary) thanks to his fake Russian passport. The second case revolves around the adventures of Nodir, an undocumented labor migrant linked to street institutions and who works as a guard and caretaker at a *dacha* (summer cottage) in Rublevka, Moscow, a property owned by a high-level official in the Russian Federal Security Service (FSB). The third case focuses on Baha, a loader at a warehouse, who experienced various hardships given his attempt to comply with Russian immigration laws. He later succeeded by using informal means of legal adaptation. The sections that follow provide the "thick descriptions" presented through these three life histories.

ZAUR: BECOMING "RUSSKIY" (RUSSIAN) THROUGH INFORMAL PRACTICES

Zaur (35, male), a migrant worker in Moscow, comes from the Fergana Valley in Uzbekistan. He arrived in Moscow in 2003 shortly after finishing secondary school in rural Fergana. Before traveling to Moscow, he worked as a broker in his home village, a seasonal summer job where he bought fruits and vegetables in large quantities from individual farmers (*dehqonlar*) and distributed them to village-based informal entrepreneurs (*rossiychilar*) at a wholesale price. Typically, *rossiychilar* export these products to different bazaars in large Russian cities. All of these transactions take place without prefinancing and rely on trust and an oral contract, whereby the *rossiychilar* are expected to sell all of the products in Russia and then pay the brokers for the products they provided. In turn, the brokers are expected to distribute the promised money to individual farmers. Zaur's brokerage business created more trouble than profit, however, since informal entrepreneurs who bought his products went bankrupt and failed to pay Zaur's expenses. As a result Zaur also found himself indebted to several individual farmers who typically relied on the summer harvests to make ends meet. These events and the resulting daily pressure placed on him by various farmers eventually forced Zaur to leave his home village and search for job opportunities in Russia.

Zaur arrived in Moscow in the autumn of 2003, when labor migration remained a new phenomenon in Russia. But Zaur quickly adapted to the new environment, given that his classmate Mirzo was already working in Moscow and helped him find a job at a furniture factory. His salary was 21,000 rubles (~US$700 based on 2003 exchange rates), and he worked at the furniture factory until 2007 without a work permit or employment contract. Given his stable monthly salary, which was considered high compared to typical wages in Uzbekistan, Zaur paid off his debts to farmers in one-year's time, allowing him to use his remittances to buy a fancy car for his parents and renovate their house in his home village. This granted Zaur and his family a higher social status and reputation in the village, which probably would not have happened so quickly if Zaur had remained in the village.

But Zaur lost his job in 2007 because of the tightening of immigration laws in Russia, which forced many employers to hire migrants with proper work permits and residence registration documents. Given his undocumented status, Zaur was forced to work in the construction sector for one year, a sector in which he could work without documents. Because construction work is considered "black work" (*qora ish*) among migrants, Zaur did not remain in this sector long. Fortunately, he had many connections from the street world through which he could "legalize" his status and, subsequently, returned to his former job at the furniture factory. In December of 2007, for a fee of 8,000 rubles (~US$250 based on 2007 exchange rates), he bought a fake Russian passport and became a "Russian citizen" with a different name and place of birth, which situated him as an Uzbek born in southern Kyrgyzstan. This removed his connection to Uzbekistan completely from his new fake Russian passport. Since his Russian passport was nicely designed and identical to an authentic passport, Zaur managed to convince his Russian boss at the furniture factory that he had indeed received Russian citizenship by bribing a high-level official at the Federal Migration Service. Thanks to this new legal status, he easily returned to his old job at the furniture factory, but he was now hired as a Russian citizen and received a monthly salary of 45,000 rubles (~US$1,500 based on 2007 exchange rates), an income level comparable to an average Muscovite's salary. Like typical Russians, he worked there only five days a week and took two days off during the weekends, although he continued to receive a salary twice as high as his covillagers, a position granting him the nickname *Russkiy* (Russian) among his village network in Moscow.

Zaur's success did not last a year. In August of 2008, on his way to his workplace, he was stopped by a police officer who asked for his identity documents. Without even thinking of the possible consequences, Zaur confidently showed him his Russian passport, proudly stating that he held Russian citizenship. But his confident voice did not convince the police officer who previously dealt with many similar cases and decided to check the authenticity of his passport at the police department. After carefully checking his passport against a database, the police officer identified his passport as a fake and informed Zaur that he had prepared an arrest report and was transferring his case to a public prosecutor, recommending that a criminal case be opened. It was highly likely that Zaur would be charged with document forgery, a criminal act according to Article 327 of the Russian Criminal Code. Not wanting to end up in prison, Zaur quickly found a Russian defense lawyer through his street connections in Moscow. His defense lawyer was street-smart and well-versed in bribery. Rather than trying to defend him in court, he asked Zaur to give him 30,000 rubles (~US$1,000), which would be given to the public prosecutor who agreed to change Zaur's case from a criminal charge to an administrative offense, resulting in a fine and deportation to Uzbekistan. The public prosecutor kept his word, and Zaur received a fine along with an administrative expulsion and deportation order. After spending three months in the temporary detention center at Dmitrievskoe Shosse in Moscow, Zaur was deported to Uzbekistan in November of 2008, with an entry ban for the next five years (until 2013).

After returning to his village, Zaur married in 2009 and started a new life. But because he had worked in Moscow for many years and was accustomed to receiving a good salary, he could not readapt to the low pay and working conditions in rural Fergana. His salary was insufficient to secure even his family's basic needs. Working as a broker was not an option given his past experience with the *rossiychilar*. In his words he had already become "Russified" (*o'rishlashib ketdim*) and longed for his migrant life in Moscow. His desire to return to Moscow prompted him to develop new strategies. In March of 2011, after long negotiations and efforts, he managed to find common ground (*til topishdi*) with an Uzbek police officer in his home district willing to assist Zaur in changing his name and obtaining a new passport for a gratuity payment of US$500. As a result, Zaur was now "clean," and he returned to Moscow in April 2011 as a migrant who had previously never been to Russia.

This time, given his previous bad experience with a forged passport, Zaur was determined to become "legal" (*qonuniy bo'lib yurish*) and follow all Russian laws. Zaur knew that his name was clean and that none of his previous offenses existed in the Russian state database because of his new name. But, going "legal" in Zaur's view meant renewing his migration card and exit-entry stamp every 90 days at the Russian-Ukrainian border. This process allowed many Central Asian migrants to remain legally within the territory of the Russian Federation, but this legal stay was limited to visitors and did not allow migrants to work in Russia.

Because Zaur was away from Moscow for nearly three years, things were different in the migrant labor market. After arriving in Moscow in April of 2011, he tried to return to his old job at the furniture factory, but he found no vacant positions there. Additionally, they knew Zaur's history with the fake Russian passport, which probably was the main reason they chose not to rehire him. Since he could not secure a stable job, Zaur had to work in many places until May of 2014, when he was again deported to Uzbekistan. Between April of 2011 and May of 2014, he worked as an electrician, a loader in a bazaar, a *dacha* caretaker, and a construction worker, earning on average of 18,000 to 20,000 rubles (~US$500–$650 based on 2011–14 exchange rates) per month. Zaur worked in all of these different jobs without a work permit since they were all based on a handshake agreement. In order to remain "legal," Zaur traveled by shared taxi to the Pogar border point (Russian-Ukrainian border) in the Bryansk province every 90 days. There he could renew his migration card and get a new exit-entry stamp in his passport, allowing him to stay another 90 days in Russia.

In May of 2014, FMS, with assistance from OMON (the Russian paramilitary police), conducted a raid at the construction site in the Moscow province where many Uzbek migrants worked. With other migrants Zaur was also apprehended during this raid. Since all of the migrants worked there without any formal contracts or work permits, their cases were transferred to the courts for trial and possible deportation. Before the court proceedings, Zaur and all of the other migrants were brought to the police department, where migrants were kept in a cell prior to trial. Knowing that all Russian police officers take bribes, Zaur offered 15,000 rubles (~US$450) to one police officer there. But the officer refused the bribe with regret, stating that FMS was involved in this case, and, therefore, the officer was not in a position to take bribes.

As expected, the next day, Zaur, like other migrants, was fined 10,000 rubles (~US$300) and received an administrative expulsion and deportation order with a five-year entry ban. He was then transferred to a temporary detention center (*Spetsial'noe uchrezhdenie vremennego soderzhaniya inostrannikh grazhdan*) in Moscow city, where he was kept for 18 days, until his deportation to Uzbekistan. Those 18 days that Zaur spent in the detention center turned out to be useful to him. Although the food and living conditions at the detention center were completely unacceptable, Zaur met a migrant worker from southern Kyrgyzstan who was street-smart and knew how to navigate around Russian laws. He told Zaur that he had a chance to return to Russia immediately if he managed to renew his passport within a month after his arrival in Uzbekistan. When Zaur asked him to explain more, he said that there was no shared database in Russia and each state institution—for instance, FMS, the police, and border control—has a separate database, and these different databases are only synchronized once a month. Even if a migrant is deported, this information exists only in the FMS database, and the border control service's database will only be updated one month later. Thus, migrants could easily enter Russia if they replace their old passport (with the deportation stamp) with a new one within 30 days. Not many migrants knew about this practice.

After being deported and arriving in rural Fergana in early June of 2014, Zaur moved quickly and secured a new passport in 12 days thanks to his connections at the district passport department. Immediately upon receiving his new passport, Zaur decided to travel to Russia by shared taxi rather than airplane, assuming that it would be safer to enter Russia through the Russian-Kazakh border, where, he believed, there was less control and more disorder. His tactic proved successful and he managed to get an entry stamp at the border, allowing him to continue his journey to Moscow, where he had good connections and knew how things worked.

Learning from his past mistakes, Zaur completely changed his strategy. He understood that he was already "illegal" in the FMS database, meaning that obtaining a real work permit and residence registration was an obvious impossibility. When Zaur worked in the wholesale bazaar, he was able to develop a friendly relationship with Mukhtar, an Azerbaijani immigrant in Moscow with Russian citizenship, who sold fruits and vegetables at a wholesale price. Coincidentally, Zaur's and Mukhtar's facial appearances were identical to the extent that a typical Russian would hardly distinguish between them. Given that Mukhtar was a Russia citizen and the similarity in their facial appearances, Zaur asked Mukhtar if he could use his Russian passport to get a job as a clerk at a supermarket, a position most Uzbek migrants in Moscow consider rather decent. This strategy rested on Zaur's understanding that for many Russians both Uzbek and Azerbaijani are *cherniy* (black) and, therefore, Russians can barely distinguish one *cherniy* from another.

In return, Zaur offered Mukhtar a 5,000-ruble *dolya* (share) per month. Because Mukhtar worked informally in the bazaar, he did not accumulate any points for his pension. Given this fact, Zaur made clear to Mukhtar that he would be registered as formally employed in the state records and receive social security and pension contributions. Based on these benefits, Mukhtar gladly accepted Zaur's business proposal and even designed a more innovative strategy. Mukhtar said that Zaur could use his original passport when applying for a job at a supermarket and opening a bank account given that the original documents are required in such situations. If these two key steps are successfully passed, then, Mukhtar suggested that Zaur would carry with him two documents to keep him out of trouble when stopped by the police or other law-enforcement authorities: (1) a notarized copy of Mukhtar's passport, and (2) the original of his *voenniy bilet* (military ID), a document testifying that Mukhtar completed his military service in the Russian army. Both Zaur and Mukhtar agreed to these arrangements.

Events unfolded exactly as Zaur and Mukhtar anticipated. Zaur approached the manager of the supermarket with Mukhtar's passport. After a follow-up conversation, Zaur's job application was accepted, and he was subsequently employed as a Russian citizen with a 45,000-ruble per month salary (~US$1,200 based on June 2014 exchange rates) and two days off each week. He also managed to open a bank account at Sberbank and received a Mastercard for payments. Zaur was known as a Russian citizen in his workplace and received his salary in a bank account, a rarity among many migrants in Russia. Zaur also began enjoying free mobility in the city since the police check was no longer a problem for him. Each time he was stopped by the police, Zaur showed the notarized copy of his passport, together with the military ID, explaining that the original passport was currently at the public notary because of a sales contract issue.

In August of 2018, the last time I met Zaur in Moscow, he was still working at the same supermarket. Zaur was not alone this time. His wife was also in Moscow, working at the same supermarket with Zaur. Since Zaur had a good relationship with the supermarket manager, his wife could work at the supermarket informally, without any contract or documents. Given his *Russkiy* status, Zaur also managed to rent a three-bedroom apartment from the housing agency for 38,000 rubles per month (~US$600 based on August 2018 exchange rate), which he used to generate revenues by subletting two bedrooms and the living room to 12 migrants. This business covered his apartment rental fees, as well as generating an additional 12,000-ruble (~US$200) profit for Zaur. To keep the apartment free from police checks, Zaur paid a monthly bribe of 5,000 rubles (~US$80) to the police officer in charge of the area near the apartment.

All in all, Zaur managed to change his social status from *cherniy* (black) to *Russkiy* (Russian) given his street smartness and his ability to develop various informal strategies to navigate the repressive legal system. Zaur used to listen to a song, "Moskva slezam ne verit" (Moscow sheds no tears), and believed that one must be creative and not afraid to take risks if s/he wanted to succeed in Moscow.

As shown above, given his street smartness and navigational skills, Zaur managed to adapt to the restrictive immigration legal regime in Russia. Because of normalized discrimination in the Russian labor market, where local workers with Russian citizenship received twice the pay migrant workers received, it was obvious that Zaur would not receive a decent salary even if he worked legally and possessed all of the required immigration documents. In addition to receiving a decent salary, Zaur also gained labor rights enabling him to complain about working conditions and claim overtime payment if he worked long hours. Hence, rather than trying to follow formal (legal) channels of legalization, which is almost unattainable given Russian realities, Zaur pursued alternative, informal paths of legal adaptation. These alternative paths provided him with greater economic security and relatively unimpeded mobility in a city notorious for police harassment and corruption.

NODIR: STREET-LEVEL ADAPTATION

Nodir (31, male) is a migrant from the Fergana Valley of Uzbekistan. He is a talkative, street-smart, physically fit individual. He has a rich experience in wrestling and street brawls, experiences confirmed by the many scars on his body. This history is also visible in his postschool career, during which he was involved in an unconventional income-earning activity. Shortly after finishing secondary school in 2004, Nodir started working as an *ellik to'rtchi* (fifty-four), a new term originating in the Fergana Valley, referring to individuals who illegally transport (or smuggle) cheap Chinese goods from Kyrgyzstan into Uzbekistan, items prohibited under Decree No. 154 of the Cabinet of Ministers of Uzbekistan[1]. While cheap Chinese products remain in strong demand, Uzbekistan continues to prohibit the importation of Chinese goods. This injunction stems from the vested interests of high-level state officials and business structures who established a monopoly over the provision of certain products by limiting the inflow of cheap Chinese products into Uzbekistan. Since these interests are formalized through a legislative act, Uzbek border guards and customs officials heavily control the inflow of these products.

As a smuggler, Nodir was to secretly transport Chinese goods and items (e.g., clothes, electronics, etc.) into the territory of Uzbekistan by means of cars provided by local entrepreneurs. He usually drove over the mountainous Kyrgyz-Uzbek border illegally through a roundabout way, a criminal act according to the Criminal

Code of Uzbekistan. Frequently, he was spotted by Uzbek border guards who tried to chase him, but he always managed to escape them. Owing to his exceptional mountain-driving skills, many villagers used Nodir's nickname "Michael Schumacher," an internationally famous German race-car driver, when referring to him. But Nodir had to stop his smuggling activity in November of 2009 when the Uzbek government intensified its control over the Kyrgyz-Uzbek border, where border guards were instructed to shoot anyone crossing the border illegally. Not wanting to risk his life, he looked for alternative means to earn money, which led him to choose Russia as a new place to seek adventures. His decision to work in Russia was largely driven by the widespread trend in his village: all young men were migrating to Russia in search of better-paying jobs.

Nodir arrived in Moscow in mid-January of 2010. Like many Uzbek migrants, he worked without a work permit and regularly renewed his exit-entry stamp in his passport at the Russian-Ukrainian border every 90 days, allowing him to extend his legal stay in Russia. With the assistance of his village networks, he quickly found a job in the construction sector in the Moscow province. His tasks included various finishing and design works, such as window fitting, painting, flooring, and wallpaper installation. His monthly income was around 15,000 to 20,000 rubles (~US$450–$600 based on 2010 exchange rates). In this position he met many migrants from different villages of the Fergana Valley and established connections with the street world. These connections served as the basis for his new job as an extortion racketeer at Moscow's Kazansky railway station (hereafter, *Kazansky vokzal*).

Kazansky vokzal, situated at Komsomolskaya square, is one of nine railway stations in Moscow, which serves the Trans-Aral railway line (among others) departing to Kazakhstan, Kyrgyzstan, Tajikistan, and Uzbekistan. Therefore, when visiting this railway station, one may spot many migrants arriving from and departing to Central Asia. Given the high concentration of migrant workers at *Kazansky vokzal*, many cafés serve Central Asian food, and many underground printing houses produce fake immigration documents.

Since Nodir had already been involved in street-based informal economic activities in Uzbekistan, it was quite obvious that his premigratory experiences influenced his labor market behavior in Moscow. In April of 2011 Nodir, together with three migrants from the Fergana Valley, started a new "job" as an extortion racketeer at *Kazansky vokzal*. The main form of their racketeering activities involved forcibly extorting money from Kyrgyz, Tajik, and Uzbek migrants (departing to Central Asia) through threats and violence. If migrants had no money, Nodir and his team either took their mobile phones or took other valuable items from their bags. In turn, Nodir sold these phones and items at a market in Moscow's Savyolovskaya metro station, where visitors were predominantly Central Asian migrants. On average, each member of the racketeering team earned a monthly income of about 50,000 to 60,000 rubles (~US$1,500–$1,800 based on 2011–13 exchange rates).

Undoubtedly, Nodir and his team's racketeering activities represented criminal acts according to Russian legislation, which could lead to a seven-year prison sentence. They knew that they needed informal approval—that is, "roofing" (*kryshevanie*) from police officers at *Kazansky vokzal*—to continue their extortionist activities there. But Nodir was street-smart and managed to strike a deal with the Russian police officers. According to their informal agreement, Nodir was expected to give a weekly *dolya* (share or fee) of 10,000 rubles (~US$300), as well as secure their daily "recreational" needs such as cigarettes and vodka. In return, the police officers ignored their extortionist activities and did not react when migrants approached them for help. This informal agreement allowed Nodir and his team to freely and openly conduct their extortionist activities within the territory of the railway station.

I note here that Nodir and his team adhered to a moral code in their daily work. Since Nodir and his team members originated from the Fergana Valley, they remained loyal to their origins and never extorted money or other items from migrants who were also from the Fergana Valley. They also did not touch migrants from Uzbekistan's capital city of Tashkent, considering the historical fact that Tashkent was part of the Kokand Khanate, an Uzbek state in the Fergana Valley that existed from 1709 until 1876 within the territory of eastern Uzbekistan. Rather than extorting money, Nodir often recalled situations in which he helped and protected Fergana migrants in Moscow, when they needed money to buy a train ticket to Uzbekistan or asked for help with recovering their salary from middlemen. Their primary targets consisted of Kyrgyz, Tajik, and Uzbek migrants originating from Uzbekistan's other regions, such as Bukhara, Kashkadarya, Khorezm, Samarkand, and Surkhandarya. In Nodir's view pure ethnic Uzbeks primarily lived in the Fergana Valley, and people living in other regions of Uzbekistan were not pure Uzbeks; that is, they were either mixed with Tajiks or Turkmens. Referring to this "ethnic impurity," Nodir and his team members did not feel guilty extorting money from their countrymen.

In December of 2013, however, Nodir and his team were forced to stop their racketeering activity. Typically, when Nodir extorted money from migrants, the police officers closed their eyes. This gave Nodir and his team absolute immunity. But an incident connected with a Kyrgyz migrant eventually put an end to their business. As usual, Nodir and his team used violence and forcibly took money and a mobile phone from a Kyrgyz migrant. In turn, the Kyrgyz migrant visited the police unit of the station, seeking redress for his grievance. Normally, the police officers did not react to such reports because Nodir paid them regularly. But this time the police officers had to react to this report since they were in the midst of an inspection from their superiors and several high-level police officials were present. The police officers quickly reacted and arrested Nodir and his team members on racketeering and extortion charges. Initially, they denied the charges. But CCTV cameras installed in the station clearly showed that they had indeed committed the crimes. It thus became apparent that Nodir and his team's case would be transferred to the prosecutor for further investigation, which would undoubtedly lead to a prison sentence. But, again, Nodir used his bribery skills and quickly offered 100,000 rubles (~US$3,000) to the head of the police, who was an ethnic Tatar. Since it was a large sum for a bribe, the Tatar police officer happily accepted the offer but on the condition that Nodir and his team would never show up at the railway station again. Otherwise, he would not forgive them if they were caught again. Nodir and his team accepted this condition and immediately ceased their racketeering activity at *Kazansky vokzal*.

This event significantly changed Nodir's behavior. In the past he would drink vodka and often had sex at different brothels, behavior considered *haram* (sinful) in Islam. As a result of this incident Nodir became religious and began praying five times a day, a practice followed by devout Muslims. He also returned to the construction sector in January of 2014, where he had begun his "migrant career" in 2010. Because Nodir did not have any immigration documents, it was easy for him to find a job in the construction sector, where employment relationships were conducted on an informal basis. In addition to construction work, Nodir also worked part-time as an "industrial alpinist" (*promyshlenniy alpinist*), a job that involves climbing trees and trimming weak or dried branches and limbs that pose a risk to pedestrians. Since this job was risky and life-threatening, Nodir received 2,000 to 3,000 rubles (~US$60–$100) for each tree he trimmed. Thus, he quickly transitioned from racketeering to daily manual labor in the construction and "alpinist" sectors, which afforded him a positive reputation among his covillagers in Moscow.

Given his street smartness and past racketeering experiences, Nodir was unafraid of facing the police and invented various tactics to avoid paying bribes. When the police stopped and asked him to show his documents, he openly told them that he had no documents and that they can do whatever they want with him. He knew that Russian police officers are only interested in money and would not keep him more than a few hours if he had no money. Since Nodir never carried his passport with him, when asked to provide his passport details, he often provided the passport details of his covillagers who had already left Russia. Thanks to his good memory, Nodir knew the serial number and expiration date of his covillager's passport. When the police checked the passport details he provided, his covillager indeed existed in the database, leading the police officers to believe that he was indeed the same person. Anecdotally, Nodir stated that he had already called his covillager and advised him not to come to Russia in the next five years since Russian police officers had fined him many times, likely resulting in an entry ban.

As an industrial alpinist, Nodir trimmed shrubs in different parts of Moscow and interacted with people from various backgrounds and social classes. In March of 2016, he met Sergey Nikolaev, a high-level official from the Russian Federal Security Service (FSB), when he was trimming shrubs in the apartment building where he lived. Because Nodir looked industrious, physically fit, and could communicate in Russian, Sergey Nikolaev offered him a job with a salary of 35,000 rubles (~US$600 based on 2016 exchange rates) per month. Sergey Nikolaev owned a *dacha* (summer cottage) in Rublevka, which he rented to tourists and guests all year round. Thus, he needed someone who could work both as a guard and a caretaker to serve the guests. Nodir happily accepted this job offer since he could receive a good salary and work and stay in an elite residential area where only wealthy people live. Because his boss, Sergey Nikolaev, was a high-level FSB official, Nodir did not need any immigration documents and enjoyed free mobility since many local police officers in the Rublevka area knew that he was under the protection of Sergey Nikolaev.

But Nodir was safe only in the Rublevka area. In September of 2016 he went to Moscow city to meet and socialize with his friends at an Uzbek café situated near the Babushkinskaya metro station. This happened to coincide with immigration service raids in the area near the metro and sweeps to catch undocumented migrants for possible deportation. Nodir was caught during this raid and was taken to the police department before court proceedings. The trial took place immediately on the next day, and Nodir received an administrative expulsion and deportation order, meaning he would be transferred to a temporary detention center, where migrants were detained until deportation. Nodir somehow managed to find a phone and quickly called his boss, explaining that he was caught during a raid and that the court had ordered his deportation. Sergey Nikolaev immediately came to the police station where Nodir was detained and had a discussion with the police and immigration officials behind closed doors. Following this, and rather surprisingly, they returned Nodir's passport to him and told him to leave Russia on his own within a 10-day period. Sergey Nikolaev blinked subtly at Nodir and told him to go to the *dacha*. Thanks to his boss's interference, Nodir was able to avoid the administrative expulsion, while all of the other migrants who were caught were sent to a temporary detention center for deportation. When Nodir reached the *dacha*, Sergey Nikolaev instructed him to hide his passport somewhere inside the *dacha*. Instead, he provided Nodir with a letter (*spravka*) from the police, stating that his passport and immigration documents were lost. With the assistance of his boss, Nodir regularly updated this letter since it provided him with valid justification for not having his documents with him. When stopped by the police or immigration officials on the street, Nodir usually claimed that he had lost his passport and immigration documents and that he would replace them as soon as possible.

I met Nodir for the last time in August of 2018 when completing my last fieldwork trip for this project. He was still working at the *dacha* under the protection of Sergey Nikolaev. But, since he was already 30 years old, he was considering returning to his home village sometime next year (in 2019) and marrying a girl his parents had found for him. When I asked him whether he was going to remain in the village, he said that he would return to Moscow with his wife shortly after the wedding, and they would both work at the *dacha*. He was confident that Sergey Nikolaev would find ways to remove his entry ban in the GUVM database and ensure his return to Russia. Recalling his racketeering work at *Kazansky vokzal* and how he changed after that experience, Nodir often compared his migrant life and adventures in Moscow to completing military service, whereby one gradually becomes more disciplined, mature, and street-smart as a result of exposure to hardships, strict rules, and hierarchies.

Being undocumented does not necessarily mean that migrants lose their agency and ability to organize their daily lives. Rather, migrants like Nodir have agency and can invent various strategies to maneuver around structural constraints. This situation results from the corrupt and weak rule-of-law environment in Russia empowering the agency of migrants to navigate the system. Nodir's bribery skills, street smartness, and knowledge of informal rules played a key role in negotiating his legal status and relationship with different law-enforcement bodies. Given that the Russian legal system does not function in accordance with rule-of-law principles and that state actors themselves break laws on a daily basis, migrants also respond to these uncertainties by inventing informal norms and practices that provide some kind of palliative mechanism to organize their precarious livelihoods. Based on Nodir's experiences, we can conclude that migrant legal adaptation in contexts characterized by hybrid regimes such as Russia is not primarily contingent on being "legal" and having authentic immigration documents. More importantly, it is about being able to quickly adjust to changing circumstances, the ability to offer bribes when necessary, to act calmly and cunningly when stopped by law-enforcement officials, and to make the right connections and use them to bend the laws. These street skills and artistic traits are as important as possessing authentic immigration documents.

BAHA: LEARNING HOW TO PERFORM "LEGALITY"

Baha (29, male) is a migrant worker in Moscow. Shortly after finishing technical college in 2009, Baha landed a job as an electricity fee collector at the district electricity department (a state-owned enterprise) in rural Fergana, Uzbekistan. His main task involved visiting households in the district on a daily basis and collecting electricity fee payments. Because of the high unemployment rate and growing poverty in rural Fergana, many households could not pay for electricity. Given these realities, Baha's job was quite challenging and rife with scandals, given that he either had to force low-income households to pay or cut their line from the power network. In addition, the nonpayment of fees was connected to frequent interruptions in electricity provision, which left people unsatisfied with the work of the district electricity department. Frustrated with the problems with electricity, many people in rural Fergana simply refused to pay. Despite these daily challenges in his work, Baha received a very low salary, which was insufficient to secure even his own basic needs. As a result, Baha invented various strategies to supplement his low salary. He helped some households with which he had a good relationship and deleted electricity usage records from their electricity meter. In return, heads of households expressed their gratitude to Baha by giving him 25 percent of the deleted electricity fees. But despite these informal income-earning opportunities, Baha decided to quit his job in June of 2013 and move to Russia as a migrant worker. This decision was driven by Baha's desire to diversify his life and seek new adventures in a new country.

Baha arrived in Moscow on June 12, 2013. Since his father was already working in Moscow, he smoothly entered the labor market. Unlike many Uzbek migrants, who failed to obtain a work permit, Baha quickly applied for and obtained a work permit for a one-year period, allowing him to secure formal employment in the Russian construction company that employed his father. This was possible given that Baha sent a copy of his passport to his father two months before his arrival, giving him sufficient time for the company to facilitate his work permit application. Thus, Baha's migrant life in Moscow began smoothly, and he started working at the construction company three days after his arrival.

Baha's primary task was to wash the tires of vehicles that serviced the construction site. Since the construction site was located in Moscow city, the company had to ensure that no dirt or wet clay was taken out of the construction site into the city, a requirement that generated a job for migrants like Baha. Baha's command of the Russian language was almost nonexistent, but he managed to learn the language quickly thanks to his talkativeness, social skills, and eagerness to communicate with Russian girls. Baha's monthly salary was 22,000 rubles (~US$700 based on 2013 exchange rates). But, his employment contract listed his official salary as 10,000 rubles (~US$300), and he received the remaining 12,000 rubles (~US$400) in a separate envelope, a typical tax evasion practice widespread in many post-Soviet countries. Each time he received his salary, Baha had to sign two different *vedomost* (payment register books): a white *vedomost* that was a public register and a black *vedomost* that was kept secretly. Since Baha was formally employed, he worked five days a week and stayed in the free accommodation (a hostel) provided by the company.

Baha's stable life came to an end in May of 2014, when his father returned to Uzbekistan. Another contributing factor to this instability revolved around tensions associated with ethnic differences. While many migrants at the construction site were from the Fergana Valley, many of them were ethnic Tajiks and did not share a common ethnic identity with Baha. This ethnic difference led to serious tensions between Uzbek migrants like Baha and ethnic Tajik migrants, who constituted the majority of workers at the construction site. Given these tensions and some brawls, Baha and several other migrants were compelled to quit their job, an event that completely changed Baha's migrant life in Moscow.

This period was the first time Baha was on his own in a foreign country. But he had extensive village networks in Moscow that he could rely on when necessary. Before contacting his covillagers, Baha visited two construction companies but was refused a job since his work permit was about to expire within a month. This meant Baha had to obtain a new work permit to continue working legally in the construction company. But, in order to prolong their working period in Russia, migrants are required to leave and reenter the territory of Russia once each year. The Russian authorities keep immigration flows under control by legally requiring migrants to renew their migration card and exit-entry stamp. Because Baha worked in Moscow, the closest border was the Pogar border checkpoint in the Bryansk province along the Russian-Ukrainian border. Thus, Baha also decided to travel to Pogar to renew his migration card and the exit-entry stamp in his passport.

Thousands of migrant workers travel to the Pogar border checkpoint by shared taxi once a year to get a new exit-entry stamp in their passport. Pogar is a small town situated on the Russian-Ukrainian border. The distance from Moscow to Pogar is about 505 kilometers, or at least an eight-hour drive. In Russia, Federal Security Service (FSB) troops are responsible for protecting the national border. FSB troops (a) administer and oversee all border control checkpoints, procedures, and infrastructures; (b) review the documents of individuals, goods, and transport vehicles crossing the Russian border; and (c) perform law-enforcement functions in the borderland.

When migrants arrive at the Pogar border crossing, they have two options. The first option is that the migrant waits in the queue at least eight hours to reach passport control in order to obtain an exit stamp and leave the Russian territory. After exiting Russia, the migrant walks toward the neutral zone between Russia and Ukraine and then walks back to the Russian passport control section in order to reenter Russia and obtain a new entry stamp in her/his passport. When reentering Russia, each migrant is required to pay a 500-ruble (~US$8) bribe to the border control official who puts an entry stamp in the passport. This is a well-established norm, whereby all migrants know about this and insert 500 rubles into their passport when handing it over to the border official.

The second option is to cross the border via a special bus, located at a nearby gas station. The fee for the bus service is 1,500 rubles (~US$25). The advantage of using the bus service is that migrants do not have to wait in the queue; thus, they obtain their exit-entry stamp within two to three hours, without even getting off the bus. The bus driver collects all of the passports and gets the stamps for everyone on the bus. On average, for each border crossing trip, this bus takes 40 passengers, and approximately 15 to 20 buses serve the border trips. Each day, at least 50 bus trips are organized, meaning at least 2,000 migrants use this bus service. This bus business generates approximately 3 million rubles (~US$47,000) per day. The profit from this service is shared between the border control officials (FSB troops) and the individuals who organize the bus service. Since this bus service is informally organized, all of the transactions described above are illegal and serve as a source of *kormushka* (a feeding trough) for border officials.

In late May of 2014, Baha, together with three migrants, traveled to Pogar via shared taxi. Each migrant-passenger paid 4,500 rubles (~US$70) for the return trip. The trip to the border took about 10 hours since the car was frequently stopped by traffic police officers who checked the driver's and the migrants' identity documents. Since one of the migrants did not have a residence registration, he had to pay a bribe to several police officers along the route.

They arrived at the border at about 8 a.m. Following the advice of their taxi driver, Baha and the other three migrants used the bus service and quickly exited the territory of Russia. But, when returning to Russia, Baha was asked to get off the bus and talk to a passport control official. After a quick conversation with the border control official, it became clear that Baha had an entry ban, meaning he was not allowed to return to Russia. It was a catch-22 situation since Baha was neither allowed to enter Russia because of the entry ban nor enter Ukraine given the tensions between Russia and Ukraine over Crimea. Baha had no option but to enter Russia, even if it was a criminal act. Not wanting to get stuck in the neutral zone, Baha approached the Ukrainian border official and asked him whether he could help him enter Russia. The Ukrainian border official answered that he could help Baha if he gave him 10,000 rubles (~US$160). The Ukrainian official said that he could provide a document that states that Baha was not allowed to enter Ukraine, thereby forcing the Russian border officials to accept him since he came to the Ukrainian border through the Russian territory.

But Baha did not have 10,000 rubles with him. Baha contacted his covillager Misha in Moscow, asking him to come to Pogar and lend him money so that he could return to Russia. Eight hours later, his friend Misha arrived at the border checkpoint with the money and contacted the Russian border guards to pass the money to Baha, who waited on the other side of the border. In response the border officials offered two options: (a) Misha himself could cross the border officially or (b) he would give the money to taxi drivers (there were taxi drivers nearby who worked for the Russian border officials), and those drivers would give the money to Baha. Since Misha also had an entry ban, he could not consider the first option. This represented a very interesting situation because the Russian border officials themselves offered the solution to the problem. Simultaneously, they made sure that they would make some money through the taxi drivers. Misha quickly made a deal with a taxi driver for 5,000 rubles (~US$80) as payment for their services and gave them 10,000 rubles to deliver to Baha. Misha knew that Baha might need more money, so he hid another 10,000 rubles inside the bread that the driver was also delivering to Baha. He did so because the taxi driver could have raised the fee if he knew that he was carrying that much money. This strategy worked well; Baha received 20,000 rubles (~US$325) and bread to sustain him.

After receiving the money, Baha passed 10,000 rubles to the Ukrainian border official, who in turn promised to get the document ready in one hour. Baha waited for more than two hours, but the official did not show up. Exhausted, given his long wait, Baha approached other Ukrainian border guards and asked them for the agreed-on certificate. The border guards told him that the official who took the money had already left for the day and would not return until two days later. Baha became angry and shouted at them, but the border guards threatened that they would shoot Baha if he did not stop immediately. Frightened, Baha returned to the neutral zone.

Baha again started looking for different ways to solve his problem. This time, he tried to negotiate with Ukrainian border guards in other ways. The guards told Baha that they could help him enter Russia through alternative roundabout ways for 7,000 rubles (~US$110). Luckily, the Ukrainian border guards kept their word and guided him to where he could enter Russia illegally. This strategy was quite risky: if the Russian border guards caught him, he could have been either shot or faced a prison sentence. Baha was lucky; he crossed the border safely and immediately returned to Moscow with Misha.

This incident designated Baha as totally "illegal" in Russia. But with Misha's assistance, Baha again became "legal" and got a fake entry stamp in his passport from *Kazansky vokzal* confirming his "official" entry to Russia. Baha also obtained a fake residence registration and work permit from *Kazanskiy vokzal*, allowing Baha to navigate situations when stopped by police officers. It was not difficult to find accommodation. Baha stayed in a shared apartment with 14 other tenants, three of whom were his covillagers. Because Baha lacked a work permit, he worked for different middlemen in the construction sector from May of 2014 through November of 2015. But he often had problems with delays or nonpayment of his salary given the handshake (informal) nature of his employment. All of the middlemen who did not pay Baha's salary typically blamed the Russian construction company or the Russian middlemen for payment problems, a justification commonly used by various middlemen. As a result, Baha could not send money home and used his meager income to cover his living expenses in Moscow, which included costs such as accommodation, food, clothes, transport, fake documents, and bribes to police officers.

In December of 2015, with the assistance of his covillagers, Baha got another job at a construction site in Balashikha, a small town in Moscow province. He joined one of the construction teams primarily consisting of his covillagers who did finishing and design work (e.g., painting, flooring, and window installation) in nearly completed residential buildings. This construction site served both as a workplace and accommodation for the migrants working there. Their boss was an Uzbek middleman, who in turn was accountable to a Russian middleman and the construction company. Although there were monthly delays, Baha and his covillagers were paid for their work. But despite this, Baha did not like working in Balashikha. This was due to the fact that Balashikha used to be a forbidden, military town during Soviet times and at that time foreigners were not allowed to work there. But this historical fact was misused by Russian police officers, who claimed that Balashikha still preserved its forbidden zone status in the post-Soviet period. Using this argument, police officers extorted bribes from the migrant workers. Therefore, many migrants did not leave the construction building and spent most of their time inside. Because Baha was an outgoing and sociable person, he liked walking outside and was often caught by a hungry police officer constantly looking for migrants to extort. Given the daily police corruption, Baha decided to quit this job in September of 2016.

Baha was the eldest son in his family, so his parents had high expectations of him. Baha knew that jumping from one job to another would not lead to success. Thus, he started exploring different possibilities to find a stable, well-paying job. Fed up with con-artist migrant middlemen, Baha tried to avoid them and work directly under Russian people who, in Baha's view, were honest and never cheated migrants (*o'ris aldamaydi*). But to find such work, he needed to have a Russian passport or at least a Kyrgyz passport that would allow him to work without a work permit given the inclusion of Kyrgyzstan in the Eurasian Economic Union. Kyrgyz migrants were, thus, in greater demand on the labor market since they could work in Russia without a work permit, a factor making them more easily employable than Tajik and Uzbek migrants.

In October of 2016 Baha bought a fake Kyrgyz passport from an underground printing house at *Kazansky vokzal*. One of his friends, a migrant from Uzbekistan's Navoiy region, also had a Kyrgyz passport, which he used to get a job as a loader at a warehouse in Moscow that supplied different wine and liquor products (both Russian and European) to many stores in Moscow. Based on his friend's recommendation, Baha also got a job as a loader at the warehouse in November of 2016. Since Kyrgyz citizens are not required to have a work permit, the manager of the warehouse did not notice that Baha and his friend had fake passports. Using his fake Kyrgyz passport, the warehouse manager quickly employed Baha with a salary of 35,000 rubles (~US$550) per month, allowing him to send money home, as well as have some money for daily expenses in Moscow. The manager also allowed Baha to use one of the empty rooms in the warehouse as accommodation.

Given these privileges, Baha's life changed considerably. He also quickly learned how to avoid paying bribes to police officers. When walking on the street and in public places, Baha usually did not carry any identity documents with him. Baha admired Chechens for their ability to "rule the street" and had several Chechen friends from Grozny, the capital of Chechnya. Like Chechens, Baha wore sport clothes and grew a long beard. When stopped by the police, Baha often introduced himself as a Chechen to the police officers. Naturally, the police officers did not initially believe him because of the absence of his identity document. But after Baha provided the passport details of his Chechen friend who resembled him and even recalled the name of the street and house in Grozny where his friend was registered, the police officers let him go. In some cases Baha presented himself as a victim of human trafficking, telling the police that he lost his passport and was exploited by Armenians who locked him in a small factory for five years. He told the police that he was waiting for a temporary identity document issued by the Uzbek embassy and would return to Uzbekistan as soon as he received it from the embassy. Baha also knew that the police officers were good psychologists and usually stopped those migrants who were not well-dressed. Therefore, Baha usually invested in decent clothes with his salary so that he would differ from those migrants who did "black work" (*qora ish*). He often stated that it was better to invest in one's clothes and appearance than paying a bribe to police officers. In short, Baha invented various strategies and stories to avoid paying a bribe to the police.

I visited Moscow for the last time in August of 2018 and found that Baha was still working at the same warehouse. But to my surprise Baha was considering marrying a Russian girl in Moscow who was originally from Orenburg, a city in southwest Russia. Already engaged then, their wedding took place in Moscow in March of 2019. Currently, Baha is trying to legalize his status in Russia using his wife's Russian citizenship. It is unclear whether he will accomplish this objective.

As Baha's brief life history shows, it is quite difficult for migrants to remain "legal" in Russia given the punitive legal environment. Instead, it is easier to adapt to the legal environment by inventing various informal and illegal strategies and tactics. Despite Baha's attempts to remain "legal" by extending his work permit, the entry ban he received for minor administrative offenses and his subsequent border adventures made it impossible for him to pursue formal paths to legal adaptation. As a result, Baha resorted to informal, street-based mechanisms of legal adaptation that provided him with more economic security and a better job even though this path carries significant risks. But given the fact that "becoming legal through illegal practices" is common in migrant Moscow, Baha's strategy represents a widespread means of legal adaptation in the Russian context. This practice is not an exception, but rather a way of life for many migrants in contemporary Russia.

Drawing from three Uzbek migrants' life histories, this chapter has demonstrated how being undocumented does not automatically deprive migrants of their agency. Instead, it encourages them to invent various informal tactics, strategies, and practices to navigate through the restrictive legal environment. These life histories illustrate how migrant workers, despite their "illegal" status, remain resilient and resourceful, displaying a significant capacity to maneuver around the structural constraints. These constraints include complicated residence registration and work permit rules, punitive laws, social exclusion, racism, and the lack of a social safety net. We have seen that migrants are not just passive, agencyless subjects constrained by a restrictive legal environment but are capable of shaping and adapting their daily routines, mundane social interactions, and "legalization" strategies to the conditions of a shadow economy, a corrupt law-enforcement system, and the lack of any rule-of-law context.

Thus, in line with Garcés-Mascareñas (2010) and Sigona (2012), I contend that researchers must recontextualize the experience of being undocumented and examine it not as an essentialized, generic, and uniform condition. Instead, we should examine this experience as a phenomenon contingent on geographical, political, and historical factors, on the one hand, and migrants' agency and experiences, on the other. Hence, we need a more context-sensitive understanding of "migrant undocumentedness" that takes into account how lacking a legal status intersects with the sociolegal environment and the broader sociopolitical context and, simultaneously, migrants' agency, experiences, and histories. In this regard "illegality" in some migration contexts may actually enable migrants to navigate around the constraints imposed by the state-regulated migrant labor system.

Informality, Migrant Undocumentedness, and Legal Adaptation in Hybrid Political Regimes

In the last two decades, Russia has emerged as one of the key immigration hubs worldwide, witnessing a massive inflow of migrants with low qualifications, no legal right to work or stay, or simply lacking the skills to quickly integrate into the local labor market. The arrival of millions of migrant workers from Central Asia, the Caucasus, and other post-Soviet republics carried significant implications for social transformation, contributing to the emergence of new informal practices and tendencies in contemporary Russian society. These new informal practices, stimulated by migratory flows, overlapped with, reshaped, and reconstituted Russia's socioeconomic tissue fed by an already existing large-scale shadow economy.

Nordstrom (2000) argues that shadow economic activities and networks are not haphazard collections of people in ad hoc groupings. Instead, they are complex chains of transactions highly coordinated and routinized, with hierarchies of deferential power, and are governed by the rules of exchanges and codes of conduct. Viewed in this light, the large shadow economy in Russia predicated on a migrant labor force is not an exception or abnormal phenomenon; rather, it is an institutionalized and routinized system with its own economy and legal infrastructure. Hence, while walking the streets and public places in contemporary Moscow, a careful observer may spot many intermediaries (with a migrant background) openly advertising and selling various fake and "clean fake" immigration documents and offering "legalization" services. It is possible to buy all types of documents from these intermediaries: residence registrations, work permits, migration cards, exit-entry border stamps, temporary and permanent residence permits, and even the much-desired Russian passport. Many underground (hidden) printing houses operate in Moscow, particularly at the Kazansky railway station, where such documents are produced. Even in authoritarian regimes, such as Uzbekistan, from whence my informants originated, it is highly unlikely to see someone openly selling fake documents on the street. It is quite obvious that the majority of these intermediaries one encounters on the streets of Moscow operate under the protection (*kryshevanie*) of Russian law-enforcement officials. Otherwise, they would not be able to operate so freely in public. True, occasionally, the Russian Federal Security Service (FSB) carries out raids and special operations to capture such intermediaries. But, the primary aim of these operations is not to eradicate the illegal document market but to gather material for a TV show on "how FSB officials worked hard" and captured a group of "radicalized Central Asian migrants who create fake documents and recruit migrants for *jihad* in Syria." These strategies satisfy the widespread antimigrant sentiments and provide the illusion to ordinary people that Russian law-enforcement bodies are working very hard to catch and punish illegal migrants. In reality, document intermediaries continue to operate under the protection of law-enforcement bodies.

A similar logic driving migrants into the realm of informality can also be observed in the interpretation and implementation of immigration laws. Whereas immigration laws in Western countries developed gradually, in the Russian context, immigration laws are often adopted at high speed, without actually considering the everyday realities of implementation. Russian authorities often enact various immigration laws and policies with the (declared) objective of reducing the number of undocumented migrants (as shown in chapter 2). But many of these legislative interventions produced contradictory outcomes given that so many laws remain ambiguous (written in general terms), far from an empirical reality, and are often accompanied by the introduction of corrections and additions that undermine the spirit of the law. As a result, state institutions and officials gain wide discretionary power to interpret and implement these laws. Typically, an institution or body responsible for implementing the laws issues an internal decree or instruction (*podzakonniy akt*) suitable for its own interests. This internal decree often remains inside the corridors of that institution. The lack of information then creates fertile ground for corruption, allowing state officials to interpret and implement laws as they wish. A migrant who wants to go "legal" often remains unaware of these internal decrees and consequently fails to comply with the laws. Thus, Russian immigration officials are more interested in producing additional undocumented migrants than in facilitating migrants to leave the shadow economy. For example, between March 24 and April 24, 2017, President Putin announced an amnesty period for undocumented migrants from Tajikistan, which would allow them to legalize their status in Russia; however, the amnesty was verbally announced with no written legislative document to accompany the announcement. Thus, the General Administration for Migration Issues of the Russian Ministry of the Interior (GUVM) was tasked with producing a formal legislative act. GUVM was also responsible for announcing the amnesty program as widely as possible in the media so that all undocumented Tajik migrants could receive information and regularize their status. But only a few news agencies announced it, and many Tajik migrants did not receive any information about the amnesty period. This likely stems from the fact that immigration officials generate no revenue from regularizing undocumented migrants. Rather, such actions would create more work for already overburdened immigration officials. If they genuinely wanted more migrants to become "legal," or if they had an alternative opportunity to generate some informal income, they would have announced it everywhere.

Accordingly, varied interpretations of laws, arbitrary enforcement, and discretionary administrative practices led to the emergence of an informal migration governance system in Russia that significantly differs from that prescribed in official immigration laws and policies. Given these circumstances, it is nearly impossible for migrants to become fully "legal" in practice. In this sense Russia seems to follow global trends in terms of producing insecure and legally ambiguous migration statuses through inconsistent and arbitrary law enforcement (Kubal 2016a), which serve to keep migrant workers submissive (Reeves 2015). Within the migration studies literature, the dominant understanding suggests that undocumentedness leads to the most subordinated, subjugated, and rightless form of existence in the host society (Holmes 2007; Peutz 2007; Rosenthal 2007; Willen 2007b; Menjívar and Abrego 2012). Susan Coutin (2003a, 30), in her study of undocumented migrants in the United States, regards undocumentedness as "a space of forced invisibility, exclusion, subjugation, and repression."

The above perspectives describing undocumentedness as a "dead end" are not surprising given the fact that the literature written in English on "migrant illegality" largely focuses on undocumented migration in Western-style democracies (Bloch and Chimienti 2011). In such contexts migrants "cannot bend the laws and produce [an] informal governance and legal order" because of the strong rule-of-law culture. But in the Russian context undocumentedness is a conscious adaptation strategy rather than a dead end. Unlike Western-style democracies, where the rule of law is embedded in the national culture, in hybrid regime contexts such as Russia migrants do not deal with the rule of law but experience the corrupt legal environment that enables them to produce various informal strategies and tactics to maneuver around legal uncertainties and arbitrary law enforcement. Thus, one of the distinctive features of the Russian migration regime rendering it different from Western migration regimes is the rampant corruption and the dependence of law-enforcement officials (e.g., immigration officials, police officers, and border guards) on informal payments generated from migrant workers. This, in turn, creates a discrepancy between formal (legal) decisions and informal (illegal) practices (Rahmonova-Schwarz 2006; Light 2010, 2016; Reeves 2015; Schenk 2018). Under these conditions, being "legal" or "illegal" becomes contingent on migrants' individual skills and contextual factors.

Given the Russian sociolegal context described above, as well as the ethnographic material presented in chapters 4, 5, 6, and 7, how should we study, understand, and theorize the legal adaptation of migrant workers in Russia? Should it be explained solely from the legal centralistic perspective (based on Western-centric literature), which emphasizes migrants' legal status (Gleeson 2010), compliance with the formal legal system of the host country (Coutin 2003b), their knowledge of immigration laws (Abrego 2011), their ability to engage in claims-making in courts (Beger and Hein 2001), or their capacity to find legal employment (Rivera-Batiz 1999)? In the context of Western-style democracies, legal adaptation is understood with reference to migrants' legal status and their ability to comply with the legal system of the host country. If we analyze the sociolegal situation of migrant workers in Russia from the perspective of the dominant immigrant (legal) adaptation and integration frameworks, millions of migrants seem "legally nonexistent" in Russia. Although I acknowledge the importance of these explanations, I suggest that we need to move beyond (Western-centric) conventional explanations and employ ethnographically embedded and legally pluralistic perspectives to understand migrant legal adaptation in Russia. Thus, in the Russian context, where even migrants with perfectly clean documents cannot be fully legal, the question is not about whether migrants comply with laws. The question, instead, revolves around how familiar migrants are with street law, informal norms, and practices, crucial factors guiding their behavior when they come into contact with police officers and immigration officials who determine who is legal and who is not depending on how migrants behave themselves.

Drawing from my ethnographic study, I have argued that it is insufficient to look at the role of the legal environment as the lens through which to understand migrant legal adaptation, since migrants experience a different legal environment in Russia. The dominant adaptation and integration frameworks might fit the context of Western-style democracies, but their application in hybrid regime contexts requires a careful recontextualization, as well as the application of a legally pluralistic framework that accounts for the informal avenues of adaptation. Hence, by using a legally pluralistic framework and accounting for the hybrid regime characteristics, we arrive at a rather different conclusion whereby migrants in Russia are active and resilient actors capable of inventing various informal strategies to adapt to the restrictive legal environment and organize their working life and tackle uncertainties and risks by producing informal legal orders. Therefore, legal adaptation in hybrid regime contexts cannot be satisfactorily explained by solely referring to the institutional and legal structures. In line with Heyman and Smart (1999), I argue that migrants' informal and illegal adaptation strategies should not be seen as deviant, subversive, or the subculture of a migrant community but rather as an option or resource migrants can use under the conditions of legal uncertainty and arbitrary enforcement.

I should stress, however, that this book is not an attempt to romanticize the role of informal norms and practices as optimal adaptation strategies. Reckoning with the advice of Ledeneva (2009), I am aware that informality plays an ambiguous role and carries both supportive and subversive functions. On the one hand, informality enables migrants to navigate around the restrictive legal environment and access many job opportunities limited to migrants with a legal status; on the other hand, that same informality produces unequal power relations between migrants and Russian employers and state actors. Many of the most exciting stories and experiences I observed during my fieldwork stemmed from legal uncertainty and complicated work permit and residence registration rules, which compelled migrants to navigate the system and invent various informal practices. The immigration laws and policies in Russia remain highly restrictive with potentially severe consequences for migrants' livelihoods. Recent studies describe migrants in Russia as victims of exploitation, corruption, and xenophobia, arguing that "the scale of the issues migrants face in the unbounded city make it extremely difficult for them to develop meaningful forms of resilience and/or resistance. Russia is an extreme example of the human rights abuses that migrants face" (Round and Kuznetsova 2016, 1030). Furthermore, Russia "may be one of the most inhospitable and even dangerous places for migrants in Europe" (Dave 2014a, 2). Yet the treatment of migrants as victims and passive actors may inhibit our looking at their actual navigational skills and experiences, an issue that motivated me to explore migrants' agency and their alternative legal adaptation strategies.

Another key contribution of this book lies in my attempt to create a new framework for understanding migrant legal adaptation in hybrid political regimes, a typology of countries characterized by a weak rule of law, corruption, a large shadow economy, widespread human rights abuses, and a state-controlled civil society. In international comparisons Russia is often portrayed as a hybrid political regime (Goode 2010a, Petrov, Lipman, and Hale 2014), with a weak rule of law (Gel'man 2004), rampant corruption and dysfunctional public administration (Ledeneva 2009), a highly controlled and weak civil society (Hale 2002), and a haphazard system of official and unofficial control (Light 2010). In this regard the empirical examples presented in this book should not be viewed as an attempt to present Russia as a deviant, exceptional migration regime or as another illustration of "how Russia really works" (Ledeneva 2006). Rather, by employing the phrase "hybrid political regime" throughout this book, I emphasize that migrant legal adaptation patterns described within the Russian context can also be identified in other hybrid political regimes.

A brief survey of the relevant literature proves rather illuminating in this respect. In Turkey, a hybrid political regime and one of the largest recipients of migrants worldwide, informality characterizes migrant workers' everyday lives (Içduygu 2006; Akalin 2007; Tolay 2012; Eder 2015; İçduygu and Millet 2016; Şenses 2016). This results from the complicated legalization requirements and arbitrariness and uncertainty in administrative practices, forcing many migrants to resort to an informal economy where they can find jobs without documents and have more flexibility and a certain degree of control over their lives (Eder 2015). A similar situation can be observed in Kazakhstan, where a weak rule-of-law environment and a large shadow economy allow many migrants to work without documents and develop multiple informal and illegal practices in order to protect their legal status, employment, and earnings (Anderson and Hancilová 2011; Dave 2014b). The Malaysian migrant labor market serves as yet another relevant example of how undocumented status actually enables migrants to escape the restraints and subordination created by state-sanctioned migrant labor arrangements (Mascarenhas 2001; Killias 2010). Olivia Killias (2010), through the narrative of Arum, an Indonesian undocumented migrant worker in Malaysia, shows how working legally leads to more subordination and exploitation, whereby migration through illegal channels represented a strategic choice and enabled Arun to circumvent the "legal," state-sanctioned migration scheme. Examples from the Gulf countries, nondemocratic contexts, also demonstrate how an undocumented status does not necessarily lead to exploitation and subordination (Fargues 2011; Pessoa, Harkness, and Gardner 2014; Fargues and Shah 2017). Fargues and Shah, in their edited volume *Skillful Survivals: Irregular Migration to the Gulf* (2017), show that for many migrants working in the Gulf countries undocumentedness is the preferred option, even though such migrants understand that it may lead to arrest, a jail term, and deportation. They do so because undocumented migrants enjoy more freedom over their working lives and can make independent choices, whereas migrants working legally are usually tied down to one specific employer for a fixed sum of money and cannot move between jobs. These examples describing different hybrid regimes and nondemocratic contexts strengthen my argument that my framework developed within the Russian context may also apply to understanding migrant legal adaptation processes in other hybrid political regimes. Thus, the book highlights the need for further research in this field to develop a deeper and more nuanced understanding of migrant legal adaptation in hybrid political regimes.

These findings from the Russian context may also have relevance for understanding the informal migrant labor market in Western-style democracies. Because the governments of Western countries continuously enhance immigration control and introduce rigid laws, additional migrant workers may resort to the informal economy. As a result, irregular migration represents a global phenomenon and has become commonplace in both developed and developing countries (Bloch and Chimienti 2011). A growing body of literature shows that migrants working in Western-style democracies may also develop various informal and illegal strategies when confronted with an increasingly restrictive and punitive immigration regime (Bean, Edmonston, and Passel 1990; Calavita 1990; Freeman 1992; Mahler 1995; Bloch, Sigona, and Zetter 2011). Bloch, Sigona, and Zetter (2011), in their study of young undocumented migrants in England, explored how young undocumented migrants moved in and out of different legal statuses through various formal and informal practices, such as regularizing their status through the asylum system or buying forged identity documents and national insurance numbers enabling them to work. Thus, insights from an analysis of the interconnections among migration, the shadow economy, and street life in Russia are relevant not only for studying migrant legal adaptation in other hybrid regimes but also in Western migration regimes.

The above arguments lead to another important contribution of this book, which is intended to move beyond the area studies approach and aims to connect the Russian case to a broader debate within migration studies. Russia and many other "non-Western" migration regimes (e.g., the Gulf states, Kazakhstan, Malaysia, Turkey, and Singapore) remain underrepresented in comparative and theoretical research on contemporary migration regimes. The undertheorization of these non-Western migration regimes within migration studies (and, more generally, in the social sciences) can be explained in part by the ongoing effects of the "three-worlds division" of social scientific labor, whereby non-Western societies were used as a foil against which the virtues of Western political systems and frameworks were tested and highlighted (Pletsch 1981). In other words the study of non-Western societies—both the "second world" (Eastern Europe, Eurasia, and Russia) and the "third world" (the developing countries of Africa, Asia, and Latin America)—relied solely on the area studies approach, largely isolated from mainstream theoretical and comparative debates in the social sciences.

This book thus attempts to overcome the limitations of the "three-worlds" approach, placing the Russian migration regime within the broader migration studies scholarship. Based on the empirical data presented herein, I have argued that the legal adaptation of migrant workers in Russia must be understood not only in terms of their knowledge of their legal status, their knowledge of immigration laws, and their legalization strategies through the formal legal system and state institutions; more importantly, these migrants must be considered in terms of their knowledge of street law, their ability to adapt to a weak rule of law and corrupt environment, and their capacity to navigate around laws and adjust to changing circumstances and situations. The migrant legal adaptation strategies explored in this book are not simply anomalies or abnormalities; they are institutionalized practices that emerged from this hybrid regime context. Thus, drawing on the legal pluralism perspective, this book provides a new framework, suggesting that the law and legal adaptation should be defined more broadly, beyond state immigration laws, policies, and institutions, and encompass informal legal orders.

NOTES

1. UNDERSTANDING MIGRANTS' LEGAL ADAPTATION IN HYBRID POLITICAL REGIMES

1. The Migrant Integration Policy Index (MIPEX) is a unique tool that measures policies aimed at integrating migrants in all EU Member-States, as well as in Australia, Canada, Iceland, Japan, New Zealand, Norway, South Korea, Switzerland, Turkey, and the US (see Huddleston et al. 2015).

2. More information about the project can be found here: https://blogs.helsinki.fi/mishamigrantproject.

2. MIGRATION, THE SHADOW ECONOMY, AND PARALLEL LEGAL ORDERS IN RUSSIA

1. In this chapter, when I refer to "Central Asian migrants," I mean specifically migrant workers from Kyrgyzstan, Tajikistan, and Uzbekistan.

2. In addition to the Main Directorate for Migration Issues, up to 16 Russian state institutions can issue an entry ban. These include the Federal Security Service, the Ministry of Defense, the Russian Financial Monitoring System, the External Intelligent Service, the Ministry of Justice, the Federal Drug Control Service, the Federal Service on Surveillance for Consumer Rights Protection and Human Well-Being, the Federal Medical Agency, and others.

3. The work permit system is preserved only for countries with which Russia has a visa regime.

4. Interview with migration expert, NGO "Tut Zhdut," May 11, 2017, Moscow.

5. Interview with an immigration lawyer, May 5, 2017, Moscow.

6. Interview with the head of the Federation of Migrants of Russia, Oct. 9, 2017, Moscow.

7. Interview with migrant rights activist, April 28, 2017, Moscow.

8. Interview with the head of the Federation of Migrants of Russia, Oct. 9, 2017, Moscow.

3. UZBEK MIGRANT WORKERS IN RUSSIA: A CASE STUDY

1. Interview with migrant rights activist, April 28, 2017, Moscow, Russia.

2. Interview with the deputy chairman of the Trade Union of Migrant Workers, May 4, 2017, Moscow, Russia.

4. UZBEK MIGRANTS' EVERYDAY ENCOUNTERS WITH EMPLOYERS AND MIDDLEMEN

1. Interview with the head of the Federation of Migrants of Russia, Oct. 9, 2017, Moscow, Russia.

2. Interview with a Radio Free Europe correspondent, August 1, 2018, Moscow, Russia.

3. The construction sector is almost completely male-dominated. For this reason I refer to individuals in this sector using the personal pronoun *he* instead of a more gender-neutral term.

4. All names used in this empirical section are pseudonyms.

5. UZBEK MIGRANTS' EVERYDAY ENCOUNTERS WITH STREET-LEVEL INSTITUTIONS

1. Interview with migrant rights activist, April 28, 2017, Moscow, Russia.

2. Interview with a Radio Free Europe correspondent, August 1, 2018, Moscow, Russia.

3. Interview with migrant rights activist, April 28, 2017, Moscow, Russia.

6. UZBEK MIGRANTS' EVERYDAY ENCOUNTERS WITH POLICE OFFICERS AND IMMIGRATION OFFICIALS

1. According to Russian legislation, only immigration officials are authorized to check the immigration documents of foreigners, while police checks are limited to exceptional circumstances, such as if a passerby looks dubious or resembles an individual suspected of committing a crime. The existence of such a clause in the legislation grants wide leverage to police officers to stop almost anyone randomly in the street who "looks dubious."

2. According to a survey conducted by the Moscow Higher School of Economics in 2011, about 70 percent of police officers explained their informal, illegal earnings in relation to their low pay (Dubova and Kosal's 2013).

3. Interview with migrant rights' activist, April 28, 2017, Moscow.

4. Interview with immigration lawyer, May 5, 2017, Moscow.

5. Interview with immigration lawyer, May 5, 2017, Moscow.

6. Interview with immigration lawyer, May 5, 2017, Moscow.

7. THE LIFE HISTORIES OF THREE UZBEK MIGRANT WORKERS IN RUSSIA

1. Decree No. 154 of the Cabinet of Ministers of Uzbekistan: "The Regulation of the Importation of Goods and Items by Physical Persons into the Territory of the Republic of Uzbekistan."

REFERENCES

Abashin, S. 2014. "Migration from Central Asia to Russia in the New Model of World Order." *Russian Politics & Law* 52 (6): 8–23.

———. 2016. "Migration Policies in Russia: Laws and Debates." In Heusala and Aitamurto 2016, 16–34.

Abrego, L. J. 2011. "Legal Consciousness of Undocumented Latinos: Fear and Stigma as Barriers to Claims-Making for First- and 1.5-Generation Immigrants." *Law & Society Review* 45 (2): 337–70.

Agadjanian, V., E. Gorina, and C. Menjívar. 2014. "Economic Incorporation, Civil Inclusion, and Social Ties: Plans to Return Home among Central Asian Migrant Women in Moscow, Russia." *International Migration Review* 48 (3): 577–603.

Agadjanian, V., C. Menjívar, and N. Zotova. 2017. "Legality, Racialization, and Immigrants' Experience of Ethnoracial Harassment in Russia." *Social Problems* 64 (4): 558–76.

Agadjanian, V., and N. Zotova. 2012. "Sampling and Surveying Hard-to-Reach Populations for Demographic Research: A Study of Female Labor Migrants in Moscow, Russia." *Demographic Research* 26: 131–50.

Aitamurto, K. 2016. "Religion and the Integration of Migrants." In Heusala and Aitamurto 2016, 110–27.

Akalin, A. 2007. "Hired as a Caregiver, Demanded as a Housewife: Becoming a Migrant Domestic Worker in Turkey." *European Journal of Women's Studies* 14 (3): 209–25.

Alba, R., and V. Nee. 2009. *Remaking the American Mainstream: Assimilation and Contemporary Immigration.* Cambridge, MA: Harvard University Press.

Alencar, A., and M. Deuze. 2017. "News for Assimilation or Integration? Examining the Functions of News in Shaping Acculturation Experiences of Immigrants in the Netherlands and Spain." *European Journal of Communication* 32 (2): 151–66.

Alexseev, M. 2015. "The Asymmetry of Nationalist Exclusion and Inclusion: Migration Policy Preferences in Russia, 2005–2013." *Social Science Quarterly* 96 (3): 759–77.

Anderson, B., and B. Hancilová. 2011. "Migrant Labour in Kazakhstan: A Cause for Concern?" *Journal of Ethnic and Migration Studies* 37 (3): 467–83.

Aslund, A. 1997. "Economic Causes of Crime in Russia." In *The Rule of Law and Economic Reform in Russia*, edited by J. Sachs and K. Pistor, 88–91. Boulder, CO: Westview Press.

Asmundo, A., and M. Lisciandra. 2008. "The Cost of Protection Racket in Sicily." *Global Crime* 9 (3): 221–40.

Ballard, R. 2006. "Ethnic Diversity and the Delivery of Justice: The Challenge of Plurality." In *Migrations, Diasporas and Legal Systems in Europe*, edited by P. Shah and W. Menski, 29–56. London: Routledge-Cavendish.

———. 2007. "When, Why and How Far Should Legal Systems Take Cognisance of Cultural Diversity?" Paper presented at the International Congress on Justice and Human Values in Europe, Karlsruhe, May 9–11.

Bauer, J. 1999. "Speaking of Culture: Immigrants in the American Legal System." In *Immigrants in Courts*, edited by J. I. Moore, 8–28. Seattle: University of Washington Press.

BBC Uzbek. 2012. "Moskva allaqachon Moskva-obodga aylanib bo'ldi." BBC O'zbek. www.bbc .co.uk/uzbek/maxsus_loyiha/2012/03/120320_cy_muslim_russia_migrants_nationalists .shtml.

Bean, F. D., B. Edmonston, and J. S. Passel, eds. 1990. *Undocumented Migration to the United States: IRCA and the Experience of the 1980s*. Washington, DC: Urban Institute.

Beger, R. R., and J. Hein. 2001. "Immigrants, Culture, and American Courts: A Typology of Legal Strategies and Issues in Cases Involving Vietnamese and among Litigants." *Criminal Justice Review* 26 (1): 38–61.

Berg-Nordlie, M., and O. Tkach. 2016. "'You are Responsible for Your People': The Role of Diaspora Leaders in the Governance of Immigrant Integration in Russia." *Demokratizatsiya* 24 (2): 173–98.

Berry, J. W. 1997. "Immigration, Acculturation, and Adaptation." *Applied Psychology* 46 (1): 5–34.

———. 2005. "Acculturation: Living Successfully in Two Cultures." *International Journal of Intercultural Relations* 29 (6): 697–712.

Bhattacharya, G. 2008. "Acculturating Indian Immigrant Men in New York City: Applying the Social Capital Construct to Understand Their Experiences and Health." *Journal of Immigrant and Minority Health* 10 (2): 91–101.

Bisson, L. 2016. *Russia's Immigration Policy: Challenges and Tools*. Ifri, Paris: Russia/NIS Center, No. 91.

Bloch, A., and M. Chimienti. 2011. "Irregular Migration in a Globalizing World." *Ethnic and Racial Studies* 34 (8): 1271–85.

Bloch, A., and L. Schuster. 2005. "At the Extremes of Exclusion: Deportation, Detention and Dispersal." *Ethnic and Racial Studies* 28 (3): 491–512.

Bloch, A., N. Sigona, and R. Zetter. 2011. "Migration Routes and Strategies of Young Undocumented Migrants in England: A Qualitative Perspective." *Ethnic and Racial Studies* 34 (8): 1286–1302.

Bobylov, S. 2014. "Glava FMS: Pochti 1 million inostrantsev zakryt v'ezd v Rossiyu." *TASS*. http://tass.ru/obschestvo/1460698.

Brednikova, O., and O. Tkach. 2010. "Dom dlia nomady (Home for the nomads)." *Laboratorium* 3: 72–95.

Brislin, R. W., D. Landis, and M. E. Brandt. 1983. "Conceptualizations of Intercultural Behavior and Training." In *Handbook of Intercultural Training: Issues in Theory and Design*, edited by D. Landis, J. Bennett, and M. J. Bennett, 1–34. New York: Pergamon.

Brownlee, J. 2009. "Portents of Pluralism: How Hybrid Regimes Affect Democratic Transitions." *American Journal of Political Science* 53 (3): 515–32.

Brubaker, R. 2003. "The Return of Assimilation? Changing Perspectives on Immigration and Its Sequels in France, Germany, and the United States." In Joppke and Morawska 2003, 39–58.

Buchanan, J. M. 1973. "A Defense of Organized Crime." In *The Economics of Crime*, edited by R. Adreano and J. Siegfried, 119–32. Washington, DC: American Enterprise Institute.

Calavita, K. 1990. "Employer Sanctions Violations: Toward a Dialectical Model of White-Collar Crime." *Law & Society Review* 24 (4): 1041–69.

———. 1998. "Immigration, Law, and Marginalization in a Global Economy: Notes from Spain." *Law & Society Review* 32 (3): 529–66.

———. 2005. *Immigrants at the Margins: Law, Race, and Exclusion in Southern Europe*. New York: Cambridge University Press.

Cameron, D. R., and M. A. Orenstein. 2012. "Post-Soviet Authoritarianism: The Influence of Russia in Its 'Near Abroad.'" *Post-Soviet Affairs* 28 (1): 1–44.

Carothers, T. 2002. "The End of the Transition Paradigm." *Journal of Democracy* 13 (1): 5–21.

Castles, S., and M. J. Miller. 2013. *The Age of Migration: International Population Movements in the Modern World*. 5th ed. Basingstoke: Palgrave Macmillan.

Chari, S., and K. Verdery. 2009. "Thinking between the Posts: Postcolonialism, Postsocialism, and Ethnography after the Cold War." *Comparative Studies in Society and History* 51 (1): 6–34.

Chavez, L. R. 1998. *Shadowed Lives: Undocumented Immigrants in American Society*. Fort Worth, TX: Harcourt Brace.

Chikadze, E., and O. Brednikova. 2012. *Migrants from Uzbekistan in Russia: Communicative Strategies and Practices of Consuming (Mass-Media) Information*. Saint Petersburg: Centre for Independent Social Research.

Chimienti, M., and C. Achermann. 2007. "Coping Strategies of Precarious Migrants in Relation to Personal Health and Health Structures: The Case of Asylum Seekers and Undocumented Migrants in Switzerland." In *Difference Sensitivity from an Organisational Perspective*, edited by C. C. Björngren and S. Cattacin, 65–74. Malmö: IMER.

Colic-Peisker, V., and I. Walker. 2003. "Human Capital, Acculturation and Social Identity: Bosnian Refugees in Australia." *Journal of Community & Applied Social Psychology* 13 (5): 337–60.

Coutin, S. B. 2003a. *Legalizing Moves: Salvadoran Immigrants' Struggle for U.S. Residency*. Ann Arbor: University of Michigan Press.

———. 2003b. "Illegality, Borderlands, and the Space of Nonexistence." In *Globalization under Construction: Governmentality, Law, and Identity*, edited by R. W. Perry and B. Maurer, 171–202. Minneapolis: University of Minnesota Press.

———. 2003c. *Legalizing Moves: Salvadoran Immigrants' Struggle for U.S. Residency*. Ann Arbor: University of Michigan Press.

Dahinden, J. 2005. "Contesting Transnationalism? Lessons from the Study of Albanian Migration Networks from Former Yugoslavia." *Global Networks* 5 (2): 191–208.

Dave, B. 2014a. "Becoming 'Legal' through 'Illegal' Procedures: The Precarious Status of Migrant Workers in Russia." *Russian Analytical Digest* 159: 2–6.

———. 2014b. "Keeping Labour Mobility Informal: The Lack of Legality of Central Asian Migrants in Kazakhstan." *Central Asian Survey* 33 (3): 346–59.

De Genova, N. 2002. "Migrant 'Illegality' and Deportability in Everyday Life." *Annual Review of Anthropology* 31: 419–47.

———. 2004. "The Legal Production of Mexican/Migrant 'Illegality.'" *Latino Studies* 2 (2): 160–85.

De Genova, N., and N. Peutz. 2010. *The Deportation Regime: Sovereignty, Space, and the Freedom of Movement.* Durham, NC: Duke University Press.

Delgado, H. L. 1993. New Immigrants, Old Unions: Organizing Undocumented Workers in Los Angeles. Philadelphia: Temple University Press.

Demintseva, E. 2017. "Labour Migrants in Post-Soviet Moscow: Patterns of Settlement." *Journal of Ethnic and Migration Studies* 43 (15): 2556–72.

———. 2019. "Migrantskie shkoly: Vliyanie gorodskogo prostranstva na shkol'nuyu segregatsiyu." Paper presented at The Anthropology of Migration: New Research in Russia international colloquium, Saint Petersburg, Russia, March 1–2. https://eu.spb.ru/news/19910-antropologiya-migratsii-novye-issledovaniya-v-rossii.

Denisenko, M. 2017. "Migration to Russia and the Current Economic Crisis." In Pikulicka-Wilczewska and Uehling 2017, 129–48.

Denisenko, M., and E. Chernina. 2017. "The Migration of Labor and Migrant Incomes in Russia." *Problems of Economic Transition* 59 (11–12): 886–908.

Diamond, L. J. 2002. "Thinking about Hybrid Regimes." *Journal of Democracy* 13 (2): 21–35.

Donato, K. M., and A. Armenta. 2011. "What We Know about Unauthorized Migration." *Annual Review of Sociology* 37 (1): 529–43.

Dubova, A., and L. Kosal's. 2013. "Russian Police Involvement in the Shadow Economy." *Russian Politics & Law* 51 (4): 48–58.

Düvell, F. 2008. "Clandestine Migration in Europe." *Social Science Information* 47 (4): 479–97.

Eder, M. 2015. "Turkey's Neoliberal Transformation and Changing Migration Regime: The Case of Female Migrant Workers." In *Social Transformation and Migration*, edited by S. Castles, D. Ozkul, and M. A. Cubas, 133–50. London: Palgrave Macmillan.

Ellermann, A. 2010. "Undocumented Migrants and Resistance in the Liberal State." *Politics & Society* 38 (3): 408–29.

Emirbayer, M., and A. Mische. 1998. "What Is Agency?" *American Journal of Sociology* 103 (4): 962–1023.

Eraliev, S. 2018. "Growing Religiosity among Central Asian Migrants in Russia." *Journal of International and Advanced Japanese Studies* 10: 137–50.

Ergashev, B., I. Iusupov, A. Pogrebniak, I. Korenev, B. Allaev, O. Gaibullaev, S. Usmanov, N. Gasanova, and R. Saifulin. 2006. "Public Administration Reform in Uzbekistan." *Problems of Economic Transition* 48 (12): 32–82.

Espiritu, Y. L. 2003. *Home Bound: Filipino American Lives across Cultures, Communities, and Countries.* Berkeley: University of California Press.

Fane, D. 1996. "Ethnicity and Regionalism in Uzbekistan: Maintaining Stability through Authoritarian Control." In *Ethnic Conflict in the Post-Soviet World: Case Studies and*

Analysis, edited by L. Drobizheva, R. Gottemoeller, C. M. Kelleher, and L. Walker, 271–302. Armonk, NY: M. E. Sharpe.

Fargues, P. 2011. "Immigration without Inclusion: Non-nationals in Nation-Building in the Gulf States." *Asian and Pacific Migration Journal* 20 (3–4): 273–92.

Fargues, P., and N. M. Shah. 2017. *Skilful Survivals: Irregular Migration to the Gulf*. Florence: European University Institute.

Fergananews.com. 2016. "Rossiya: Astrahanskie Uzbekistansy trebuyut nakazat' odnogo iz liderov Kongressa Uzbekov." Fergananews.com Information Agency. www.fergananews .com/news/25348.

Fiorentini, G., and S. Peltzman. 1995. *The Economics of Organised Crime*. Cambridge: Cambridge University Press.

Flynn, D. M. 2007. "Reconstructing 'Home/lands' in the Russian Federation: Migrant-Centred Perspectives of Displacement and Resettlement." *Journal of Ethnic and Migration Studies* 33 (3): 461–81.

FMS. 2015. "Statistics on Foreign Nationals Residing in the Russian Federation, Nov. 2015." www.fms.gov.ru/about/statistics/data/ details/54891.

Foner, N. 1997a. "What's New about Transnationalism? New York Immigrants Today and at the Turn of the Century." *Diaspora* 6 (3): 355–75.

———. 1997b. "The Immigrant Family: Cultural Legacies and Cultural Changes." *International Migration Review* 31 (4): 961–74.

Freeman, G. P. 1992. "Migration Policy and Politics in the Receiving States." *International Migration Review* 26 (4): 1144–67.

Friedman, L. M. 1975. *The Legal System: A Social Science Perspective*. New York: Russell Sage Foundation.

Frisby, T. 1998. "The Rise of Organised Crime in Russia: Its Roots and Social Significance." *Europe-Asia Studies* 50 (1): 27–49.

Frye, T. 2002. "Private Protection in Russia and Poland." *American Journal of Political Science* 46 (3): 572–84.

Frye, T., and E. Zhuravskaya. 2000. "Rackets, Regulation, and the Rule of Law." *Journal of Law, Economics, and Organization* 16 (2): 478–502.

Fujiwara, L. 2008. *Mothers without Citizenship: Asian Immigrant Families and the Consequences of Welfare Reform*. Minneapolis: University of Minnesota Press.

Fumagalli, M. 2007. "Introduction: Stability, Sovereignty, and the Resilience of Politics under Authoritarian Rule." *Central Asian Survey* 26 (1): 1–6.

Furnham, A., and S. Bochner. 1986. *Culture Shock. Psychological Reactions to Unfamiliar Environments*. London: Methuen.

Gabdulhakov, R. 2019. "In the Bullseye of Vigilantes: Mediated Vulnerabilities of Kyrgyz Labour Migrants in Russia." *Media and Communication* 7 (2): 230–41.

Gambetta, D. 1993. *The Sicilian Mafia: The Business of Private Protection*. Cambridge, MA: Harvard University Press.

Gans-Morse, J. 2012. "Threats to Property Rights in Russia: From Private Coercion to State Aggression." *Post-Soviet Affairs* 28 (3): 263–95.

Garcés-Mascareñas, B. 2010. "Legal Production of Illegality in a Comparative Perspective: The Cases of Malaysia and Spain." *Asia Europe Journal* 8 (1): 77–89.

Geertz, C. 1973. *The Interpretation of Cultures*. New York: Basic Books.

Gel'man, V. 2004. "The Unrule of Law in the Making: The Politics of Informal Institution Building in Russia." *Europe-Asia Studies* 56 (7): 1021–40.

Gilbert, L., and P. Mohseni. 2011. "Beyond Authoritarianism: The Conceptualization of Hybrid Regimes." *Studies in Comparative International Development* 46 (3): 270–97.

Gimpelson, V., and R. Kapeliushnikov. 2014. "Between Light and Shadow: Informality in the Russian Labour Market." SSRN Scholarly Paper No. ID 2462711. Rochester, NY: Social Science Research Network.

Gleeson, S. 2010. "Labor Rights for All? The Role of Undocumented Immigrant Status for Worker Claims Making." *Law & Social Inquiry* 35 (3): 561–602.

Goldring, L., C. Berinstein, and J. K. Bernhard. 2009. "Institutionalizing Precarious Migratory Status in Canada." *Citizenship Studies* 13 (3): 239–65.

Golunov, S. 2014. "Ethnic Migration and Crime." *Russian Politics & Law* 52 (6): 42–60.

Gonzales, R. G. 2011. "Learning to Be Illegal: Undocumented Youth and Shifting Legal Contexts in the Transition to Adulthood." *American Sociological Review* 76 (4): 602–19.

Goode, J. P. 2010a. "Redefining Russia: Hybrid Regimes, Fieldwork, and Russian Politics." *Perspectives on Politics* 8 (4): 1055–75.

Gordon, M. M. 1964. *Assimilation in American Life: The Role of Race, Religion, and National Origins.* New York: Oxford University Press.

Gorenburg, D. 2014. "The Adaptation of Migrants in Russia: Editor's Introduction." *Russian Politics & Law* 52 (6): 3–7.

Griffiths, J. 2003. "The Social Working of Legal Rules." *Journal of Legal Pluralism and Unofficial Law* 35 (48): 1–84.

Hagan, J. M. 1994. *Deciding to Be Legal: A Maya Community in Houston.* Philadelphia: Temple University Press.

Hale, H. E. 2002. "Civil Society from Above? Statist and Liberal Models of State-Building in Russia." *Demokratizatsiya* 10 (3): 306–21.

Hallett, M. C. 2014. "Temporary Protection, Enduring Contradiction: The Contested and Contradictory Meanings of Temporary Immigration Status." *Law & Social Inquiry* 39 (3): 621–42.

Handelman, S. 1995. *Comrade Criminal: Russia's New Mafiya.* New Haven, CT: Yale University Press.

Hannerz, U. 1996. *Transnational Connections: Culture, People, Places.* London: Routledge.

Hansen, R. 2000. *Citizenship and Immigration in Postwar Britain.* Oxford: Oxford University Press.

Hendley, K. 2012. "The Puzzling Non-consequences of Societal Distrust of Courts: Explaining the Use of Russian Courts." *Cornell International Law Journal* 45, 517–67.

Hendley, K., P. Murrell, and R. Ryterman. 2000. "Law, Relationships and Private Enforcement: Transactional Strategies of Russian Enterprises." *Europe-Asia Studies* 52 (4): 627–56.

———. 2001. "Law Works in Russia: The Role of Law in Interenterprise Transactions." In *Assessing the Value of Law in Transition Economies,* edited by P. Murrell, 56–93. Ann Arbor: University of Michigan Press.

Heusala, A.-L. 2018. "The Soviet Legacy of 'National Security' in Russian Migration Policy." *Russian Politics* 3 (3): 430–50.

Heusala, A.-L., and K. Aitamurto, eds. 2016. *Migrant Workers in Russia: Global Challenges of the Shadow Economy in Societal Transformation.* London: Routledge.

Heyman, J., and A. Smart, eds. 1999. *States and Illegal Practices.* Oxford: Berg.

Hiwatari, M. 2016. "Social Networks and Migration Decisions: The Influence of Peer Effects in Rural Households in Central Asia." *Journal of Comparative Economics* 44 (4): 1115–31.

Holmes, S. M. 2007. "'Oaxacans Like to Work Bent Over': The Naturalization of Social Suffering among Berry Farm Workers." *International Migration* 45 (3): 39–68.

Hondagneu-Sotelo, P. 1994. *Gendered Transitions: Mexican Experiences of Immigration.* Berkeley: University of California Press.

Hook, J. V., and F. D. Bean. 2009. "Explaining Mexican-Immigrant Welfare Behaviors: The Importance of Employment-Related Cultural Repertoires." *American Sociological Review* 74 (3): 423–44.

Howard, M. M., and P. G. Roessler. 2006. "Liberalizing Electoral Outcomes in Competitive Authoritarian Regimes." *American Journal of Political Science* 50 (2): 365–81.

Huddleston, T. 2008. "From Principles to Policies: Creating an Evidence Base for a European Approach to Migration Management." Heinrich Boel Stiftung. https://heimatkunde .boell.de/2008/09/01/principles-policies-creating-evidence-base-european-approach -migration-management.

Huddleston, T., O. Bilgili, A.-L. Joki, and Z. Vankova. 2015. *Migrant Integration Policy Index 2015.* http://mipex.eu/what-is-mipex.

Human Rights Watch. 2009. *"Are You Happy to Cheat Us?" Exploitation of Migrant Construction Workers in Russia.* New York: Human Rights Watch.

Humphrey, C. 1999. *Russian Protection Rackets and the Appropriation of Law and Order.* New York: Berg.

———. 2012. "Favors and 'Normal Heroes': The Case of Postsocialist Higher Education." *HAU: Journal of Ethnographic Theory* 2 (2): 22–41.

Humphrey, C., and D. Sneath. 2004. "Shanghaied by the Bureaucracy: Bribery and Post-Soviet Officialdom in Russia and Mongolia." In *Between Morality and the Law: Corruption, Anthropology, and Comparative Society,* edited by I. Pardo, 85–99. Aldershot: Ashgate.

Içduygu, A. 2006. "The Labour Dimensions of Irregular Migration in Turkey." Technical Report, [Migration Policy Centre], [CARIM-South], CARIM Research Report, 2006/05. http://hdl.handle.net/1814/6266.

Içduygu, A., and E. Millet. 2016. "Syrian Refugees in Turkey: Insecure Lives in an Environment of Pseudo-integration." *Global Turkey in Europe,* Working Papers 13. Rome: Istituto affari internazionali. www.iai.it/en/pubblicazioni/syrian-refugees-turkey-insecure-lives -environment-pseudo-integration.

Ilkhamov, A. 2004. "The Limits of Centralization: Regional Challenges in Uzbekistan." In *The Transformation of Central Asia: States and Societies from Soviet Rule to Independence,* edited by P. Jones Luong, 159–81. Ithaca, NY: Cornell University Press.

———. 2013. "Labour Migration and the Ritual Economy of the Uzbek Extended Family." *Zeitschrift für Ethnologie* 138 (2): 259–84.

IMF. 2012. *Republic of Uzbekistan and the IMF.* International Monetary Fund.

Interfax. 2016. "Olga Kirillova, the Head of the General Administration for Migration Issues of the Interior Ministry of Russia: Two Million Violators of the Migration Regime Will Never Be Able to Return to Russia." *Interfax.ru.* www.interfax.ru/interview/516300.

Ivakhnyuk, I. 2006. "Migration in the CIS Region: Common Problems and Mutual Benefits." Paper presented at the International Migration and Development symposium, UN Population Division, Department of Economic and Social Affairs, Turin, June 28–30.

———. 2013. "Conceptualizing Migration Policy in Russia." In *Migration in Russia 2000–2013*, edited by I. Ivanov, 78–91. Moscow: Russian International Affairs Council.

Johnson, E. J. 2007. "Post-Soviet Welfare Provision: State or Society?" Paper presented at the Annual Meeting of the American Political Science Association, Chicago, August 30–Sept. 2.

Joppke, C., and E. Morawska, eds. 2003. *Toward Assimilation and Citizenship: Immigrants in Liberal Nation-States*. Basingstoke: Palgrave Macmillan.

Jordan, B., and F. Düvell. 2002. *Irregular Migration*. London: Edward Elgar.

Kandiyoti, D. 2007. "Post-Soviet Institutional Design and the Paradoxes of the Uzbek Path." *Central Asian Survey* 26 (1): 31–48.

Kandiyoti, D., and N. Azimova. 2004. "The Communal and the Sacred: Women's Worlds of Ritual in Uzbekistan." *Journal of the Royal Anthropological Institute* 10 (2): 327–49.

Karimov, I. 1993. *Building the Future: Uzbekistan—Its Own Model for Transition to a Market Economy*. Tashkent: Uzbekiston.

Kelly, P., and T. Lusis. 2006. "Migration and the Transnational Habitus: Evidence from Canada and the Philippines." *Environment and Planning A* 38 (5): 831–47.

Kibria, N. 1995. *Family Tightrope: The Changing Lives of Vietnamese Americans*. Princeton, NJ: Princeton University Press.

Killias, O. 2010. "'Illegal' Migration as Resistance: Legality, Morality and Coercion in Indonesian Domestic Worker Migration to Malaysia." *Asian Journal of Social Science* 38 (6): 897–914.

Kingsbury, M. A. 2017. "Beyond Attitudes: Russian Xenophobia as a Political Legitimation Tool." In Pikulicka-Wilczewska and Uehling 2017, 178–95.

Kondakov, A. 2017. "Queer Coalitions: An Examination of Political Resistance to the Russian Migration Law." *Europe-Asia Studies* 69 (8): 1222–41.

Korobkov, A. V. 2007. "Migration Trends in Central Eurasia: Politics versus Economics." *Communist and Post-Communist Studies* 40 (2): 169–89.

Krasinets, E. 2009. "Nelegal'naya migratsiya v Rossii." In *Demograficheskie perspektivy v Rossii*, edited by G. Osipova and S. Ryazantsev, 194–98. Moscow: Ekon-Inform.

Kubal, A. 2013a. *Socio-legal Integration: Polish Post-2004 EU Enlargement Migrants in the United Kingdom*. Farnham: Ashgate.

———. 2013b. "Migrants' Relationship with Law in the Host Country: Exploring the Role of Legal Culture." *Journal of Intercultural Studies* 34 (1): 55–72.

———. 2013c. "Conceptualizing Semi-legality in Migration Research." *Law & Society Review* 47 (3): 555–87.

———. 2016a. "Entry Bar as Surreptitious Deportation? Zapret na v'ezd in Russian Immigration Law and Practice: A Comparative Perspective." *Law & Social Inquiry* 42 (3): 744–68.

———. 2016b. "Spiral Effect of the Law: Migrants' Experiences of the State Law in Russia—a Comparative Perspective." *International Journal of Law in Context* 12 (4): 453–68.

Kubal, A. M. 2009. "Why Semi-legal? Polish Post-2004 EU Enlargement Migrants in the United Kingdom." *Journal of Immigration, Asylum and Nationality Law* 23 (2): 148–64.

Kurkchiyan, M. 2011. "Perceptions of Law and Social Order: A Cross-National Comparison of Collective Legal Consciousness." *Wisconsin International Law Journal* 29: 366–92.

Kuznetsova, I. 2017. "Dangerous and Unwanted: Policy and Everyday Discourses of Migrants in Russia." In Pikulicka-Wilczewska and Uehling 2017, 149–62.

Kuznetsova, I., and J. Round. 2018. "Postcolonial Migrations in Russia: The Racism, Informality and Discrimination Nexus." *International Journal of Sociology and Social Policy* 39 (1/2): 52–67.

Laruelle, M. 2007. "Central Asian Labor Migrants in Russia: The 'Diasporization' of the Central Asian States?" *China and Eurasia Forum Quarterly* 5: 101–19.

Ledeneva, A. 2009. "From Russia with Blat: Can Informal Networks Help Modernize Russia?" *Social Research* 76 (1): 257–88.

Ledeneva, A. V. 2006. *How Russia Really Works: The Informal Practices That Shaped Post-Soviet Politics and Business*. Ithaca, NY: Cornell University Press.

———. 2013. *Can Russia Modernise? Sistema, Power Networks and Informal Governance*. Cambridge: Cambridge University Press.

Levi, S. 2007. "Turks and Tajiks in Central Asian History." In *Everyday Life in Central Asia: Past and Present*, edited by J. Sahadeo and R. Zanca, 15–31. Bloomington: Indiana University Press.

Levitsky, S., and L. Way. 2002. "The Rise of Competitive Authoritarianism." *Journal of Democracy* 13 (2): 51–65.

Levitt, P. 2001a. "Transnational Migration: Taking Stock and Future Directions." *Global Networks* 1 (3): 195–216.

———. 2001b. *The Transnational Villagers*. Berkeley: University of California Press.

Levitt, P., and N. G. Schiller. 2004. "Conceptualizing Simultaneity: A Transnational Social Field Perspective on Society." *International Migration Review* 38 (3): 1002–39.

Light, M. 2010. "Policing Migration in Soviet and Post-Soviet Moscow." *Post-Soviet Affairs* 26 (4): 275–313.

———. 2016. *Fragile Migration Rights: Freedom of Movement in Post-Soviet Russia*. Abingdon: Routledge.

Lim, S.-L., and E. Wieling. 2004. "Immigrant Chinese American Women: Negotiating Values and Perceptions of Self in the Cultural Borderlands of East and West: A Qualitative Study." *Family Journal* 12 (2): 148–58.

Lindahl, H. 2010. "A-Legality: Postnationalism and the Question of Legal Boundaries." *Modern Law Review* 73 (1): 30–56.

Lucassen, L., D. Feldman, and J. Oltmer. 2006. *Paths of Integration: Migrants in Western Europe*. Amsterdam: Amsterdam University Press.

Mahler, S. J. 1995. *American Dreaming: Immigrant Life on the Margins*. Princeton, NJ: Princeton University Press.

Malakhov, V. S. 2014. "Russia as a New Immigration Country: Policy Response and Public Debate." *Europe-Asia Studies* 66 (7): 1062–79.

———. 2015. *Integratsiia migrantov: Kontseptsii i praktiki* [Integration of migrants: Concepts and practices]. Moscow: Fond "Liberalnaia missiia."

Malakhov, V. S., and M. E. Simon. 2018. "Labour Migration Policy in Russia: Considerations on Governmentality." *International Migration* 56 (3): 61–72.

Marat, E. 2009. *Labor Migration in Central Asia: Implications of the Global Economic Crisis*. Silk Road Studies Program, Institute for Security and Development Policy.

Markovska, A., A. Serdyuk, and V. Sokurenko. 2019. "Corruption, Policing and Migration: Exploring the Interaction between Migrant Workers and Police in Russia, Ukraine and the UK." *International Migration* 57 (1): 145–62.

Mascarenhas, M. 2001. "Farming Systems Research: Flexible Diversification of a Small Family Farm in Southeast Michigan." *Agriculture and Human Values* 18 (4): 391–401.

Massey, D. S., J. Durand, and N. J. Malone. 2002. *Beyond Smoke and Mirrors: Mexican Immigration in an Era of Economic Integration*. New York: Russell Sage.

Matusevich, Yan. 2015. "Understanding Migrant Mobilization in Post-Soviet Russia: Do Existing Theoretical Frameworks Apply?" Master's thesis, Oxford University.

McAulley, M., A. Ledeneva, and H. Barnes. 2006. *Dictatorship or Reform? The Rule of Law in Russia*. London: Foreign Policy Centre.

McConnell, E. D. 2013. "Who Has Housing Affordability Problems? Disparities in Housing Cost Burden by Race, Nativity, and Legal Status in Los Angeles." *Race and Social Problems* 5 (3): 173–90.

Megoran, N. 2017. *Nationalism in Central Asia: A Biography of the Uzbekistan-Kyrgyzstan Boundary*. Pittsburgh, PA: University of Pittsburgh Press.

Menjívar, C. 2006. "Liminal Legality: Salvadoran and Guatemalan Immigrants' Lives in the United States." *American Journal of Sociology* 111 (4): 999–1037.

Menjívar, C., and L. Abrego. 2012. "Legal Violence: Immigration Law and the Lives of Central American Immigrants." *American Journal of Sociology* 117 (5): 1380–1421.

Menski, W. F. 1993. "Asians in Britain and the Question of Adaptation to a New Legal Order: Asian Laws in Britain?" In *Ethnicity, Identity, Migration: The South Asian Context*, edited by M. Israel and N. Wagle, 238–68. Toronto: University of Toronto Press.

———. 2008. "Angrezi Shariat: Glocalised Plural Arrangements by Migrants in Britain." *Law Vision*, no. 10, 10–12.

Merry, S. E. 1990. *Getting Justice and Getting Even: Legal Consciousness among Working-Class Americans*. Chicago: University of Chicago Press.

Messina, C. 1994. "From Migrants to Refugees: Russian, Soviet and Post-Soviet Migration." *International Journal of Refugee Law* 6 (4): 620–35.

Moore, S. F. 1973. "Law and Social Change: The Semi-autonomous Social Field as an Appropriate Subject of Study." *Law & Society Review* 7 (4): 719–46.

Morawska, E. T. 1999. *The New-Old Transmigrants, Their Transnational Lives and Ethnicization: A Comparison of 19th/20th and 20th/21st C. Situations*. Florence: European University Institute.

Morlino, L. 2009. "Are There Hybrid Regimes? Or Are They Just an Optical Illusion?" *European Political Science Review* 1 (2): 273–96.

Morris, J., and A. Polese. 2015a. *Informal Economies in Post-Socialist Spaces: Practices, Institutions and Networks*. New York: Palgrave Macmillan.

———. 2015b. "My Name Is Legion: The Resilience and Endurance of Informality beyond, or in spite of, the State." In Morris and Polese 2015a, 1–25.

Morris, L. 2003. *Managing Migration: Civic Stratification and Migrants' Rights*. London: Routledge.

Moscow Times. 2016. "Deadly Moscow Cemetery Feud Raises Concern of Return to 90s." *Moscow Times*. www.themoscowtimes.com/2016/05/18/deadly-moscow-cemetery-feud -raises-concern-of-return-to-90s-a52928.

———. 2017. "Moscow Metro Construction Workers Strike over 5 Months Unpaid Wages." *Moscow Times*.https://themoscowtimes.com/news/moscow-metro-construction-workers-strike-over-5-months-unpaid-wages-52139.

Mukomel, V. 2012. *Labour Migration and the Host Country: Russian Case*. Florence: European University Institute.

———. 2013. *Integratciya migrantov: Rossiiskaya Federatciya* [Integration of migrants: Russian Federation]. San Domenico di Fiesole, Florence: CARIM-East RR, Robert Schuman Centre for Advanced Studies, European University Institute.

Munck, G. L. 2006. "Drawing Boundaries: How to Craft Intermediate Regime Categories." In *Electoral Authoritarianism: The Dynamics of Unfree Competition*, edited by A. Schedler, 27–40. Boulder, CO: Lynne Rienner.

Nelken, D. 2004. "Using the Concept of Legal Culture." *Australian Journal of Legal Philosophy* 29: 1–28.

Ngai, M. M. 2014. *Impossible Subjects: Illegal Aliens and the Making of Modern America*. Princeton, NJ: Princeton University Press.

Niekerk, M. 2004. "Afro-Caribbeans and Indo-Caribbeans in the Netherlands: Premigration Legacies and Social Mobility." *International Migration Review* 38 (1): 158–83.

Nikiforova, E., and O. Brednikova. 2018. "On Labor Migration to Russia: Central Asian Migrants and Migrant Families in the Matrix of Russia's Bordering Policies." *Political Geography* 66: 142–50.

Noori, N. 2006. "Delegating Coercion: Linking Decentralization to State Formation in Uzbekistan." PhD diss., Columbia University.

Nordstrom, C. 2000. "Shadows and Sovereigns." *Theory, Culture & Society* 17 (4): 35–54.

Nuijten, M., and G. Anders. 2007. *Corruption and the Secret of Law: A Legal Anthropological Perspective*. Farnham: Ashgate.

O'Flynn, K. 2009. "Market Closure Still Reverberates in Moscow." RadioFreeEurope/RadioLiberty. www.rferl.org/a/Market_Closure_Still_Reverberates_In_Moscow/1795488.html.

Ozodlik Radiosi. 2015. "Ulan-Udeda O'zbeklar guruhi yurtdoshlariga tinchlik bermayotir." *Озодлик радиоси.* www.ozodlik.org/a/27279439.html.

———. 2016. "Rossiyadagi O'zbeklar jamiyatlari liderlari orasida yangi mojaro boshlandi." *Radio Free Europe Uzbek Service.* www.ozodlik.org/a/28009246.html.

———. 2018. "Moskvada maoshini ololmagan O'zbek muhojirlari va ish beruvchi yarashdi." www.ozodlik.org/a/29378412.html.

Pardo, I. 1996. *Managing Existence in Naples: Morality, Action, and Structure*. Cambridge: Cambridge University Press.

Park, R. 1964. *Race and Culture: Essays in the Sociology of Contemporary Man*. Glencoe, IL: Free Press.

Park, R. E. 1928. "Human Migration and the Marginal Man." *American Journal of Sociology* 33 (6): 881–93.

Pashkun, D. 2003. "Structure and Practice of the State Administration in Uzbekistan." Discussion Paper No. 27. Budapest: Open Society Institute.

Perlman, B. J., and G. Gleason. 2007. "Cultural Determinism versus Administrative Logic: Asian Values and Administrative Reform in Kazakhstan and Uzbekistan." *International Journal of Public Administration* 30 (12–14): 1327–42.

Pessoa, S., L. Harkness, and A. Gardner. 2014. "Ethiopian Labor Migrants and the 'Free Visa' System in Qatar." *Human Organization* 73 (3): 205–13.

Petrov, N., M. Lipman, and H. E. Hale. 2014. "Three Dilemmas of Hybrid Regime Governance: Russia from Putin to Putin." *Post-Soviet Affairs* 30 (1): 1–26.

Peutz, N. 2007. "Out-Laws: Deportees, Desire, and 'The Law.'" *International Migration* 45 (3): 182–91.

Pikulicka-Wilczewska, A., and G. Uehling, eds. 2017. *Migration and the Ukraine Crisis: A Two-Country Perspective*. Bristol: E-International Relations.

Pilkington, H. 1998. *Migration, Displacement, and Identity in Post-Soviet Russia*. London: Routledge.

Pilkington, H., and M. Flynn. 2006. "A Diaspora in Diaspora? Russian Returnees Confront the 'Homeland.'" *Refuge: Canada's Journal on Refugees* 23 (2): 55–67.

Pipia, K. 2016. *Интолерантность и ксенофобия* [Intolerance and xenophobia]. Moscow: Levada Center.

Pirie, F. 2006. "Legal Complexity on the Tibetan Plateau." *Journal of Legal Pluralism and Unofficial Law* 38 (53–54): 77–99.

Pletsch, C. E. 1981. "The Three Worlds, or the Division of Social Scientific Labor, circa 1950–1975." *Comparative Studies in Society and History* 23 (4): 565–90.

Pochuev, M. 2015. "Law Imposing 10-Year Entry Ban on Violators of Sojourn Procedures Comes into Force." TASS. http://tass.ru/en/russia/770591.

Poliakov, S. 1992. *Everyday Islam: Religion and Tradition in Rural Central Asia*. New York: M. E. Sharpe.

Pomfret, R. 2000. "The Uzbek Model of Economic Development, 1991–99." *Economics of Transition* 8 (3): 733–48.

Portes, A., and R. Bach. 1985. *Latin Journey: Cuban and Mexican Immigrants in the United States*. Berkeley: University of California Press.

Portes, A., and J. Böröcz. 1989. "Contemporary Immigration: Theoretical Perspectives on Its Determinants and Modes of Incorporation." *International Migration Review* 23 (3): 606–30.

Portes, A., L. E. Guarnizo, and P. Landolt. 1999. "The Study of Transnationalism: Pitfalls and Promise of an Emergent Research Field." *Ethnic and Racial Studies* 22 (2): 217–37.

Portes, A., and R. G. Rumbaut. 2006. *Immigrant America: A Portrait*. Berkeley: University of California Press.

Portes, A., and M. Zhou. 1993. "The New Second Generation: Segmented Assimilation and Its Variants." *Annals of the American Academy of Political and Social Science* 530 (1): 74–96.

Putin, V. 2005. "Vstupitel'noe slovo na zacedanii soveta bezopasnosti po migratsionnoi politike" [Opening remarks at the Security Council meeting on migration policy]. http://kremlin.ru/events/president/transcripts/22861.

Rahmonova-Schwarz, D. 2006. "Destination Russia: Migration Policy Reform and Reality." *Handbook of the Organisation for Security and Cooperation in Europe (OSCE)*, 289–99.

RANEPA. 2019a. "Yezhemesyachniy monitoring sotsial'no-ekonomicheskogo polozheniya i samochuvstviya naseleniya" [Ежемесячный мониторинг социально-экономического положения и самочувствия населения]. www.ranepa.ru/images/News/2019–05/23 –05–2019-monitoring.pdf.

———. 2019b. "Monitoring Ekonomicheskoi Situatsii v Rossii: Tendentsii i Vizovi Sotsial'no-Ekonomicheskogo Razvitiia, No 12 (95)" [Monitoring of economic situation in Russia: Trends and challenges of socioeconomic development, No. 12 (95)]. www.ranepa.ru/images/News/2019-07/22-07-2019-monitoring.pdf?fbclid=IwAR3R2UU3QJS847KvzqS9VeAbDK-ZrZSCoqFGqnFZBzYEZAR2RT0YSUxzPVw.

Rasanayagam, J. 2002. "Spheres of Communal Participation: Placing the State within Local Modes of Interaction in Rural Uzbekistan." *Central Asian Survey* 21 (1): 55–70.

RBK. 2016. "Rost chisla migrantov v Rossii vyshel na dokrizisnii uroven' iz-za Ukrainy" [Number of migrants in Russia increased to pre-crisis level due to Ukraine events]. www.rbc.ru/politics/06/12/2016/5846d3b89a79470b6f8738fa.

Read, J. G. 2004. "Family, Religion, and Work among Arab American Women." *Journal of Marriage and Family* 66 (4): 1042–50.

Redfield, R., R. Linton, and M. J. Herskovits. 1936. "Memorandum for the Study of Acculturation." *American Anthropologist* 38 (1): 149–52.

Reeves, M. 2011. "Staying Put? Towards a Relational Politics of Mobility at a Time of Migration." *Central Asian Survey* 30 (3–4): 555–76.

———. 2013. "Clean Fake: Authenticating Documents and Persons in Migrant Moscow." *American Ethnologist* 40 (3): 508–24.

———. 2015. "Living from the Nerves: Deportability, Indeterminacy, and the 'Feel of Law' in Migrant Moscow." *Social Analysis* 59 (4): 119–36.

———. 2016. "Diplomat, Landlord, Con-Artist, Thief: Housing Brokers and the Mediation of Risk in Migrant Moscow." *Cambridge Journal of Anthropology* 34 (2): 93–109.

Rigo, E. 2010. "Citizens despite Borders: Challenges to the Territorial Order of Europe." In *The Contested Politics of Mobility: Borderzones and Irregularity*, edited by V. Squire, 219–35. London: Routledge.

Rivera-Batiz, F. L. 1999. "Undocumented Workers in the Labor Market: An Analysis of the Earnings of Legal and Illegal Mexican Immigrants in the United States." *Journal of Population Economics* 12 (1): 91–116.

Roberts, S. 2005. "After Government? On Representing Law without the State." *Modern Law Review* 68 (1): 1–24.

Robertson, G. B. 2007. "Strikes and Labor Organization in Hybrid Regimes." *American Political Science Review* 101 (4): 781–98.

Robinson, L. 2005. "South Asians in Britain: Acculturation, Identity and Perceived Discrimination." *Psychology and Developing Societies* 17 (2): 181–94.

Romodanovski, K., and V. Mukomel. 2015. "Regulation of Migration Processes: Problems of Transition from Reactive to System Policy" [Regulirovanie migratsionnykh protsessov: problem perekhoda ot reactivnoi k sistemnoi politike]. *Obschestvennye nauki i sovremennost* 5 (10): 5–18.

Rosenthal, A. 2007. "Battling for Survival, Battling for Moral Clarity: 'Illegality' and Illness in the Everyday Struggles of Undocumented HIV+ Women Migrant Workers in Tel Aviv." *International Migration* 45 (3): 134–56.

Round, J., and I. Kuznetsova. 2016. "Necropolitics and the Migrant as a Political Subject of Disgust: The Precarious Everyday of Russia's Labour Migrants." *Critical Sociology* 42 (7–8): 1017–34.

Ruget, V., and B. Usmanalieva. 2008. "Citizenship, Migration and Loyalty towards the State: A Case Study of the Kyrgyzstani Migrants Working in Russia and Kazakhstan." *Central Asian Survey* 27 (2): 129–41.

———. 2010. "How Much Is Citizenship Worth? The Case of Kyrgyzstani Migrants in Kazakhstan and Russia." *Citizenship Studies* 14 (4): 445–59.

Ruhs, M., and B. Anderson. 2010. "Semi-compliance and Illegality in Migrant Labour Markets: An Analysis of Migrants, Employers and the State in the UK." *Population, Space and Place* 16 (3): 195–211.

Ruziev, K., D. Ghosh, and S. C. Dow. 2007. "The Uzbek Puzzle Revisited: An Analysis of Economic Performance in Uzbekistan Since 1991." *Central Asian Survey* 26 (1): 7–30.

Sahadeo, J. 2007. "Druzhba Narodov or Second-Class Citizenship? Soviet Asian Migrants in a Post-Colonial World." *Central Asian Survey* 26 (4): 559–79.

Sakwa, R. 1995. "Subjectivity, Politics and Order in Russian Political Evolution." *Slavic Review* 54 (4): 943–64.

Sam, D. L., and J. W. Berry. 2010. "Acculturation When Individuals and Groups of Different Cultural Backgrounds Meet." *Perspectives on Psychological Science* 5 (4): 472–81.

Sayegh, L., and J.-C. Lasry. 1993. "Immigrants' Adaptation in Canada: Assimilation, Acculturation, and Orthogonal Cultural Identification." *Canadian Psychology/Psychologie canadienne* 34 (1): 98–109.

Schedler, A. 2015. "Electoral Authoritarianism." In *Emerging Trends in the Social and Behavioral Sciences: An Interdisciplinary, Searchable, and Linkable Resource*, edited by T. Landman, and N. Robinson, 381–94. London: Sage.

Schenk, C. 2017. "Labour Migration in the Eurasian Economic Union." In Pikulicka -Wilczewska and Uehling 2017, 164–77.

———. 2018. *Why Control Immigration?* Toronto: University of Toronto Press.

Schiller, N. G., L. Basch, and C. Blanc-Szanton. 1992. "Towards a Definition of Transnationalism." *Annals of the New York Academy of Sciences* 645 (1): ix–xiv.

Schiller, N. G., L. Basch, and C. S. Blanc. 1995. "From Immigrant to Transmigrant: Theorizing Transnational Migration." *Anthropological Quarterly* 68 (1): 48–63.

Schmidt, M., and L. Sagynbekova. 2008. "Migration Past and Present: Changing Patterns in Kyrgyzstan." *Central Asian Survey* 27 (2): 111–27.

Schneider, J., and M. Crul. 2010. "New Insights into Assimilation and Integration Theory: Introduction to the Special Issue." *Ethnic and Racial Studies* 33 (7): 1143–48.

Schuck, P. 1998. *Citizens, Strangers, and In-Betweens: Essays on Immigration and Citizenship.* Oxford: Westview Press.

Şenses, N. 2016. "Rethinking Migration in the Context of Precarity: The Case of Turkey." *Critical Sociology* 42 (7–8): 975–87.

Sewell, W. H. 1992. "A Theory of Structure: Duality, Agency, and Transformation." *American Journal of Sociology* 98 (1): 1–29.

Shah, P. 2005. *Legal Pluralism in Conflict: Coping with Cultural Diversity in Law.* London: Glasshouse.

———. 2009. "Transnational Hindu Law Adoptions: Recognition and Treatment in Britain." *International Journal of Law in Context* 5 (2): 107–30.

Shnirel'man, V. 2008. "Migrantofobiya i kul'turnyi rasizm." *Ab Imperio* 2: 287–324.

Sievers, E. W. 2002. "Uzbekistan's Mahalla: From Soviet to Absolutist Residential Community Associations." *Journal of International and Comparative Law at Chicago-Kent* 2: 91–158.

Sigona, N. 2012. "'I Have Too Much Baggage': The Impacts of Legal Status on the Social Worlds of Irregular Migrants." *Social Anthropology* 20 (1): 50–65.

Skoblikov, P. 2001. "Imushchestvennye spory i kriminal v sovremennoi Rossii" [Property disputes and criminals in modern Russia]. Moscow: Publishing House DELO.

Solomon, P. H. 2004. "Judicial Power in Russia: Through the Prism of Administrative Justice." *Law & Society Review* 38 (3): 549–82.

Spechler, M. C. 2002. "Free at Last? Uzbekistan and Russia." *Problems of Post-Communism* 49 (1): 63–67.

Spoor, M. 1995. "Agrarian Transition in Former Soviet Central Asia: A Comparative Study of Uzbekistan and Kyrgyzstan." *Journal of Peasant Studies* 23 (1): 46–63.

Stonequist, E. V. 1937. *The Marginal Man: A Study in Personality and Culture Conflict.* New York: Charles Scribner's Sons.

Streltsova, Y. 2014. "The Adaptation of Immigrants in Russia: The Language Aspect." *Russian Politics & Law* 52 (6): 24–41.

Súilleabháin, A. Ó. 2013. "Discrimination, Often Violent, Impacts Thousands of Central Asian Migrants in Russia." IPI Global Observatory. http://theglobalobservatory .org/2013/02/discrimination-often-violent-impacts-thousands-of-central-asian -migrants-in-russia.

Swidler, A. 1986. "Culture in Action: Symbols and Strategies." *American Sociological Review* 51 (2): 273–86.

Ta, T. V. 1999. "Vietnamese Immigrants in American Courts." In *Immigrants in Courts*, edited by J. I. Moore, 140–57. Seattle: University of Washington Press.

Takei, I., R. Saenz, and J. Li. 2009. "Cost of Being a Mexican Immigrant and Being a Mexican Non-citizen in California and Texas." *Hispanic Journal of Behavioral Sciences* 31 (1): 73–95.

Tamanha, B. Z. 2000. "A Non-essentialist Version of Legal Pluralism." *Journal of Law and Society* 27 (2): 296–321.

Tolay, J. 2012. "Discovering Immigration into Turkey: The Emergence of a Dynamic Field." *International Migration* 53 (6): 57–73.

Tolipov, F. 2016. "The Problems and Possible Scenarios of Labor Migration in Uzbekistan." *CABAR.asia.* http://cabar.asia/en/farkhod-tolipov-the-problems-and-possible-scenarios -of-labor-migration-in-uzbekistan.

Triandis, H. C. 2018. *Individualism and Collectivism.* New York: Routledge.

Troitskii, K. 2016. "Administrativnye vydvoreniia iz Rossii: Sudebnoe razbiratel'stvo ili mas- sovoe izgnanie?" [Administrative expulsions from Russia: Court case or mass deportation?]. Moscow: Civic Assistance Committee.

Tubergen, F. V. 2006. *Immigrant Integration: A Cross-National Study.* Amsterdam: LFB Scholarly.

Tucker, N. 2015. "Islamic State Messaging to Central Asian Migrant Workers in Russia." *CERIA Brief,* no. 6, 1–8.

Turaeva, R. 2018. "Imagined Mosque Communities in Russia: Central Asian Migrants in Moscow." *Asian Ethnicity* 20 (2): 131–47.

Twining, W. 1999. "Globalization and Comparative Law." *Maastricht Journal of European and Comparative Law*, no. 6, 217–43.

Tyuryukanova, E. 2008. "Illegal, Trafficked, Enslaved? Irregular Migration and Trafficking in Persons in Russia." In *Political Violence, Organized Crimes, Terrorism, and Youth*, edited by M. D. Ulusoy, 104–29. Amsterdam: IOS Press.

———, ed. 2011. *Migrant Women from the Commonwealth of Independent States in Russia.* Moscow: Maks Press.

Umidbek, B. 2015. "Sverdlovskda ish haqini ololmagan O'zbeklarni sudlaladilar." Ozodlik Radiosi/Radio Free Europe/Radio Liberty, Sept. 16.

UNPD. 2015. *International Migration Stock 2015.* New York: United Nations Population Division.

Urinboyev, R. 2013. "Living Law and Political Stability in Post-Soviet Central Asia: A Case Study of the Ferghana Valley in Uzbekistan." PhD diss., Lund Studies in Sociology of Law, Lund University.

———. 2014. "Is There an Islamic Public Administration Legacy in Post-Soviet Central Asia? An Ethnographic Study of Everyday Mahalla Life in Rural Ferghana, Uzbekistan." *Administrative Culture* 15 (2): 35–57.

———. 2016. "Migration and Transnational Informality in Post-Soviet Societies: Ethnographic Study of 'Po rukam' Experiences of Uzbek Migrant Workers in Moscow." In Heusala and Aitamurto 2016, 70–93.

———. 2017a. "Establishing an 'Uzbek Mahalla' via Smartphones and Social Media: Everyday Transnational Lives of Uzbek Labor Migrants in Russia." In *Constructing the Uzbek State: Narratives of Post-Soviet Years*, edited by M. Laruelle, 119–48. Boulder, CO: Lexington Books.

———. 2017b. "Arbeitsmigration und Schattenwirtschaft in Russland" [Labor migration and shadow economy in Russia]. *Religion und Gesellschaft in Ost und West* 7 (8): 18–19.

———. 2018a. "Migration, Transnationalism, and Social Change in Central Asia: Everyday Transnational Lives of Uzbek Migrants in Russia." In *Eurasia on the Move: Interdisciplinary Approaches to a Dynamic Migration Region*, edited by L. Marlene and S. Caress, 27–41. Washington, DC: George Washington University Central Asia Program.

———. 2018b. "Mahalla." In *The Global Encyclopaedia of Informality*, edited by A. Ledeneva, 69–72. London: UCL Press.

Urinboyev, R., and A. Polese. 2016. "Informality Currencies: A Tale of Misha, His Brigada and Informal Practices among Uzbek Labour Migrants in Russia." *Journal of Contemporary Central and Eastern Europe* 24 (3): 191–206.

Urinboyev, R., and M. Svensson. 2013a. "Corruption in a Culture of Money: Understanding Social Norms in Post-Soviet Uzbekistan." In *Social and Legal Norms*, edited by M. Baier, 267–84. Farnham: Ashgate.

———. 2013b. "Living Law, Legal Pluralism, and Corruption in Post-Soviet Uzbekistan." *Journal of Legal Pluralism and Unofficial Law* 45 (3): 372–90.

———. 2017. "Corruption, Social Norms and Everyday Life in Uzbekistan." In *Corruption and Norms: Why Informal Rules Matter*, edited by I. Kubbe and A. Engelbert, 187–210. Basingstoke: Palgrave.

Varshaver, E., and A. Rocheva. 2014. "Migrant Communities in Moscow: Their Origins, Functionality, and Maintenance Mechanisms." SSRN. https://ssrn.com/abstract=2426477.

Varshaver, E., A. Rocheva, E. Kochkin, and E. Kuldina. 2014. "Киргизские мигранты в Москве: результаты количественного исследования интеграционных траекторий" [Kyrgyz migrants in Moscow: Results of a quantitative research on integration tracks]. Rochester, NY: Social Science Research Network, SSRN Scholarly Paper No. ID 2425312.

Vertovec, S. 1999. "Conceiving and Researching Transnationalism." *Ethnic and Racial Studies* 22 (2): 447–62.

———. 2001. "Transnationalism and Identity." *Journal of Ethnic and Migration Studies* 27 (4): 573–82.

Viladrich, A. 2012. "Beyond Welfare Reform: Reframing Undocumented Immigrants' Entitlement to Health Care in the United States, a Critical Review." *Social Science & Medicine* 74 (6): 822–29.

Volkov, V. 1999. "Violent Entrepreneurship in Post-Communist Russia." *Europe-Asia Studies* 51 (5): 741–54.

———. 2000. "Between Economy and the State: Private Security and Rule Enforcement in Russia." *Politics & Society* 28 (4): 483–501.

———. 2002. *Violent Entrepreneurs: The Use of Force in the Making of Russian Capitalism.* Ithaca, NY: Cornell University Press.

———. 2004. "Hostile Enterprise Takeovers: Russia's Economy in 1998–2002." *Review of Central and East European Law* 29 (4): 527–48.

Ward, C., and A. Kennedy. 1994. "Acculturation Strategies, Psychological Adjustment, and Sociocultural Competence during Cross-Cultural Transitions." *International Journal of Intercultural Relations* 18 (3): 329–43.

Warikoo, K., and D. Norbu. 1992. *Ethnicity and Politics in Central Asia.* New Delhi: South Asian Publishers.

Weine, S., A. Golobof, M. Bahromov, A. Kashuba, T. Kalandarov, J. Jonbekov, and S. Loue. 2013. "Female Migrant Sex Workers in Moscow: Gender and Power Factors and HIV Risk." *Women & Health* 53 (1): 56–73.

White, J. B. 1994. *Money Makes Us Relatives: Women's Labor in Urban Turkey.* Austin: University of Texas Press.

Wigell, M. 2008. "Mapping 'Hybrid Regimes': Regime Types and Concepts in Comparative Politics." *Democratisation* 15 (2): 230–50.

Willen, S. S. 2007a. "Toward a Critical Phenomenology of 'Illegality': State Power, Criminalization, and Abjectivity among Undocumented Migrant Workers in Tel Aviv, Israel." *International Migration* 45 (3): 8–38.

———. 2007b. "Exploring 'Illegal' and 'Irregular' Migrants' Lived Experiences of Law and State Power." *International Migration* 45 (3): 2–7.

Williams, C. C., J. Round, and P. Rodgers. 2013. *The Role of Informal Economies in the Post-Soviet World: The End of Transition?* Abingdon: Routledge.

World Bank. 1999. *Uzbekistan: Social and Structural Policy Review.* World Bank Report No. 19626. Washington, DC: World Bank.

———. 2011. *Migration and Remittances Factbook.* Washington, DC: World Bank.

Yakimov, A. 2015. "Uzbekskiy Peterburg" [Uzbek Saint Petersburg]. YouTube video, Feb. 17, 2016. www.youtube.com/watch?v=qn6kBJHmPlU.

Yusupova, G., and E. Ponarin. 2016. "Social Remittances in Religion." *Problems of Post-Communism* 65 (3): 188–200.

Zabyelina, Y. 2016. "Between Exploitation and Expulsion: Labour Migration, Shadow Economy and Organised Crime." In Heusala and Aitamurto 2016, 94–109.

Zakaria, F. 1997. "The Rise of Illiberal Democracy." *Foreign Affairs*, no. 76, 22.

Zanca, R. 2003. "'Take! Take! Take!' Host-Guest Relations and All That Food: Uzbek Hospitality Past and Present." *Anthropology of East Europe Review* 21 (1): 8–16.

Zayonchkovskaya, Z. 2000. "Recent Migration Trends in the Commonwealth of Independent States." *International Social Science Journal* (*UNESCO*) 52 (3/165): 343–55.

Zayonchkovskaya, Z., and E. Tyuryukanova, eds. 2010. *Migration and Demographic Crisis in Russia* [Migratsiia i demograficheskii krizis v Rossii]. Moscow: INP RAS.

Zettelmeyer, J. 1998. "The Uzbek Growth Puzzle. Working Paper of the International Monetary Fund." *International Monetary Fund*, WP/98/133.

Zhou, M. 1997. "Segmented Assimilation: Issues, Controversies, and Recent Research on the New Second Generation." *International Migration Review* 31 (4): 975–1008.

Zlolniski, C. 2006. *Janitors, Street Vendors, and Activists: The Lives of Mexican Immigrants in Silicon Valley*. Berkeley: University of California Press.

STATUTES CITED

The Federal Law on Refugees, 1993.

The Federal Law on Forcibly Displaced Persons, 1993.

Russian Law on the Rules of Entry and Exit from the Territory of the Russian Federation, with amendments, No. 114-ФЗ, 1996.

Russian Citizenship Law, 2002.

Federal Law on the Legal Status of Foreign Citizens and Stateless Persons in the Russian Federation, No. 115-ФЗ, adopted July 25, 2002.

The Code of Administrative Offenses of the Russian Federation as of December 30, 2001, No. 195-ФЗ (edited as Federal Law No. 116-ФЗ as of June 22, 2007).

Russian Law on the Rules of Entry and Exit from the Territory of the Russian Federation, with amendments, Federal Law No. 321-ФЗ, 2012.

Russian Law on the Rules of Entry and Exit from the Territory of the Russian Federation, with amendments, Federal Law No. 224-ФЗ, 2013.